Intelligent
Software Agents

Springer
Berlin
Heidelberg
New York
Barcelona
Budapest
Hong Kong
London
Milan
Paris
Santa Clara
Singapore
Tokyo

Walter Brenner   Rüdiger Zarnekow
Hartmut Wittig
in co-operation with Claudia Schubert

Intelligent
Software Agents

Foundations and Applications

With 211 Figures

Springer

Walter Brenner
Lehrstuhl für Wirtschaftsinformatik
TU Bergakademie Freiberg
Gustav-Zeuner-Str. 8-10
D-09599 Freiberg, Germany

Rüdiger Zarnekow
Hartmut Wittig
Multimedia Software GmbH Dresden
Risaer Straße 5
D-01129 Dresden, Germany

Title of the Original German Edition:
Intelligente Softwareagenten
© Springer-Verlag Berlin Heidelberg, 1998

Translated from the German by Anthony S. Rudd

Library of Congress Cataloging-in-Publication Data

Brenner, Walter.
    [Intelligente Software Agenten. English]
    Intelligent software agents: foundations and applications/
  Walter Brenner, Rüdiger Zarnekow, in co-operation with Claudia
  Schubert
        p.   cm.
    Translation of: Intelligente Software Agenten.
    Includes bibliographical references and index.
    ISBN 3-540-63411-8 (alk. paper)
    1. Intelligent agents (Computer software)   I. Zarnekow, Rüdiger.
  II. Wittig, Hartmut.   III. Title.
  QA76.76.I58B74   1998
  006.3'3-dc21   98-14462
                                                           CIP

ISBN 3-540-63411-8 Springer-Verlag Berlin Heidelberg New York

© Springer-Verlag Berlin Heidelberg 1998
Printed in Germany

Typesetting: perform k + s textdesign GmbH, Heidelberg
Cover Design: Künkel + Lopka, Heidelberg
Printed on acid-free paper   SPIN 10638156 33/3142 – 5 4 3 2 1 0

Contents

1 Introduction[1]

This book is concerned with intelligent software agents. As with James Bond, agent 007, who, in the service of Her Majesty, the Queen of Great Britain, solves difficult problems by himself and never loses sight of the task at hand, intelligent software agents help private and business users in their search for information and performance of tasks in a networked, digital world. The Internet today provides us with an introductory view of how this digital and networked world will look. Intelligent agents in future will develop into an important tool for private and business users. Many experts believe they provide a new category of software that will gain greatly in importance in the coming years.

Although the development of intelligent agents is just at the beginning, a number of agents are available on the Internet as prototypes. The BargainFinder and Firefly agents (bf.cstar.ac.com/bf/ and www.firefly.com) provide the reader with a first impression of how intelligent agents can be used and what benefits they can bring.

This book provides the fundamental concepts of intelligent agents and makes use of specific examples to show their practical capabilities as far as can be judged at the moment. A positioning of agents as instruments for the information society follows the introduction in the second chapter. Examples for potential usage from the business and private areas provide a first impression of the power of intelligent agents and of the expected economic benefits. The third chapter is concerned with the basic concepts of the definition and characteristics of this new software. The fourth chapter investigates the basic modules of intelligent agents. A description of areas of influence, such as artificial intelligence and nets is followed by a discussion of the architecture of intelligent agents and descriptions of cooperation and communication in multi-agent systems. This chapter closes with sections on learning and planning, security, and the demands made on the IT infrastructure. The fifth chapter concentrates on the development methods and tools for intelligent agents. The chapter describes the analysis and design techniques, and the various programming languages in which intelligent agents can be programmed. The sixth

---

[1] This chapter was written by Walter Brenner.

chapter contains examples of intelligent agents, arranged according to their application areas. Chapter 7 closes with a prospective view of the future development of intelligent agents.

Everyone concerned with the Internet and the new possibilities of information and communication technology knows that nowadays there is no area that is developing faster. The authors are aware of the dynamics of this research area and its effects when they describe such a fast developing area in a slow, traditional medium like a book. One thing is sure today: when the book appears on the market, new intelligent agents will already exist and some of the hypotheses made by this book will have been shown to be incorrect. Why, despite this, does it make sense to write a classical book on this subject? Is there an alternative? Experience shows that the majority of the people in business and public life who make decisions on the use of new technologies continue to prefer books and articles in periodicals rather than electronic sources such as the Internet. Or is there some other reason for the enormous success of Nicolas Negroponte's book *Being Digital*, which we thank for multimedia and many concepts of the digital and networked world, and even intelligent agents?

Today, a book is still the only way to establish a new area. The authors are sure, however, that the information habits of the leading decision-making bodies will change in the coming years. Probably, as a consequence, in the medium-term future, books on the new developments in information and communication technology will appear only in digital form and on media such as the Internet.

Parallel to this book, we have produced our own homepage: www.softagent.com. Under this address you can find a summary of our book, the references for the examples used in the book, and a discussion platform. We will continually update this page so that interested readers can always use our homepage to overcome the "slowness" of the book medium and also to inform themselves on the latest state in the development of intelligent agents.

The authors appreciate any help and suggestions, and, in particular, experience on the use of intelligent agents. Please send any comments to: Professor Dr. Walter Brenner, TU Freiberg, Gustav-Zeuner Strasse 10, D-09596 Freiberg, Germany, or get in touch via the Internet under the e-mail address: brenner@bwl.tu-freiberg.de.

Before you begin with the contents of this book, a note on its form: Part I is concerned with the fundamentals of intelligent agents; Part II discusses the applications. Those readers with a knowledge of computer science can read the book sequentially, that is, starting with Chapter 3 and then working through the book. We recommend those readers with limited computer science knowledge to first study Chapters 2 and 3, and then continue with Chapter 6. They can read Chapters 4 and 5 if they have further interest.

Following this short introduction, we hope you enjoy reading the book. We would like to pass on to you the experience we have gained from our long-term work with the Internet and intelligent agents: while you are reading, try to reserve some time to test for yourself the examples in the Internet. In this way you will gain a personal impression of the power of these new tools in the digital, networked world.

A note of thanks

We could not have written this book without the help of our co-workers, friends and colleagues.

Our special thanks go to the two Executive Directors of Multimedia Software GmbH Dresden, Joachim Niemeier and Friedhelm Theis, and their employees. We also thank Torsten Fritsch and Jan Fiedler. Furthermore, we thank Hermann Brenner, Georg Wilking and Thomas Lemke, together with Sandra Kutschki and Michael Klaas for their unfailing help in the production of this book. We also thank Hermann Engesser and Dorothea Glaunsinger from Springer-Verlag for their excellent cooperation.

Freiberg, Dresden, March 1998   The authors

Part I: Fundamentals

The first part of this book is concerned with the theoretical basis and the basic components of intelligent software agents, and discusses both the pertinent development methods and tools for agent-based systems. The design and architectures of intelligent agents are discussed, as are methods and strategies for communication and cooperation in multi-agent systems. Learning and planning in multi-agent systems, security and confidentiality in agent systems, the requirements made on the basic system, and descriptions of development tendencies form other central aspects. The three development languages Java, Telescript, and Tcl are introduced as representatives of popular agent languages at the end of the discussion of agent-oriented analysis and design methods. This part of the book ends with a short introduction to the principles of component-based software development.

2 Agents as Tools of the Information Society[1]

2.1 On the Way to the Information Society

Business and society find themselves in transition to an information society. The continuing digitization of content and the networking of business, administration, and private households form the basis of the information society. In the future, an ever increasing number of businesses and government bodies will be connected to electronic networks, over which they will obtain information in digital form and provide information for others (see Figure 2.1/1).

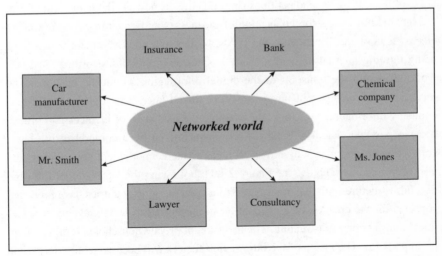

Figure 2.1/1: Information society structures

---

[1] This chapter was written by Walter Brenner.

We understand **digitization** to be the transformation of information, for example available on paper, into a form that permits electronic processing. For example, the use of a word processing system to write a letter on a personal computer results in the digitization of its contents. In the 1960s and 1970s, the digitization of formalized information took highest priority. The origins of today´s large business databases that contain information on employees, customers, suppliers, or products stem from this time. The 1980s were particularly characterized by the digitization of text and graphics. The word processing and graphics programs that evolved in parallel to the development of the personal computer permitted the digitization of text and graphics with limited effort. The term "multimedia" appeared at the start of the 1990s. It represents the expansion of digitization into pictures, sound (audio) and moving pictures (video). In the last few years, the increasingly extensive and cheaper forms of digitization have produced an unbounded amount of digital content. For example, the current availability of digital books in the form of CD-ROMs is enormous, and also the contents in the Internet are no longer manageable. Digital television will produce new dimensions. In future it will be possible to use electronic networks to transfer television programs in the same way as data today. Some countries began very early with the digitization of whole industries or government departments. For example, the city-state Singapore started in the latter part of the 1980s with the systematic digitization of the legal system. A complete archive of laws, verdicts, and petitions since this time is now available in digital form.

Networking means the connection of businesses and government bodies using electronic networks. Even since the 1970s, businesses and government bodies have being forming internal networks. Many businesses in the 1980s formed local networks to permit the transport of the digital information within the business. The local networks of different businesses were linked later. The first forms of intercompany information exchange, for example the exchange of invoices and orders, became possible. The 1990s have been characterized by a comprehensive interconnection of workplaces in almost all areas of the economy and government, and also of private households (see Figure 2.1/1). Following the US National Information Infrastructure initiative, many industrial and emerging countries have produced concepts for the creation of a national or, in the European Union, even a supranational information infrastructure. The inclusion of private households is of a particular importance. The vision of the information society will become reality only when large numbers of private users also connect to the networks.

The **Internet** provides a first impression how information will be used in the future information society. Even today, the Internet as part of a global interconnecting of business, government, and private households permits any point of the

Earth to be reached with relatively limited effort. The Internet then can be used to transfer information, for example, using e-mail or the World Wide Web (WWW). Even today, the amount of digital information available worldwide is no longer manageable, and is increasing daily. Whereas primarily text and graphics were available on the WWW at the start of the 1990s, nowadays increasingly digitized audio and video content is placed on the Internet. Concepts that permit telephoning or television broadcasting over the Internet will greatly change the telecommunications and media industries in the future.

Even today, the Internet makes information from a wide range of knowledge areas available for business, government and private households. The spectrum ranges from information about institutions, such as businesses or universities (e.g., www.mms-dresden.de or www.wiwi.tu-freiberg.de), over electronic shopping (e.g., www.internet-mall.com), in which a wide range of products is offered, and ending with games (e.g., www.sega.com). The history of the Amazon bookstore (www.amazon.com) provides an impression of the business potential that even today is available in the Internet. It permits the purchasing of books over the Internet. Amazon describes itself as already being the largest bookstore in the world. Amazon went public in Spring 1997 after only three years in existence. The shares had a value of approximately 30 million US dollars when the company went public.

2.2 Tools of the Information Society

The use of the new possibilities of the information society requires new tools and aids. **Browsers** are an example of a new tool (see Figure 2.2/1). Browsers form the interface between the user and the Internet. Because their use is largely intuitive, they permit the user to access the Internet with relatively limited learning effort. For example, Netscape's Communicator browser (www.netscape.com) provides access to the WWW or the e-mail capabilities of the Internet.

Figures for the PointCast company, as example, provide an indication of the business volumes that can be attained with tools for the information society. More than one million people regularly use the PointCast network services. This represents more than 30 to 50 million viewer-hours monthly and is equivalent to the average of a mid-sized television network [Wildstrom 1997].

Figure 2.2/1: Netscape Communicator browser

Search engines represent another category of information society tools. They support the user in the guided search for information. For example, if a user requires information about a country or a company, he uses a search engine, such as AltaVista (www.altavista.com), to determine what information is available in the Internet (see Figure 2.2/2).

Search engines represent information retrieval tools that permit the individual user to extract relatively quickly information he requires to solve a specific business or private problem out of the almost unlimited information offering.

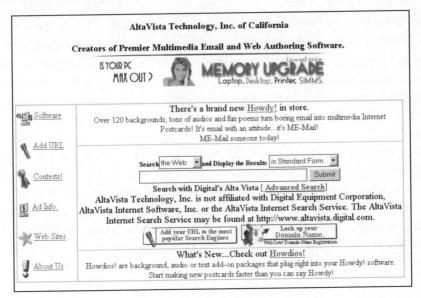

Figure 2.2/2: The AltaVista search engine

2.3 Intelligent Software Agents

Intelligent agents are a new category of information society tools. As a first working definition, we understand intelligent agents to be software programs that independently perform tasks on behalf of a user in a network environment. Chapter 3 of this book contains a more detailed definition of intelligent agents. The operation of an intelligent agent is best explained using a specific example. We describe intelligent agents in both the business and private areas in the following section.

2.3.1 Intelligent Agents in the Business Area

Place yourself in the position of an employee in a large company who is responsible for the purchase of office materials such as pencils, ball-point pens, and writing pads. Previously he had a business relationship with a number of local suppliers, with each of which he negotiated once a year a skeleton agreement and from whom he then received the office materials.

If the purchase of office materials is transferred to the digitized and networked world, and the capabilities of intelligent agents are used, there is a completely new procedure. In the first instance, the buyer would use a search engine, for example AltaVista (see Figure 2.2/2), to attempt to find a company who offers office material in the Internet. However, the search turns out to be relatively time consuming; AltaVista provides the buyer with the addresses of the individual suppliers. In a second phase, he or she must "visit" each of these suppliers in the Internet and determine whether they offer the office materials he requires and at what price. Despite using a search engine, you cannot be sure, as early experiences using search engines in Internet have shown, whether you have really found the cheapest supplier.

A special intelligent agent could help at this point. The buyer would first inform his intelligent agent which office materials he or she requires. The intelligent agent would then independently start the search in the Internet for suppliers of office materials and request from each of these suppliers whether they have the required office materials in stock and what they cost. In the third step, the intelligent agent informs the buyer of the price quotes it found in the network. The buyer in a fourth step then can go directly via the Internet to the cheapest supplier and purchase the required goods.

This first example of an intelligent agent shows how the intelligent agent supports a user to master the complexity of the Internet. It independently searches for the required information and saves the user from performing repetitive and time-consuming tasks. A first working definition of **intelligence** means that the agent is provided with knowledge of the user's wishes and also makes use of this knowledge. The more intelligence an agent has available, the greater the extent to which it can reduce the load on the user and provide other benefits.

Using the example of the office material purchasing, an increase in the intelligence of the agent could mean that the agent systematically monitors the office material suppliers in the Internet and then informs the user when prices change, sale-price items become available, or new products have been added to a supplier's range that provide an alternative to the user's wishes.

A further increase to the intelligence of the agent could mean that it not only searches for special offers or changed prices, but purchases products on behalf of the user. The user provides the agent with his purchasing strategy before the search starts. Conceivable strategies, for example, would be that the agent should buy only when a specific price limit is reached, or that the agent buys the required items at any price but with delivery by a specific date, or that the agent negotiates with a supplier over price and quantity. Depending on the programming, the agent itself completes the business or informs its user before completing the business whether he still wants to buy at these conditions.

In a following stage, the agent could not only search in the Internet for goods and also buy these, but itself determine the requirement for office material from the company's internal applications. The intelligent agent is linked with the company's storeroom for office material and itself monitors the stock levels. When specific stock levels become too low, the agent itself uses the Internet to obtain the replacements.

The examples show the application areas that currently can be imagined for agents. These range from relatively simple search tools with limited intelligence, through to agents that can replace a buyer for certain product groups. There are not really any limits to the capabilities of agents in a digitized and networked world. The more content available in the Internet, in the case of our example, the larger the number of suppliers who offer their products in the Internet, the more capable the network infrastructure becomes, and thus the greater the areas of use for intelligent agents. Consequently, it is easy to see why several computer science experts consider intelligent agents to be one of the most important future developments.

The examples of intelligent agents for private households described in the next section support this forecast. Indeed, we expect that the decisive stimulus for the development of intelligent agents in future will no longer come from the business area but from the private area.

2.3.2 Intelligent Agents in the Private Area

Germany had only two television channels 30 years ago. The addition of the 'third programs' at the beginning of the 1970s and the private programs in the 1980s were revolutionary steps. As more television programs are provided, the search for interesting broadcasts becomes more time-intensive. If we assume that an average household nowadays can receive approximately 30 television programs, it takes between 60 and 90 minutes at minimum before those broadcasts of particular interest have been selected from the following week's program.

The availability of television programs will be greatly extended in the information society. Media experts forecast that shortly after the new millennium, every household will be able to receive between 300 and 500 television programs. A quick estimate shows that a systematic search for interesting television programs would take so much time that there would be hardly any time left to view the selected broadcasts.

An intelligent agent can help here. The user informs the agent of his television preferences. For example, one of the authors of this book would tell his agent that he is particularly interested in sport broadcasts involving the New York Giants football team and Formula 1 racing. The intelligent agent would search the television programs available in digital form on behalf of the user and then inform him what will be shown on television concerning New York Giants and Formula 1 in the near future. The agent will save the user from having to make the tedious search through hundreds of television programs.

An intelligent agent that continuously follows the new broadcasts and television programs could provide the user with new information on his areas of interest. For example, if New York Giants has just won a decisive game in the National Football League, the agent could use the SMS technology to send the result of the game and the current standings to the user's mobile GSM telephone and inform him in which television program the summary of the game can be seen.

In a further stage, the agent could learn from a person's television habits. It registers, for example, that the viewer not only watches broadcasts New York Giants but also those with Denver, but the same viewer just glances at broadcasts involving San Francisco 49ers. The intelligent agent deduces from this behavior that the viewer is not just interested in New York Giants and Formula 1 as it was originally informed, but he also wants to be informed about Denver. The tendency can be recognized from this example how the agents through their intelligence, which can be expressed as a certain learning capability, become in the course of time a "mirror image" of the user in the Internet. The intelligent agent filters that information of interest for a specific person from the enormous amount of information available in the Internet.

An example from the car travel area shows a further potential use. The dense traffic has the result that there is hardly any long trip nowadays that does not meet with a traffic jam somewhere. An intelligent agent could support the driver here. The driver informs his intelligent agent some time before the start of the trip of his destination and desired time of arrival. The agent then starts to produce a picture using information available in the Internet: what routes could be used, what is the state of these roads, have traffic jams already been reported on the routes, or can traffic jams be expected, for example due to large events. As a result of the first analysis, the intelligent agent informs the driver with a first suggestion for route and the latest possible departure time. The intelligent agent continually monitors the situation along the route. When a change occurs, the intelligent agent uses a pager, for example, to inform the driver of important changes, if, for example, the trip should be started earlier. The agent continues to monitor the situation even after the journey has started. GPS is used to continually inform the agent of the current location. If, for example, a traffic jam occurs that it identified in the Internet, it can immediately suggest possible detours. The intelligent agent is in effect a digital co-driver that helps the user to reach his destination as fast as possible.

An example from the area of the private finance management shows how intelligent agents can be used to earn money in the financial markets. An ever increasing number of private persons place their money in shares and securities. There is much evidence that the Telekom share will become a new "people's share" in the same way as the shares in Volkswagen AG once were. There are already a number of possibilities in the USA to conduct stock market business using the Internet (www.lombard.com). Private people who speculate have as central problem the time needed daily to obtain information on the stock market prices and company developments, and to conduct the appropriate transactions. An intelligent agent can help with the information acquisition. On behalf of its user, it continually monitors the prices of those shares in its user's portfolio and informs him when the share prices go outside a previously defined price range. For example, intelligent agents could inform a user that it wants to sell his shares. As part of a "sales strategy", the user can inform the agent that he will sell within a specified period or when a certain price is exceeded. The agent then monitors the price development and informs the user when he can sell or the agent sells the shares by itself.

The examples from the private area show that intelligent agents will become a central tool of the information society. They represent a new category of instruments to simplify the private household's use of the digital networked world.

2.4 Economic Potential

Before we start in the next chapter with the concepts and specific application examples for intelligent agents, we will first consider their economic potential. We divide the representation of the benefits of the agents into the two categories: potential benefit from the user's viewpoint, and potential benefit from the viewpoint of the information and communications industry. However, we must make the restriction, the potential benefit cannot currently be proved, rather these are forecasts, because the current software agents are often available only as prototypes.

2.4.1 Potential Benefit from the User's Viewpoint

Although users of intelligent agents will be private and business persons in future, it is already apparent that the innovative agents will be developed first for private users. The solutions in the private area will be transferred to the business area. The capability to show measurable benefits for the users will be decisive for the use of intelligent agents as tool of the information society.

The following potential benefits from the viewpoint of business and private users are already apparent:

- **Improvement of efficiency**. Intelligent agents improve the efficiency of working with the Internet. They undertake work in the Internet on behalf of the user and return the result. Instead of spending a large amount of time to go from one Internet address to the next, the user informs its agent of his wish and the agent solves the problem more or less independently depending on its own intelligence. A further effect that improves the efficiency is the increase in the speed of arriving at a solution to the problem in the Internet. The first tests with the prototypes show that agents get the required results significantly faster than experienced Internet users. Agents permit an individualization of the information from the Internet. The user informs his agent of his wishes and the agent provides him only with that information that meets his wish. Irrelevant information is reduced to a minimum.

- **Improvement of effectivity**. Intelligent agents improve the effectivity of working with the Internet. That is, they help to find the required information with less effort. The Internet, although still at the start of its development, already contains an enormous amount of information, and every day more information is being added. Even experienced users can no longer retain an overview of the Internet. When a search for specific information is made, there is the danger that no information is found even though it is present in the Internet. The agent increases the effectivity of the network use by being programmed to independently search in the Internet and attempt to include as many sources as possible in the search. Furthermore, agents counteract the characteristics of human problem solving. The Nobel prize winner Simon has already shown that a person does not search for the optimum solution, but rather accepts the first best solution for his problem [March/Simon 1958]. With regard to the Internet, this means that a user continues to search only until he finds something generally appropriate and then he terminates the search. This human problem solving mechanism has the effect that a normal user, especially when he is subject to time pressure, cannot profit from the magnitude of the Internet. An agent masters these limits. It searches the complete network on behalf of its user. Consequently, an agent can find completely new sources that may only just recently have been added to the network and include these in the search. This improves the effectiveness of the use of the Internet. The user profits from the work of his intelligent agent using the complete offering in the Internet. The independent task-related search with an intelligent agent is the only economical facility currently known that can keep pace

with the rapid growth of the Internet. Only an intelligent agent with its independent and task-related search is capable of taking the new offerings in the Internet into consideration in a systematic manner.

- **Increase in the transparency and optimizations**. Intelligent agents increase the
  transparency of the contents of the Internet by comparing information from various sources. Chapter 6 of this book describes examples of intelligent agents involved in purchasing a specific product in the Internet, for example a CD or a
  book, in which all available offerings with the price and delivery conditions are
  listed and so provide a relatively comprehensive transparency of the market. As
  part of an optimization, the user can select the most favorable quote for him. The
  'invisible hand' postulated by Adam Smith has been made visible in the electronic business world with the help of the intelligent agents.

2.4.2 Potential Benefit from the Viewpoint of the Information and Communications Industry

Intelligent agents are creating a new business field that promises large growth potential in the coming years. OVUM, an English consultancy, in its latest study on
intelligent agents came to the following results: the sales for intelligent agents will
increase from approximately 19 million US dollars in 1996, to 357 million US
dollars in 1998 and 4.6 billion US dollars in 2006. OVUM forecasts that the service
providers and developers of intelligent agents will take the largest part of these
sales [Guilfoyle et al. 1997].

OVUM forecasts that intelligent agents will achieve approximately 5% of the
sales made in the Internet. However, OVUM makes the assumption that ever more
intelligent agents will appear on the market during the coming years but many of
them will prove to be business failures. Furthermore, OVUM expects that the
agents for private households will become the primary innovation factor and from
the start of the next millennium the sales with private households will exceed those
of business and government. OVUM forecasts that of the 4.6 billion US dollars in
2006, only a third of the sales will be made to business and government.

The examples for the use of intelligent agents in both business and private areas
show us their wide range of future application areas. The representation of the economic potential also underscores the future importance of intelligent agents. Despite these impressive examples and figures, a residual risk that should not be un-
derestimated remains for intelligent agents. Will they be successful in the market?
Too many developments in the information and communications technology in the
past were greeted euphorically and then faded into unimportance or realized the

originally forecast effects only after long delays. In this context, one only has to remember the discussions on computer-supported software development or expert systems in the first half of the 1980s.

2.5 State of the Research and the Practical Applications

Intelligent agents, even though they are almost 30 years old, have attained a certain importance only with the growth of the Internet. Although intelligent agents can be found in science and in practical applications, they are still at the start of their development. Almost all intelligent agents that we present in Chapter 6 of this book are prototypes. Consequently, many statements, such as the discussions of the economical potential in the previous section, contain a risk factor.

However, large efforts can be observed worldwide in research and in practical applications that are intensively concerned with intelligent agents. The interested reader can inform himself at the homepage of the book (see Section 1) on the state of the research and application areas for intelligent agents.

2.6 Summary

Intelligent agents represent software programs that independently perform requests on behalf of a user in a networked and digital world, for example, the search for information. Intelligent agents provide tools for the information society, without which work in a digital networked world would not be possible. Agents have been developed for both business and government bodies, and for the private households. Future innovation for intelligent agents will emanate from the private households. Worldwide, the research on intelligent agents and their application is still at the beginning.

3 Fundamental Concepts of Intelligent Software Agents[1]

3.1 Definition of Intelligent Software Agents

It has not yet been possible to agree on a generally accepted, comprehensive, definition of an intelligent agent. This is evidence of the inter-disciplinary character of agents, which on the one hand are subject to the effects of different scientific research directions, and, on the other hand, reflect the requirements demanded in practical applications. If one approaches the area of agents primarily from the direction of the artificial intelligence, there are different criteria than those seen from the point of view of the information and communications systems. Similarly, the demands of a social scientist differ from those of the more technically oriented observations made by a computer scientist.

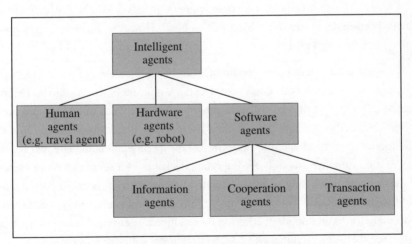

Figure 3.1/1: Categories of intelligent agents

---

[1] This chapter was written by Rüdiger Zarnekow.

For these reasons, the different goals of all the scientific disciplines must be analyzed and combined with the demands made on practical applications to form a consistent set and so achieve an appropriate definition of intelligent agents.

At the highest level, three major categories of agents can be distinguished: human agents, hardware agents and software agents (see Figure 3.1/1). All agent categories have the common feature that they to a large extent independently perform tasks on behalf of their contracting party or user for which specialized knowledge is needed or which consist of many time-intensive individual steps. We meet human agents almost every day. If, for example, you want to book a journey, you request a travel agent to do this for you. You expect him to perform reliably, independently and quickly all tasks concerned with booking the journey. This includes gathering information from a wide range of information sources, for example travel offerings from various providers, the identification of the best travel components, the avoidance of inconsistencies or contradictions in the selection of individual components, and finally producing the complete journey. The work of the travel agent not only saves the customer from acquiring the specialized knowledge required to book a journey, but also saves a significant amount of time. If these concepts are is transferred to the area of computer science, this immediately produces the main tasks of hardware and software agents. Using the analogy of human agents, hardware and software agents should perform certain tasks for their users that they cannot undertake themselves because of insufficient time or lack of knowledge. The following considerations are primarily concerned with software agents, because these are the subject of this book. However, many concepts apply equally to hardware agents.

An agent always requires a certain amount of intelligence to perform its tasks. Consequently, one refers to intelligent agents. A non-intelligent agent can be considered to be any traditional software program, because even traditional programs perform a specific task and provide their users with a direct time saving. Only the intelligence permits an agent to perform its task largely autonomously and require intervention from the user only for important decisions. An agent that is not capable of independent processing is only of limited use for its user, because only a minimal time saving results from the frequent intervention. Consequently, autonomous processing forms an important criterion for intelligent agents and is one of the main differences between intelligent agents and traditional software programs.

An agent must interact with its environment to achieve its goals. It must be capable of gathering information on its environment and making decisions based on this information, and then initiate specific actions based on the decisions. This working process of a software agent is directly analogous to that of a human agent. Just a response to incoming information does not normally suffice for an effective interaction with the environment. A direct communication or even cooperation with other objects is often required, for example, with other agents or human users. Software agents should possess the appropriate capabilities, that is, they should have a communications language and be able to cooperate with other objects. This is the only way of solving complex problems.

If the two central aspects of intelligence and interaction are integrated in the existing considerations, this produces the following basic understanding: Intelligent software agents are defined as being a software program that can perform specific tasks for a user and possesses a degree of intelligence that permits it to perform parts of its tasks autonomously and to interact with its environment in a useful manner.

This definition provides us with a number of different application scenarios for intelligent software agents. Depending on the general task area, differentiations can be made between information agents, cooperation agents, and transaction agents (see Figure 3.1/1). The primary task of an information agent concerns the support of its user in the search for information in distributed systems or networks. The information agent must be capable of the following tasks: locate information sources; extract information from the sources; filter the information of relevance for the user from the total quantity of found information using the user's interest profile; prepare and present the results in an appropriate form. An agent provides useful assistance for its user only when it performs all these individual steps. An information agent must be supplied with knowledge of all available information sources, the problem area to be considered and the semantics of the information [Fiedler 1997]. Only then can it perform the requested task reliably, independently and, in particular, faster than a human user.

Cooperation agents have a different focus. Their main task is to solve complex problems by using communication and cooperation mechanisms with other objects, such as agents, humans or external resources. Cooperation agents are used when a problem exceeds the capabilities of an individual agent or agents already exist that already have a solution and whose knowledge can be used by other agents. The demands on the intelligence of a cooperation agent are higher than that of a pure information agent, because the development of problem solution strategies and the cooperation between several agents is a significantly more complex and less predictable task than the pure search for information.

The third large application area of intelligent software agents lies in the transaction-oriented application environments. Both in classical database environments and in the areas of network management and electronic commerce, the main task of intelligent agents is the processing and monitoring of transactions. Transaction agents are especially suitable for these tasks. Security, data protection, robustness and trustworthiness are aspects that play a central role in the design of transaction agents. Such agents normally operate in very sensitive areas and represent their users for tasks that demand a high degree of responsibility, for example in the purchase of products using a user's credit card. Incorrect behavior or the loss of confidential information can have grave consequences and is not acceptable for transaction agents.

The three discussed categories of intelligent software agents do not fully exclude each other. Although the categories are quite different, it is possible that an agent, because of its tasks, can be counted in two or even all three categories. The transaction capability, in particular, can be combined with the other two groups. For example, an information agent that has identified information for its user can also perform the purchase of the information, that is, accept responsibility for the actual purchase transaction. If it must contact other agents during its search for information, it can be assigned to the group of cooperation agents. However, only initial forms of such complex agents are currently available. The existing agents can generally be assigned to one of the three areas.

In addition to our division of intelligent agents into information, cooperation, and transaction agents, a number of other divisions exist in the literature. Reference is made here to the agent categories collaborative, interface, mobile, information/Internet, reactive, hybrid, and smart agents from [Nwana 1996], and the interface, task, and information agents from [Sycara et al. 1996].

3.2 Characteristics of Intelligent Software Agents

To obtain a basic understanding of the tasks and functioning of intelligent agents, it is necessary first to discuss the characteristic properties that differentiate an intelligent agent from traditional software programs. The following section describes in detail the most important characteristics from the wide range of characteristics discussed in the literature; some of these have already been discussed in the previ-

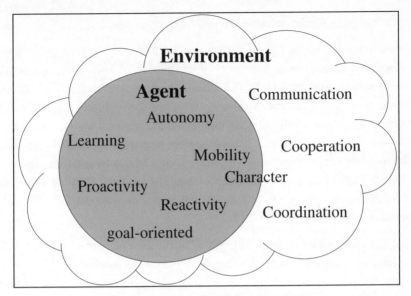

Figure 3.2/1: Characteristics of intelligent agents

ous section. It should be noted that not every agent must have all the listed properties. Indeed, there are many practical systems with significant differences of complexity; whereas simple agents with very low complexity may have only one or two
of the listed characteristics, highly-complex agent systems in the ideal situation can
support (at least partially) all the mentioned properties.

The characteristics of intelligent agents can be grouped into the two large categories of internal and external properties (see Figure 3.2/1). Internal properties are
those that form the 'internal being' of an agent, that is, the properties that determine
the actions within the agent. Internal properties include the ability to learn, reactivity , autonomy and goal-orientedness.

The external properties include all those characteristics that affect the interaction
of several agents or human-agent communication. For example, these are capabilities such as communication or cooperation. Not all characteristics can be assigned
to just one of the two groups, rather parts can belong to both groups. The character
of an agent for which significant parts determine the internal behavior of an agent
but which also plays an important role in the external communication is such a
property.

The following section describes the individual characteristics.

- **Reactivity**. Reactivity (or situated) designates that an agent must be capable of reacting appropriately to influences or information from its environment. This environment can consist of other agents, human users, external information sources or physical objects. Reactivity forms one of the fundamental requirements for an intelligent agent and should be supported to some extent by all agents. The agent must have suitable sensors or possess its own internal model of its environment (from which it can draw conclusions by itself) in order to be able to react to changes in the environment. The first case is called a true reactive agent, whereas agents with an internal environment model are called deliberative agents (see Section 4.2.1).

  The many watcher agents currently available are examples of simple reactive agents (see Section 6.3). Such agents have the task to monitor specific information sources, for example Internet servers, and to inform their user when the contents change. Watcher agents possess a simple sensor with which they can perform the required monitoring functions, such as the monitoring of a WWW page. If a change occurs, the agent can re-read the corresponding information source and search it for new information.

- **Proactivity/goal-orientation**. The property proactivity is a level above the reactivity. If an intelligent agent does not just react to changes to its environment but itself takes the initiative under specific circumstances, this is called proactive behavior. The characteristic of goal-orientation is closely related. The capability for an agent itself to take the initiative requires that the agent has well-defined goals or even a complex goal system. Only then does it make sense for an agent to influence its environment and so achieve its own goals. The comprehensiveness and complexity of the associated goal system are important here. For example, if an agent only has the general goal to gather information in a specific area, then it cannot do much more than monitor the specific information sources and react to changes, in this case the arrival of new information from the area of interest. True proactive behavior occurs only to a very limited extent here. In contrast, a more comprehensive goal system would not just consist of a generalized overall goal, but also be composed of a number of sub-goals, each of which permits the agent to perform its tasks much more precisely. A truly proactive behavior is possible only with such complex goal systems.

- **Reasoning/learning**. Every agent must have a certain minimum degree of intelligence in order to be designated as being an agent. However, a very wide variation in the area of intelligence can be envisaged that ranges from simple agents with limited intelligence through to complex, highly-intelligent systems. The intelligence of an agent is formed from three main components: its internal knowledge base, the reasoning capabilities based on the contents of the knowledge base, and the ability to learn or to adapt to changes to the environment (adaptive behavior). The agent's reasoning powers should have a certain amount of rationality. An agent acts rationally when its processing brings it nearer to satisfying its overall goal or one of its sub-goals. Consequently, rational processing requires the existence of a goal system. Classical AI techniques, such as rule-based systems, knowledge-based systems or neural networks (see Section 4.6) are well-suited for reasoning, however even purely agent-oriented concepts exist. These include an artificial evolution model in which agents create new generations of agents that have increasingly complex reasoning mechanisms [Belgrave 1995].

Reasoning capability puts an agent in the position of being able to observe its environment and to make specific decisions when changes occur in this environment. However, the ability to learn from previous experiences and to successively adapt its own behavior to the environment is just as important for the intelligent behavior of an agent. This applies both for the communication with users and other agents, and for the available resources. For example, if an agent has gathered information for its user and the user has informed it that he is not interested in the found information, then the agent must learn from this, that is, it must modify its knowledge base in such a manner that the next search for information will not return information from the area not of interest to the user. The same applies for the available information resources. If, after a certain period of time, some resources prove to be of limited use or the agent detects new resources, it is expected to learn and adapt its behavior accordingly. In the course of time, this produces a user profile that takes account of the user's specific areas of interest and peculiarities, and which permits the agent to perform a qualitative, valuable, personalized information search. As with the reasoning process, the agent's learning process should have rational aspects, that is, it should always help the agent in meeting its goals.

- **Autonomy**. One of the important differences between agents and traditional software programs is the capability of an agent to follow its goals autonomously, that is, without interactions or commands from the environment. An agent does not need to have each of its steps approved by its user or other agents, rather it is capable of acting alone. Autonomous action does not only relieve load on the user, because he no longer needs to make many decisions by himself, rather it has the external effect of an increase in the intelligence. The intelligence of an agent affects the user in that he can give it commands, ideas and areas of interest that the agent then can use to independently solve the required task.

To permit autonomous behavior, an agent must have both control over its actions and internal states [Wooldridge/Jennings 1995] and be provided with those resources and capabilities required to perform its tasks. These include, for example, the availability of an electronic network, the capability to navigate through the network (see "mobility" property) or the capability to make contact with other agents (see "communication" property). Goal-orientation and, to a limited extent, the ability "to" learn are also prerequisites for a truly autonomous behavior. An agent must agree each of its steps with its user if it does not have any goals that it attempts to achieve.

The user frequently specifies the degree of the agent's autonomy. Situations can be envisaged in which an agent is capable of a complete autonomous behavior although its user does not wish this. In particular, many users are not prepared to delegate the decision-making process when the agent is to make decisions for its user that have legal or financial consequences. For example, a purchasing agent is fully capable of not only finding the required object at the cheapest price but also buying it directly. However, the user normally would like to make the purchase decision himself and so instruct his agent not to make a purchase without referring back to him.

- **Mobility**. Mobility describes the ability of an agent to navigate within electronic communications networks. Mobile agents are capable of wandering from one computer of an electronic network to another. In contrast, stationary agents are bound to a specific computer. Although the may be able to send messages using an existing network or to contact other agents in the network, they cannot themselves move within this. Mobile agents place high demands on the network environment and raise many questions regarding security, data privacy, and management. Every associated computer must be capable of both packaging mobile agents and sending them to other computers and also receiving, validating and executing agents. Section 4.2 2 contains a detailed description of the technical and organizational aspects of the development of mobile agents.

Only mobility makes apparent several of the significant advantages of intelligent agents. It reduces the network loading for example, because a mobile agent does not need to gather the information it requires to fulfill its tasks by sending a series of messages over the network. It can, instead, go to the computer or agents with the required information, which causes just a single network load, and then perform all tasks locally on the target computer. Although it is possible to envisage such an asynchronous communication without agents, the use of intelligent agents raises it to a higher level. An agent with its intelligence can much better benefit from the advantages of asynchronous communication compared with traditional software programs or client-server architectures.

Combined with mobile agents, the previously described autonomy characteristic provides a further advantage. If a mobile agent acts autonomously, its user is not required to maintain a continuous network connection. Instead, it can provide the agent with a task, send it over the network and then remove the network connection. As soon as the agent has achieved the required results, it automatically reports back by establishing a network connection to its user or it waits for the user's next network selection. This allows a reduction of the user's connection costs. Only mobile agents permit an agent to be sent into a network and the subsequent removal of the network connection. In addition, mobile agents can go to specific meeting points, also known as agencies, where they can make contact with other mobile agents with similar interests, and then conduct conversations or negotiations with them. An agency can also provide a range of services and data that may be of interest for the associated agent. Thus, it serves as marketplace or discussion and communications forum for a specific area of interest. Stationary agents can realize such a structure only to a limited extent.

- **Communication/cooperation**. An agent often requires an interaction with its environment to fulfill its tasks. Human users, in particular, and other agents and arbitrary information sources belong to the environment. Two complementary properties can be differentiated as part of the interaction: communication and cooperation. An agent can use the communications capability to make contact with its environment. An agent communications language that provides a standardized protocol for the exchange of information permits agents to communicate with each other (see Section 4.3). The agent is provided with a precisely defined range of queries that it can use to communicate with other agents, and from whom it also receives a precisely defined range of responses.

The described communications mechanism is normally adequate only for simple agent systems and for the communication between agents and external resources. It is not adequate for a dialog between several agents with the goal of providing a common solution for a task. Here, a more extensive property, the cooperation, must augment the communications capability. Cooperation of several agents permits faster and better solutions for complex tasks that exceed the capabilities of a single agent. Every agent profits from the cooperation, because its own goals are reached in a shorter time or even can be solved completely by other agents. Those agents that cooperate with each other must use an extended agent communications language, because they not only require a pure communications language, but must be able to exchange their goals, preferences and knowledge.

For example, if several agents want to achieve the same sub-goal, an agent that is particularly suitable for this task can solve this sub-goal for all the agents. As soon as this is done, the agent can pass its newly won knowledge to the other agents. The capability for cooperation thus increases the power of all associated agents, solves existing conflicts, corrects inconsistent information states and consequently improves the efficiency of the complete system [Sycara et al. 1996]. A frequent discussion is made on the extent to which cooperating agents are dependent on a social behavior of the associated agents. An agent should be aware that it is part of a group and the success of the group also depends on its own behavior. If this is not the case, this means that an agent does not act as part of a group and it places its goals in the foreground and may even intentionally attempt to hinder other agents in the pursuance of their goals, for example by providing incorrect information. In this case there is a limit to the usefullness of the results that can be achieved through cooperation.

- **Character**. It is often desirable that an agent demonstrates an external behavior with as many human traits as possible. For example, if an agent appears to its users as a virtual person, then it must have certain human characteristics to satisfy this role in a useful manner. An agent's most important characteristics are honesty, trustworthiness and reliability. No user would trust an agent with important tasks if he feared that it would not be trustworthy and would intentionally follow a goal that had not been agreed or would pass confidential information to another agent or persons. Furthermore, agents are often used in areas that demand a high degree of trustworthiness and absolute reliability. This is the case in aeronautics and in the space industry, in military systems, and, to a lesser extent, also in electronic malls. A user will prefer to perform critical tasks himself or use traditional software as long as an agent has not gained adequate trust, even when this means additional effort.

It is important that agents with a high degree of interaction with people exhibit emotional states, such as joy, sadness, frustration. Because misunderstandings can easily occur, an agent without emotion cannot realistically present many situations and results. Emotional states play a central role, in particular, in the entertainment area in which agents often take the external form of a virtual (three-dimensional) person. Only with their help can the actual identity of the other party, namely just a software program, remain largely hidden from the human communication partner.

If the listed characteristics are compared with any existing agent, it is apparent that very few of the agents currently available or in development have all the mentioned properties. The theoretical and development effort required to implement such 'perfect' agents normally exceeds the available resources several times over. Even the scientific foundation is still missing or just at the beginning in many areas. In particular, the current developments for the capability of performing intelligent actions and the development of human characteristics are available in only rudimentary form.

3.3 Classification

Following the definition of intelligent software agents and a discussion of their characteristics, a classification of agents now follows. A useful classification must have the goal of categorizing existing agent systems and future developments within a standardized scheme. An ideal classification can be made using the characteristics defined in the previous section. All agents can be assigned to the multi-dimensional matrix that results from the characteristics. However, the matrix has only limited practical value for the reader, because a clear representation is hardly possible. For this reason, we have limited ourselves in the following section to the three classification criteria that we consider to be the most significant. These we can use to show in a clear form the assignment of intelligent software agents in a three-dimensional space. The three selected criteria are fully adequate to make a useful classification of current and future agents. They also permit all the characteristics mentioned in the previous section to be represented in one or more criteria. They provide the further advantage that not only single agents, but also complete applications, can be assigned to individual areas of the matrix.

As shown in Figure 3.3/1, agent systems can be classified according to the three criteria: intelligence, mobility and number of agents. Because two of the three clas-

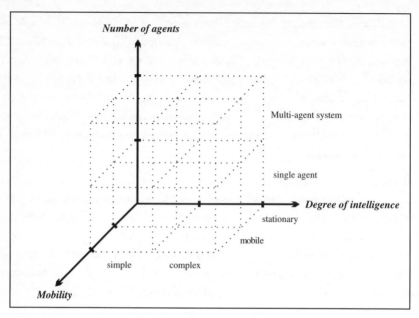

Figure 3.3/1: Classification matrix for agent systems

sification criteria, intelligence and mobility, have already been discussed in detail in the previous section, they are not described here.

For simplicity and clarity, we use the expressions simple and complex agent to describe the degree of intelligence. Simple agents have only a limited amount of intelligence, whereas complex systems demonstrate a highly intelligent behavior. Two types of mobile agents can be differentiated within the classification criterion of mobility: mobile scripts and mobile objects. Mobile scripts are sent to another computer prior to their execution. In contrast, mobile objects can change their position at any time, namely at any time during their execution. In this case, not only is the actual object transferred, but also its current state and system environment. Mobile objects place significantly higher demands on the associated computer systems.

The number of agents associated with a system forms the third classification criterion. A differentiation is made between individual agents and multi-agent systems. Single agents move in an environment that does not contain any other agents. More correctly, they are not capable of contacting other agents, even when they are in their environment. Single agents contact just their user and other information sources, such as databases. In contrast, multi-agent systems consist of a number of agents that can communicate or even cooperate with each other (see Section 4.3).

All characteristics of the previous section can be placed in the three dimensions of the matrix: reactivity, proactivity, reasoning, learning, and character are properties that significantly determine the intelligence of an agent. Communication is needed in both single agents and in multi-agent systems, and can be assigned to the category of the number of agents. The capability of cooperation affects both the intelligence criterion and the number of agents. Autonomous behavior influences both the intelligence and the mobility of agent. The operation of a mobile agent is useful only when it has a certain degree of autonomy. If it must refer back to its user before every decision and so return to his computer or send a message, it makes little sense to leave the user's computer in the first place.

The general task areas of intelligent software agents introduced in Section 3.1 (information, cooperation and transaction agents) can be assigned to the fields of the classification matrix.

Information agents (see Figure 3.3/2) normally have only a relatively limited amount of intelligence and so belong to the area of simple agents. Furthermore,

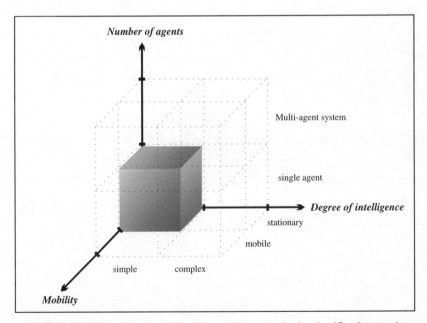

Figure 3.3/2: The assignment of the information agents in the classification matrix

they are almost always agents that operate individually, because they do not need any extensive cooperation of several agents to perform their search for information. The majority of the information agents that currently exist have a stationary nature. However, it would be especially desirable for information agents to be realized as mobile agents. This increases both their autonomy and also leads to a reduction in the network load. Consequently, a rapidly increasing proportion of mobile information agents can be expected when the infrastructure needed for them becomes available.

Cooperation agents must have a relatively high degree of intelligence and so fall into the area of the complex agents (see Figure 3.3/3). The second classification criterion is specified because they must be active in multi-agent environments. Mobility is not essential, because cooperation-oriented agent systems concentrate on the actual problem solving process and they are often developed and conceived for operation within a computer system. However, it should be appreciated that mobility can be a desirable criterion for cooperation agents. For example, the previously presented concept for agencies (see Section 3.2) can be realized only using mobile agents.

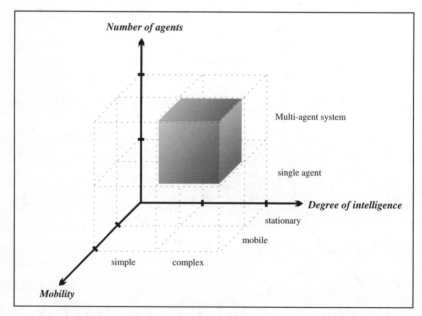

Figure 3.3/3: The assignment of the cooperation agents in the classification matrix

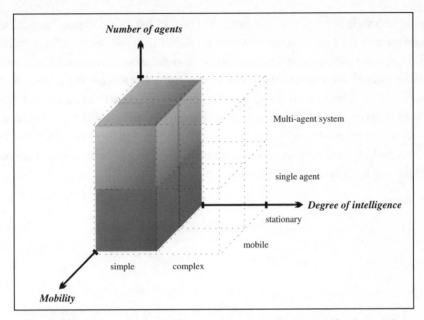

Figure 3.3/4: The assignment of the transaction agents in the classification matrix

Transaction agents can be used both as single agents and as multi-agent systems (see Figure 3.3/4). For example, a number of different agents that close transactions with each other are involved in agent-based electronic markets. On the other hand, agents are used to monitor transactions within a communications network as single systems. No particularly high demands are made on their intelligence, rather the robustness of the agent's architecture has primary importance. The use of transaction agents in multi-agent systems can form an exception. If, for example, complex negotiations take place between several agents, and must an agent consequently have a clever negotiating strategy, then this is linked with the corresponding demands on its intelligence. Transaction agents can be realized as both stationary and mobile agents. The decision depends on the associated application scenario.

3.4 Summary

Intelligent software agents can be differentiated into three general task areas: information, cooperation and transaction agents. All three forms are software systems that perform specific tasks for their owners and possess a degree of intelligence that makes it possible for them to perform parts of their tasks autonomously and to interact with their environment. In contrast to classical software programs, intelligent software agents have a number of typical characteristics, such as autonomy, ability to learn, reactivity, proactivity, mobility, goal-orientation, communication, cooperation, coordination and character. Not every agent needs to have all the mentioned properties in order to be designated as being an agent. Agents and agent systems can be differentiated in a basic classification matrix on the basis of the three classification criteria: number of agents, degree of intelligence and mobility. Both single agents and all three general task areas (information, cooperation and transaction agents) can be assigned in this matrix.

4 Base Modules of Agent Systems[1]

4.1 Areas of Influence

Even during the definition of intelligent agents, it became apparent that the influences of various research directions are reflected in the development of an agent. Figure 4.4/1 emphasizes this fact by comparing the areas of influence with the characteristics assigned to an agent.

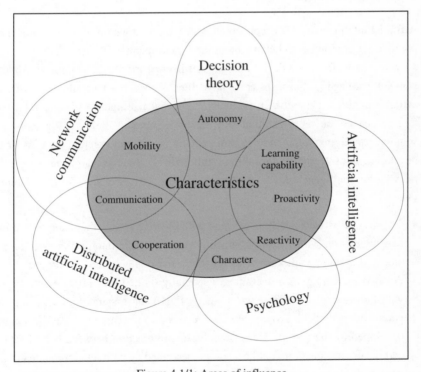

Figure 4.1/1: Areas of influence

[1] Sections 4.1 to 4.5 were written by Rüdiger Zarnekow. Sections 4.6 and 4.7 were written by Hartmut Wittig.

It is easy to recognize that almost every property is associated with a different scientific discipline. Reactivity, proactivity, and learnability are classical research areas of artificial intelligence, although the results of control theory play an important role in reactivity. Distributed artificial intelligence is primarily concerned with questions of communication and cooperation in multi-agent systems. Developments in the area of distributed network and communications systems provide the basic prerequisites for the mobility and communications capability of an agent. Decision theory concepts make it possible for an agent to act autonomously, because they provide the capability for it to make independent decisions. Psychology is concerned with an agent's character and also, to a limited extent, with its reactivity.

The following section describes the three most important areas of influence. These are classical artificial intelligence, distributed artificial intelligence, and network or communications systems.

4.1.1 Artificial Intelligence

Artificial intelligence (AI) is concerned with the investigation of ideas that make it possible for computers to behave in an intelligent manner [Winston 1987]. Consequently, results from classical AI are also of interest for the development of intelligent software agents, because, as we have already seen, these should demonstrate a certain intelligent behavior. In particular, artificial intelligence is concerned with topics such as the representation and the understanding of knowledge, problem solution paradigms, logic and theorem proving, speech and picture analysis or the development of learning algorithms. Although all these research areas are also relevant for intelligent software agents, there are a number of significant differences [Maes 1994b].

- Classical AI is particularly concerned with closed systems that have only a limited interaction with the environment. Although their internal knowledge provides AI systems with knowledge of their environment, they are not capable of directly interacting with it. Rather, a specially trained user provides the system with knowledge about the environment, often using a symbology that only experts can understand. Experts are also required to interpret and use the solution developed by the system. Consequently, this interaction between the AI system and the environment, that at best can be described as indirect communication, is performed exclusively in the form of a human expert. In contrast, agents must be able to communicate and interact directly with their environment. Because they are frequently used in very dynamic environments, they must be capable of detecting changes directly and with a minimum of delay. A direct communication with other agents is also required for the solution of complex problems.

- Classical AI systems normally possess highly complex, extensive knowledge within a very limited field. In contrast, intelligent agents are often build from many, less complex modules. The total intelligence of an agent system is the result of the cooperation of many simple agents and not the result of the development of individual, highly-complex systems. Another factor to be taken into consideration is the requirement that untrained users must be able to use an agent. Complicated input mechanisms and complex procedures for knowledge or problem determination are not practicable for this reason.

- The standardized knowledge representation mechanisms used by traditional AI systems permit them to process and solve special tasks. However, because the majority of their components are static, the problem must be known in advance. It is not normally possible to change goals dynamically during program execution, for example to take account of new situations. Intelligent agents choose a completely opposite approach. Their internal structure must be designed for dynamic environments. Only this makes it possible for them to formulate new problems and goals (proactivity) that do not need to be specified by their user.

The combination of these reasons has the result, that, although traditional AI can help solve a number of problems in the development of intelligent agents, it can provide only limited impulses for the improvement of its central components and tasks.

4.1.2 Distributed Artificial Intelligence

Distributed artificial intelligence (DAI) attempts to compensate for the deficiencies of classical AI with regard to the development of intelligent agents. It is concerned with the design of distributed, interacting systems and associated questions. Consequently, it concentrates on the development of organization structures, problem solution strategies, and cooperation and coordination mechanisms for a range of distributed, knowledge-based problem-solving modules. In analogy to the human problem-solving process, DAI makes use of teams of experts who can use constructive cooperation to solve problems that for reasons of their complexity would exceed the capabilities of every individual team member.

The widely used classification of DAI developed by Bond/Gasser in 1988 differentiates three significant subareas: parallel AI, distributed problem solving, and multi-agent systems (see Figure 4.1/2) [Bond/Gasser 1988]. Parallel AI primarily investigates the extent to which complex problem situations can be accelerated by their distribution to a larger number of resources. Distributed hardware and software are used to attempt to divide traditional AI systems into a number of parallel processes and so increase to the speed of processing. Because distributed problem solution strategies or cooperation and coordination mechanisms play only a minor role here, parallel AI has not achieved any great importance for the development of intelligent agents.

Within the area of distributed problem solving, the attempt is made to find solution methods to the question to the extent to which complex problems can be solved by the assignment to modules that cooperate with each other by exchanging their knowledge. In contrast to parallel AI, distributed problem solving concentrates on the cooperation aspect. The solution process chosen as part of the distributed problem solution consists of the three individual steps: problem division, solution of the subproblems using independent modules, and combining the subsolutions into a complete solution (see Section 4.3.2). Every module processes its assigned subproblem and can make use of other modules' knowledge. The development of algorithms has proven to be an exacting task for which it is useful to divide and allocate problems, and that permits a goal-oriented cooperation of the individual modules. The algorithms and procedure models of distributed problem solving are based on the assumption that the agents operating within the complete system have been designed by a central developer [Green et al. 1997]. Thus, they always follow complementary goals, because the efficiency of the complete system has priority

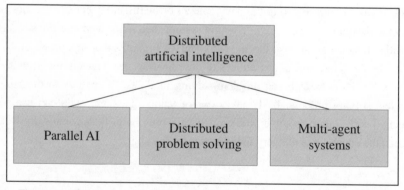

Figure 4.1/2: Subareas of distributed artificial intelligence [Bond/Gasser 1988]

for its developer and the agent is designed appropriately. For this reason, it can be assumed that all agents are prepared to cooperate, which is designated in technical terminology as 'benevolent agent assumption'.

Distributed problem solving requires that the problems are known at the start of the development. This is the only way of ensuring the design of the appropriate number of modules and the processing of the subproblems by experts. This is called a top-down methodology, because the system to be developed is designed for the current problem. The third areas of DAI, the multi-agent systems, choose an opposite approach here. They extend existing agents with communication and interaction capabilities; this is then a bottom-up process. This has the advantage that multi-agent systems can solve problems that have not been envisaged during system development. Consequently, they are not developed for a specific task, but have been designed generally for the common solution of problems. Instead of being primarily concerned with the division of problems, the multi-agent systems concentrate on the form of the actual agents. Consequently, this area concentrates on topics such as conflict recognition and rectification, the creation of non-contradictory goal-systems and the strategic behavior of agents [Kirn 1996].

In contrast to distributed system solving, different people normally develop the agents of multi-agent systems, which are then included in the complete system. Thus, it cannot be assumed that all agents are interested in achieving an overall goal in the most efficient manner. Indeed, conflicting goals occur in reality, and every agent of a multi-agent system is primarily interested in achieving its own particular goal. The 'benevolent agent assumption' does not apply in this case.

DAI has developed a number of paradigms and methods. These include, in particular, the blackboard principle, the contract-net system and the partial global planning method. Because all three methods are described in detail in Section 4.3, only a brief classification is made here. A blackboard provides distributed problem-saving modules with a common data area in which they can save all required information. The blackboard assumes full responsibility for the communication of the modules, the exchange of knowledge and the gathering of partial solutions. The special procedure used for the coordination as part of the contract net system permits those modules involved in solving the problem to divide the individual subproblems in the most efficient manner. Any module can offer its services to solve those subproblems for which it considers itself to be particularly capable. A manager module provided with the appropriate authorizations selects that module from all interested modules it considers to be most qualified. This permits every subproblem to be solved in the shortest possible time and makes optimum use of the knowledge available in the complete system. In partial global planning, every module itself has responsibility for the solution of its subproblem. However, it has access to the communications and interaction processes between all modules of the system and can form the appropriate conclusions for its own situation.

Within DAI, in particular in the area of multi-agent systems, there are three basic questions of interest that also determine this book's structure [Müller 1993]:

- What are intelligent agents and how do they differ from traditional software modules (see Sections 4.3 and 4.2)?

- Which capabilities for cooperation exist for systems of several agents (see Sections 4.3 and 4.4)?

- Which application areas are suitable for agent systems, that is, which problems can be solved efficiently using intelligent agents (see Section 4.6)?

DAI provides initial answers to all three questions, although developments, in particular for the last two items, can by no means be considered to be complete. In contrast to classical AI, DAI does not define an agent as a software program that is just a combination of classical AI modules (knowledge base, learning module, communications module). Rather, it makes clear that other emphases must be set for the development of intelligent agents, and, in extreme situations, the use of classical AI components must be fully rejected. The division of intelligent agents into reactive and deliberative agents (see Section 4.2.1) typical nowadays is the primary result of this discussion. Reactive agents possess no explicit internal knowledge representation. They react to specific, standard events, by using sensors to monitor their environment and to look for specific situations that agree with their internal recognition patterns. If one of the known situations occurs, the handling algorithm associated with this situation is performed and so produces a response from the agent. In contrast to reactive agents, deliberative agents possess explicit knowledge of their environment. Consequently, a deliberative agent is not dependent on just recognizing changes but can make independent decisions concerning the environment based on its internal knowledge.

Once the basic architecture of an intelligent agents has been clarified, it remains to make decisions on the various types of cooperation between one the many agents of existing systems. Questions on the organization form, communication, but also on the cooperation and coordination, take priority here. Similarly to human work groups, it is possible to envisage multi-agent systems that have different organization forms, such as hierarchical, peer, self-organizing, or market-oriented structures. Communication is performed using blackboards or through the direct exchange of messages. It is possible to envisage special cases of agent systems without any communication [Rosenschein et al. 1986]. The cooperation and coordination strategies build on the base formed by the communications capability. They form a significant capability of multi-agent systems and actually decide over the possible degree of complexity of the problems to be solved.

The questions fundamental for the practical use are part of the definition of useful application areas and scenarios for intelligent agents. DAI has also supplied here a range of knowledge that is primarily concerned with the determination problems particularly suitable for agent systems. However, it must be appreciated that many of the practical application areas of intelligent agents did not originate as a result of DAI knowledge but mainly as the result of user demands and structures of the current information landscape.

4.1.3 Network and Communications Systems

In addition to AI/DAI knowledge, developments in the area of networks and communications systems play the most important role in the design of intelligent agents. Almost every agent or every multi-agent system is dependent on the existence of a functioning network infrastructure to fulfill its tasks. For example, if an agent requires specific information which it does not itself possess and is not currently available on its computer system, it can use a communications network to access remote information sources. Also contact to other agents is normally performed using a network, because multi-agent systems are often distributed systems whose individual components, agents, are active on different computers.

The two described scenarios for information acquisition and inter-agent communication represent the classic usage scenarios of a network. The area of intelligent agents adds a further important aspect. A mobile agent uses the available communication network to move itself between various points within the network. The network transmission of a complete program object during its runtime is almost unknown in classical software applications. This means that the functionality and reliability of the communication medium are of existential importance for the mobile agents.

The communications demands and capabilities of intelligent agents are high. Thus, an agent should not consider the communications network to be purely passive, as is normally the case for traditional applications systems, but should actively follow its status and react independently to changes. [Ranganathan et al. 1996] in this context speak of network-aware systems. For example, a mobile agent must continually monitor the network it uses for changes with regard to the bandwidth of certain subconnections or the specific number of accessible computer systems. If a mobile agent determines that a specific computer no longer belongs to the network or that a specific transmission link is temporary overloaded, the mobile agent makes allowance for this in its planning. Because of the central importance of the network for its activities, it is not sufficient to rely passively on the functionality of other components, such as a router.

To separate agents from the implementation-specific details of a communication network, they are based on a multi-level service model such as the seven layer Open System Interconnection (OSI) model of the International Standards Organization (ISO) shown in Figure 4.1/3. In the OSI model, every layer provides specific services to the above layer. For example, the physical layer provides the data link layer with a service to transfer individual bits over a communications channel. Consequently, the data link layer no longer needs to concern itself with the transfer and conversion of bits at the network card of the system, but can use the bit transmission layer service provided for this purpose.

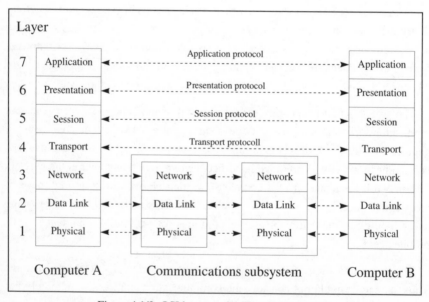

Figure 4.1/3: OSI layer model [Tanenbaum 1989]

The data link layer itself provides the next-higher layer, in this case the network layer, with a service for the secure transmission of data frames. Whereas the data link layer provides only services for the transmission of individual bits, the network layer can use a more powerful service for the transmission of complete data packets. Each higher layer continues this increasing level of abstraction until the application layer is reached. The application layer implements functions such as e-mail, file transfer or directory services, which are almost completely hidden from the details of the network infrastructure and communications mechanisms.

The protocols provided by the OSI layer model (see Figure 4.1/3) perform an important role in its practical use. A precisely defined protocol exists between two corresponding layers of the OSI model. This specifies how to form the communication between two applications based on a particular layer using the services of the next-lower layer. Only the existence of protocols makes possible the understanding between two remote applications. For example, the presentation protocol is available if two program objects of the presentation layer wish to communicate with each other. The presentation protocol uses services of the session layer to specify the procedure to be used for the communication and which functionality is to be provided. [Tanenbaum 1989] contains a detailed introduction of the principles of the OSI layer model and the tasks of the individual layers.

The application protocols provided by the model assume particular importance for intelligent agents (which are normally part of the application layer). Consequently, the application layer in agent-based systems is often divided into several further layers each with a different degree of abstraction. The base software of mobile agents described in Section 4.2.2.3 provides protocols and components for all agent-specific functionalities, that exceed the usual communications mechanisms, in the form of layers is an example.

Intelligent agents and multi-agent systems are usually realized as client-server systems. In the classical client-server architecture, a computer, the server, provides specific services that are used by one or more other computers, the clients. This rigid partitioning is not appropriate in agent systems, rather the agent's role changes according to the situation. For example, an agent can provide services at one time, that is, adopt the role of a server, and request services at another time, that is, act as a client. It is even possible to envisage the concurrent client and server. In addition, agents, because of their autonomy property, can never be comparable with classical servers. Even an agent that acts as server is not a passive service provider, such as the server within a classical client-service system, rather it can always decide whether it wants to continue or change its role. An agent can also change the service offering significantly more dynamically and individually. For these reasons, extended communications mechanisms based on the concepts of the classical client-server systems must be implemented in agent systems.

4.2 Architecture

The aim of this section is to present the central, architectonic components and the various forms of intelligent agents. The influences of the previously discussed research directions, that are reflected in the agent architecture, make this task more difficult. The consideration of an agent as a black-box system, based on the generally accepted model for software modules (see Figure 4.2/1), is a minimum layer.

An agent in the black-block concept receives a range of inputs that it accepts using a perception component. It uses its intelligence to process these inputs and produces an output, usually in the form of initiated actions. In contrast to the classical input-processing-output principle of data processing, an agent must possess intelligent processing mechanisms. An agent requires its intelligence to provide its significant characteristics, such as autonomy, cooperation or proactivity, and so differ from traditional software programs.

The representation of an agent as a black box is accepted in all scientific disciplines, because the model is kept sufficiently general and so can satisfy all special requirements. However, from the architectonic viewpoint, it provides only very rudimentary information on the specific internal structure of an intelligent agent. Figure 4.4/2 goes one step further and shows the agent's work processes in a form that can be used later as basis for the development of concrete, task-specific mod-

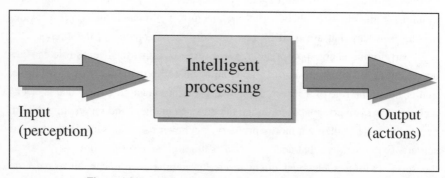

Figure 4.2/1: Agent as black box (based on [Müller 1996])

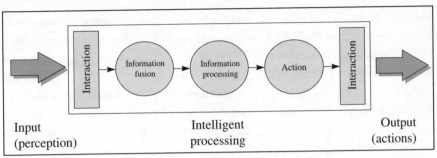

Figure 4.2/2: Work processes of an intelligent agent

ules and components. An agent possesses one or more interaction modules for the communication and cooperation with its environment. An agent's environment can consist of other agents, human users or any information sources. For every environment object type an agent normally has its own interaction module that is specially matched to the capabilities and particularities of the corresponding interaction partner. The agent uses the interaction modules to obtain information and changes within its environment, and also to initiate its own actions. Thus, the interaction modules provide both its input and output interface

The central task of most agents is not to interact with the environment but rather process and interpret the perceived information and to achieve its own goals. For this purpose, all incoming information must be first integrated in an appropriate manner and accepted in the agent's knowledge base. This process is designated as information fusion in the diagram. The information fusion assumes particular importance when observations arrive from various interaction modules that may be contradictory or present in different forms of representation. For example, the information provided by a human user may differ in both form and content from that of an agent, event though they may apply to the same topic. The information fusion process must recognize and correct such inconsistencies.

Once the agent has accepted the new external information, this can be processed in the next step. The information processing process forms the central component of an agent, because it reflects the agent's true functionality. The aim of the information processing is to interpret the available data and to form specific plans. Because every agent follows a specific goal, the effects of the new situations on the internal goals must be determined as part of the interpretation of the effects. The agent must act if effects are recognized. The new situation provides it with the possibility of getting nearer to its goal or confronts it with a problem that stands in the way of reaching its goal and so needs to be solved. The agent can specify its knowledge in the form of a plan that contains the specific processing steps as reaction to the new situation. However, this is not essential, because an agent can react without a previous planning. The agent passes those actions it considers appropriate to the action module, which then performs them. The action module uses the services of the appropriate interaction modules when an action requires the interaction with an object of the environment. The monitoring of the execution also belongs to the action module's task.

Not all the agent's actions need to represent the reaction to new situations. Rather, an agent can also act proactively and create new plans itself. For example, if an agent knows that one of its important information queries can be started only at a specific time, it performs it at this time itself without having to wait for the occurrence of a specific situation. The prerequisite here is an internal representation of the agent's environment, in this case the knowledge that the appropriate information provider can be contacted only at a specific time. This knowledge results directly in the central differentiation between deliberative and reactive agents; the following section describes this topic in detail.

4.2.1 Deliberative and Reactive Agents

Deliberative agents assume an explicit symbolic model of the environment and the capability of logical reasoning as basis for intelligent actions, and so maintain the tradition of the classical AI. The modeling of the environment is normally performed in advance and forms the main component of the agent's knowledge base. The actual conversion process and the selection of a suitable representation language are particularly difficult. A procedure must be found that permits a correct, internal model of the agent's environment that has sufficient content to be created with an acceptable effort but which also selects a representation form that provides an adequate degree of modeling functionality. Because of the high complexity of such representations, deliberative agents have only limited suitability for use in dynamic environments. Because the necessary knowledge and the required resources are not normally available, it is difficult for such agents during their execution to add in their existing model new information or knowledge about their environment.

Deliberative agents have as a second significant property, in addition to their internal symbolic environment model, their capability to make logical decisions. The agent, as part of the decision making process, uses the knowledge contained in its

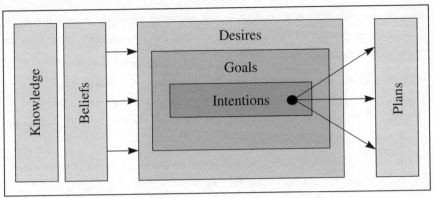

Figure 4.2/3: BDI structure (based on [Rao/Georgeff 1995])

model to modify its internal state. This internal state is often termed the mental state, and is composed of the three base components: belief, desire and intention [Rao/ Georgeff 1995]. Consequently, deliberative agents are often called BDI (belief, desire, intention) agents.

New concepts extend the classical BDI concept with goals and plans, which then provide the five factors that constitute the mental state of a deliberative agent (see Figure 4.2/3) [Müller 1996].

- **Beliefs** contain the fundamental views of an agent with regard to its environment. An agent uses them, in particular, to express its expectations of the possible future states.

- **Desires** are derived directly from the beliefs. They contain the agent's judgments of future situations. For example, an agent can have the desire that a specific future state (contained in its beliefs) occurs but another does not occur. An agent with its formulation of desires has not yet made any statement on the extent to which these are realistic. Thus an agent may well have an unrealistic desire, even though it knows that this will very probably never occur. Even desires that conflict or contradict are possible.

- **Goals** represent that subset of the agent's desires on whose fulfillment it could act. In contrast to its desires, an agent's goals must be realistic and must not conflict with each other. The goals form the agent's potential processing scope, because they represent those processing alternatives available at a specific time.

- **Intentions** are a subset of the goals. If an agent decides to follow a specific goal, this goal becomes an intention. Because an agent does not possess the necessary resources, it cannot normally follow all goals at the same time. Consequently, it must assign priorities to the outstanding goals and process them in accordance with their weighting.

- **Plans** combine the agent's intentions into consistent units. There is a close connection between intentions and plans: intentions constitute the subplans of an agent's overall plan, and, conversely, the set of all plans reflects the agent's intentions.

The results of the BDI model have an effect on the architectonic design of a deliberative agent. Figure 4.2/4 shows the central components of an agent.

The agent's knowledge base contains, in particular, the symbolic model. The desires, goals and intentions are derived from the knowledge base, a task for which the reasoner adopts a central importance. The planner takes the intentions and combines them into a consistent overall plan. This is a dynamic, incremental process. The planner tests new intentions for dependencies with existing plans. For example, the results of an intention can represent the input values of another intention. The planner recognizes and makes allowance for this form of dependency. Existing plans are continually adapted to the situations that result from the arrival of new intentions.

The scheduler receives the current plans from the planner. Every plan consists of a number of single actions that must be processed sequentially or in parallel. The scheduler must decide when specific actions are to be made available for execution.

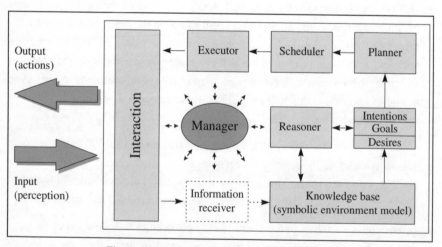

Figure 4.2/4: Architecture of a deliberative agent

For this purpose, it requires a continuous overview of all resources available for the agents. The scheduler assigns an optimum and a latest execution time to every action. The scheduler also specifies details on the maximum runtime and resource usage. The action is passed with this supplementary information to the execution components. The executor executes the next outstanding action, monitors its correct processing, and terminates its execution. The executor can terminate an action if it requires more computer time than provided by the scheduler. The executor returns the action to the scheduler or planner if it cannot be started before the latest specified time.

Figure 4.2/4 shows that a dynamic modification of the internal model is possible only to a limited extent. Although a deliberative agent has access to information receivers, these are infrequently used to extend the knowledge base. The interaction with other agents primarily concerns the pure communication or cooperation.

For reasons of their complexity, deliberative agents cause a range of problems. The central problems of classical AI is reflected almost unchanged also in the use of deliberative agents. The main criticism lies in their rigid structure. Agents work in very dynamic environments. Consequently, they should be capable of making their decisions on the basis of the current situation. However, this is possible only to a very limited extent for deliberative agents. Their intentions and plans are based on the symbolic model that was developed at some specific time in the past and only then minimally updated. The relatively rigid structure of plan-based systems increases this disadvantage. Because the transition of the intentions to the planner, scheduler and executor is very time-extensive, the situation has often already changed to a greater or lesser extent when the time comes to execute a plan. The symbolic algorithms for deliberative agents are normally designed to achieve perfect, provable results, which always leads to a high degree of complexity. A fast reaction with a result of satisfactory quality for the associated situation is often more appropriate in dynamic environments than striving for optimum plans. In contrast, deliberative agents often prefer the mathematical proof of a plan over the efficiency of the planning process.

These considerations lead to a concept diametrically opposed to deliberative agents, so-called reactive agents. Reactive agents do not possess an internal symbolic model of their environment. Even the capability to perform complex reasoning processes is largely omitted. The reason for these restrictions lies in the creation of compact, error-tolerant and, above all, flexible agents. Unlike deliberative agents, reactive agents do not obtain their intelligence from internal models but from the interaction with their environment. The importance of the interaction process is correspondingly high. Supporters of the reactive school in this context even claim that intelligence does not exist within individual systems, such as deliberative agents, but is implicitly part of the complete environment [Brooks 1991]. The intelligence exists and increases only through the continuing interaction of systems.

A reactive agent must not necessarily have a complex structure to be able to act within a complex environment. It suffices to precisely observe the environment and to recognize a range of simple principles or dependencies. This knowledge is used to develop task-specific modules that are capable of continuously checking their environment for the occurrence of specific situations and to initiate a direct reaction when such a situation occurs.

Figure 4.2/5 shows the fundamental architecture of reactive agents that corresponds to a simple stimulus/response system. Sensors record information, forward it to the task-specific competence modules and so produce a reaction of the competence module, which actuators transfer to the environment.

Classical robots are a simple example of a reactive agent. A robot possesses a number of sensors that permit it to observe its environment. For example, it can determine whether it has hit an obstacle, whether objects have changed their position, or whether another robot is active in its vicinity. This information is passed to the robot's competence modules. For example, a competence module with the task of changing the motion direction is always active when a sensor detects an obstacle in the current travel direction. If the motion module has the task of avoiding obsta-

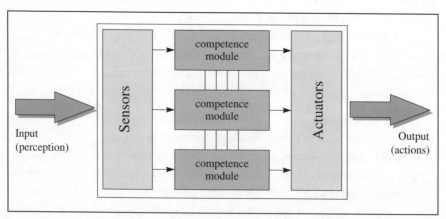

Figure 4.2/5: Architecture of reactive agents (based on [Brooks 1986])

cles, it must change the travel direction of the robot in this example. The required actuators in this case are the front wheels, the alignment of which is changed by the competence module. Other competence modules, for example, could be concerned with the task of moving specific objects, of finding a route to a defined position, or of removing obstacles.

In general, it can be seen that the sensors of a reactive agent permit it to obtain information on its environment and to recognize the occurrence of changed situations. The specific form of the sensors (and also the actuators) depends very heavily on the objects monitored by the sensor. For example, sensors for information recording from people can concentrate on speech or text recognition, whereas sensors that monitor other agents can use simple communications procedures for their work.

The information gathered by a sensor is passed to the corresponding competence module. The transfer is normally made in raw format, that is, no higher communications languages or symbolic representations are used. Every competence module is responsible for a clearly defined, but not particularly complex, task. An information agent, for example, must have modules that search for information sources, collect search results, and present the result. All the properties required to fulfill its tasks are contained within the competence modules. There are no central components, such as the planner or the reasoner of deliberative agents. Every competence module must possess all the capabilities it requires to process its tasks. This architectonic design has a consequence that a reactive agent does not possess any generally usable functionality. A competence module has a precisely specified task and provides a precisely specified solution. A reactive agent cannot solve any task for which no competence module exists. In contrast, deliberative agents are more comprehensively defined. Their central components (reasoner, planner, scheduler) have not been designed with regard to the processing of special tasks, but, depending on the knowledge base content, can be used for a range of general problems.

Because the competence modules work in parallel, many dependencies occur. For this purpose, competence modules can communicate both directly amongst each other or with each other using its environment. The direct communication takes the form of a one-to-one relationship between two components. The communication is based on simple communications mechanisms and not on a complex language. Direct communication has the principal advantage of fast reaction capability. No intermediate modules exist between two competence modules, that is, the receiving competence module accepts and processes a communication invocation without delay. The second case of communication over the environment is realized when a module causes a change in its environment that in turn is observed by another module, which then initiates a response. Although this variant is slower than the direct communication, it permits a reaction to more complex situations.

The decentralized structure of the competence modules increases the fault tolerance and robustness of a reactive agent. If a module fails or operates incorrectly, the agent most probably can continue to perform the majority of its tasks. In contrast, the failure of a central component of a deliberative agent almost always results in the failure of the complete system.

Reactive agents normally do not possess any capabilities to create plans. The extent to which this negatively affects its tasks to be performed cannot be fully determined. Although plans can be used to optimize an agent's behavior and level of objective-attainment, there are factors that play a role, especially in practical applications, that speak against the processing of optimized plans. For example, an agent often possesses only incomplete information on its environment and its own objectives. Its environment is highly dynamic and subject to continuous changes, its own objectives change dynamically, and the resources for the creation of optimum plans are usually not available. This raises the question whether a planning process is appropriate under such conditions.

A further discussion item is concerned with the question whether, and, if yes, to what extent, reactive agents are capable of demonstrating a goal-oriented behavior. The competence modules have at best implicit goals that are defined by their functionality and cannot be changed. Unlike deliberative agents, they cannot use their internal knowledge base to dynamically generate and follow new goals. However, despite these restrictions, many people have the opinion that reactive agents are capable of goal-oriented actions. Similar to intelligence, the goal-orientation results implicitly from the interaction with the environment, and not from the central evaluation or planning. For example, every competence module of the mentioned information agent follows an implicit goal that results from its task. These goals always become apparent when interaction is made with objects of the environment, for example, when an intelligent agent's search query module passes a concrete query for an information source or when a result module presents the user with its results.

The discussion on the advantages and disadvantages, and the different focal points of deliberative and reactive agents, results in the creation of systems that use the advantages of both concepts and attempt to integrate them in a uniform architectonic platform. Such systems are called hybrid architectures or agents. Hybrid agents possess both a reactive and a deliberative component. Whereas the reactive component is primarily used for the interaction with the environment, the deliberative systems (with their symbolic model and complex reasoning capability) concentrate on the area of planning and decision making. The system architect is responsible for the weighting of the individual components and what assumes priority for the decisions. Hybrid systems are normally designed as a hierarchical architecture with an increasing degree of abstraction. The lower levels are formed by reactive systems and are used for the acquisition of raw information. Deliberative components for long-term goal determination and planning are used in the upper levels. Section 4.2.3 contains concrete examples for all three categories of agents (deliberative, reactive, hybrid).

4.2.2 Stationary and Mobile Agents

One of the most important architectonic decisions during the design of intelligent agents is reflected in the distinction between stationary and mobile agents. The criterion of mobility influences not only the agent's internal architecture but also has consequences for the way in which the complete agent system works. Mobile agents are capable of moving freely within an electronic network and the computers contained within it; mobile agents can also communicate with objects of the environment, such as information sources or other agents. The type of the network plays only a subordinate role. It can be, for example, a company-internal LAN, a national WAN or networks that cover the whole world, such as the Internet. It is important that a mobile agent can move from one computer of the network to another without affecting its method of operation. This is called the ability to migrate. In contrast, stationary agents are not capable of leaving their original environment, which is normally the computer system on which they were created. Although they can send messages to remote objects, they do not possess the functionality needed to move themselves to another computer.

Even when the image of intelligent agents provided by popular scientific literature almost always corresponds to mobile agents, mobility is only an optional capability. It is neither an essential nor a necessary requirement for an intelligent agent. Mobility by itself does not turn a software program into an intelligent agent. The other characteristics of intelligent agents, such as autonomy, communication, cooperation and reactivity have the same importance, and only the combination of as many of these characteristics as possible can create a true intelligent agent. It should also be noted that almost all tasks of mobile agents can also be performed by stationary agents, however, not always with an appropriate effort. The following example illustrates this.

We assume that an intelligent agent has been assigned the task to search within the Internet for information concerning a particular book. Although this task can be potentially performed by either a stationary or a mobile agent, there are fundamental differences in the resulting method of operation. A stationary agent proceeds as follows: it first searches a suitable database for the addresses of the most important virtual bookstores present in the Internet. The stationary agent must use the network to pass a search query to the database and receives the corresponding address details as result from the network. Its next step is to question each of the determined bookstores with the information required by the user. To perform this task, the stationary agent must use the network to send the queries to every book dealer and then receive the results back over the network. The situation will frequently arise in which significantly more information is returned from the book dealer than the agent really wanted. Even less relevant search results must be transported over the network, because only the agent can decide whether a specific information item matches the user's wishes. It is obvious that a stationary agent not only generates an unnecessary high network load to perform its book search, but also requires a continuous network connection. It must continuously send and receive information. The communication costs for its user for the simple search are correspondingly high.

A mobile agent can solve the described task more flexibly and elegantly. It goes directly to the computer that contains the addresses of the book dealers as soon as it has received the information it needs for its search from its user. Once it has arrived there, the connection of its user to the network can be terminated, and the mobile agent is now capable of performing locally all queries to the database. Once the mobile agent has determined the book dealers of interest, it goes directly to each of the dealer's servers. It makes its query for the user's information on each of the servers and collects the corresponding results. These are also local transactions because no data needs to be transferred over the network. In contrast to its stationary counterpart, the mobile agent is able to directly reject any information that is not relevant and only take the data of real importance, that is, to transport these data over the network. Once it has questioned the last book dealer, the mobile agent returns to its original computer. Only now does the connection between the original computer and the network need to be reestablished; and this only for the relatively short time needed to transfer the agent.

To summarize, the use of mobile agents brings a number of benefits for the user. His communications costs are significantly lower; for reasons of the low data transmission volumes, the low transmission speeds typical between end-users and public networks become less important; there is insignificant load on the resources of the original computer, because all work steps are executed and processed on other computers within the network. Obviously, the resource demands made on the associated server systems increase at the same time, because these must execute and support the mobile agents.

4.2.2.1 Introduction

Both traditional software programs and stationary agents use primarily the Remote Procedure Call (RPC) for remote work. The communication between two program modules with RPC is the same as the call of a procedure of a remote module (see Figure 4.2/6).

For example, if a stationary agent wants to use the services of a different software program within the network, it uses a message, the so-called request, to pass his intention to invoke a specific procedure. The required procedure is then processed on the remote computer and the results, also in the form of a message (reply), are returned to the agent.

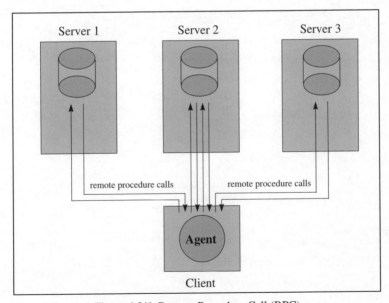

Figure 4.2/6: Remote Procedure Call (RPC)

The communication using RPC is always performed in accordance with the client-server principle. A computer, the client, uses a service of another computer, the server. All messages sent over the network are either request or reply messages and travel using standardized protocols. The protocols must be known in advance, that is, the available services and the call parameters required for every service must be fully defined before the start of the communication. If a specific service is to be used more than once, a separate RPC is required for each invocation. For example, if a client wishes to use a search provided by the server to search a server's data files for various criteria, it must generate an RPC for every search query. The resulting high network load, together with the rigid protocol structures, limits the practical usefulness of the RPC for many application scenarios.

The principle of remote programming (RP) forms the technical basis for all mobile agents. In contrast to the classical Remote Procedure Call, the communication between two objects in RP does not take the form of the exchange of request and reply messages. Instead, the client's calling procedure itself is transferred to the server in question and then executed locally there (see Figure 4.2/7). Thus, the remote procedure calls become local procedure calls at the remote computer. The required data parameters are passed with the procedure. Instead of the request and reply messages of the RPC, the network traffic for RP consists of messages that

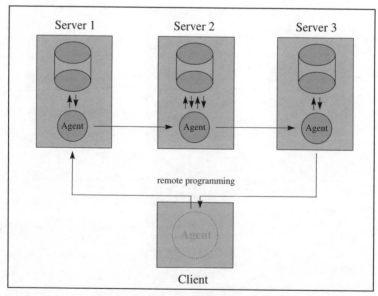

Figure 4.2/7: Remote programming (RP)

Communication	Properties	Agents
remote programming	high intelligence flexible	mobile
remote procedure call SQL queries	low intelligence proprietary protocols closed environment	stationary

Figure 4.2/8: Comparison between RP and RPC

contain the procedure and the associated data structures. Such messages correspond in their conduct to a mobile agent. RP´s primary advantage lies in its greater flexibility and the lower network load. It is no longer necessary to be limited to fixed procedure calls defined in advance. Instead, only a general mechanism needs to be defined that is used to transfer procedures and to execute on remote computers. The network load is also reduced, because the interaction between client and server no longer takes place exclusively over the network, but contains only a single transmission action and subsequent local procedure calls.

Figure 4.2/8 provides a final comparison between RP and RPC. RP distinguishes itself from RPC primarily through its higher intelligence. Although RPC or classical SQL queries can be used to perform information filtering on the server, mobile agents that adhere to the principles of RP have a significantly higher intelligence and flexibility in this regard.

4.2.2.2 Advantages and Disadvantages of Mobile Agents

The unquestionable advantages of mobile agents are counteracted by a number of important disadvantages. The major disadvantages are the unsolved security problems and the high demands made on the technical infrastructure. The aim of this section is to provide in structured form the arguments for and against the use of mobile agents.

Mobile agents that use the principles of remote programming inevitably accept with this decision the associated advantages and disadvantages. The following points, in particular, have shown themselves to be advantageous:

- **Reduced network load**. The reduction in network traffic provides one of the significant advantages of mobile agents and has already been mentioned in previous discussions. Because mobile agents can perform most of their tasks locally on the appropriate server, the volume of data transferred over the network is reduced to a minimum. In addition to the actual agents, only that information needs to be transported that is really of interest to the user of the agent. In particular for storage-intensive media, such as picture, video or audio data, it can be a decisive advantage that not every graphic investigated in the course of an inquiry needs to be transferred over the network, but on completion of the inquiry only those that have been classified as being relevant. The reduced network load brings advantages for the private users of mobile agents. Their communications costs are lower, because they are normally billed either for the duration of the connection time or according to the volume of transferred data. Both values are lower when mobile agents are used.

- **Reduced resource usage of the client**. Mobile agents use the capacities and resources of the remote server to process their tasks. A user of mobile agents may detect a significant reduction of load on his own computer system. On the other hand, the capacity of the server will need to be increased correspondingly, because they are loaded not just with the invocations and processing of their own procedures but must also provide additional resources for the operation of mobile agents.

- **Asynchronous processing**. In contrast to stationary agents that do not need to operate asynchronously, mobile agents always operate asynchronously. Their users provide them with specific tasks, they move to various servers to solve the tasks, and then return later with the appropriate results. The user does not need to monitor the agent during its work. He can even terminate the connection to the network in an optimum situation. A network reconnection must be established only when the mobile agent is ready to return to the original computer. This connection is needed for the time to transfer the agent. The asynchronous, autonomous operation of a mobile agent brings its user time savings and also reduced communications costs.

- **Reconfigurable services**. Traditional software programs that use RPC for communication provide only very limited capabilities to adapt to the user's individual requirements; both the range of callable procedures of the remote server, and the type and number of the invocation parameters are predefined. Special user requirements, for example the wish for an individual search query, can be realized only when the appropriate procedure is developed and offered on the server. The use of mobile agents avoids this problem. A mobile agent contains procedures specific for the user and can itself go to a remote server. The procedures do not have to be developed and provided by the server operator, but are provided by the agent itself. The action takes place fully dynamic, because the agent can be installed and executed on the remote server. If, for example, a server of a book dealer provides procedures to search its data files for either authors or book titles, the traditional usage does not offer any possibility to perform more complex searches, unless they have been explicitly provided by the dealer. In contrast, a mobile agent can contain procedures for more complex search transactions that are built on the basis of the simple procedures provided by the server, for example a combined author and title search. Because the mobile agent goes to the book dealer's server where it is also executed, it appears to its user that the server offers the complex search provided by the agent. The user is not concerned with who provides the extended functionality, but only that it is made available. Mobile agents permit reconfigurable, personalized services that would not be conceivable with traditional RPCs.

- **Active behavior**. The capability of mobile agents to go to remote computer systems makes active behavior scenarios conceivable. A provider can use mobile agents to directly provide new services for potential customers by developing the appropriate agents and then sending them to the customer's computers [Magedanz et al. 1996]. For example, mobile agents can be used for the distribution of software or the automatic installation of new software versions in a way that is largely transparent for the user. Mobile agents provide customers not only with spontaneous access to new services but no longer require that the customers themselves become active. The involved providers also have advantages. In addition to the possibility of active customer involvement, the main advantages can be seen in the significantly more flexible and more dynamic distribution capabilities of new services and service offerings.

- **Decentralized structure**. Mobile agents support the classical client-server paradigm. However, their mobility permits them to create decentralized structures to a significantly greater extent than traditional software programs. Unlike the RPC, processing is not distributed over only two computers. A mobile agent can with skillful planning distribute its work to different servers. If an intelligent network management system is available that can recognize any overloading of individual network nodes and free capacity on other nodes, the mobile agent can be guided appropriately to perform its resource-intensive work on those servers that are currently less busy. A delay is also possible, for example, when temporary peak loads cause a short-term full load of the complete network. The mobile agent in this situation can delay the further processing of its work or advance those substeps that cause only a low network load.

The use of mobile agents raises a number of questions. These concern both the general problems of the mobility of program objects, for example, the security aspect, and the restrictions that result from the still-young development history of mobile agents that currently occur in the practical implementation and relate, in particular, to the areas of migration, efficiency, standardization and billing systems. The central problem of mobile agents is the security problem that remains unsolved in significant aspects. This central problem is composed of several subproblems: the identification and authentication of the associated components; the protection from virus-related mobile agents with malicious and destructive program functions; and ensuring the agent's ability and willingness to pay. Section 4.5 contains a detailed description of all three subareas as part of the general security discussion.

In addition to the security problem, mobile agents are currently subject to a number of technical hurdles. The most important of these are:

- **Transport/migration**. High demands are made on the software environments used by the clients and servers for the migration of agents. A number of complex software modules and layers are needed to transport an agent and to perform the listed security validations. Because such components are currently available only in preliminary form, the practical use of mobile agents is limited.

- **Efficiency**. It cannot yet be predicted what actual load will be produced by a large number of mobile agents. For example, currently only limited information is available how servers should be designed on which hundreds or even thousands of agents are concurrently active and which network load a large number of agents would actually produce.

- **Standards/interoperability**. Mobile agents are only appropriate when they have a large number of access points. This makes the definition and agreement of standards very necessary. Every involved server must provide the mobile agent with a standard system environment in which it can be executed. Furthermore, standards must be developed for the management of agents, the creation of common user directories and the communication between agents. Standards are also important for stationary agents, however not to the same degree as within the heterogeneous, distributed environments in which mobile agents are normally used.

- **Billing systems**. The costs incurred by mobile agents cannot be recorded without detailed facilities for measuring and billing resource consumption. In this regard, standards must be produced for the accounting systems within the server, and financial billing systems to efficiently invoice the resulting costs must be made available.

4.2.2.3 Technical Implementation

Figure 4.2/9 shows the design of the software architecture of a server that supports the execution of mobile agents.

Every computer system can build on the operating system to provide a base software that performs the integration of the mobile agents in the complete system and provides sufficient base functionality for the operation of mobile agents. The base software forms the interface between the mobile agents and the actual operating system of the computer. The agents are built on top of the base software. They possess different degrees of functionality depending on the task.

From the communications viewpoint, a number of communications paths and capabilities must be differentiated in such an architecture. For example, a mobile agent can communicate directly with the base software by invoking one of the procedures provided by the base software. It receives the answer in the form of return parameters of the associated procedure. An inter-agent communication is conceivable if several agents are concurrently active in a system that have the ca-

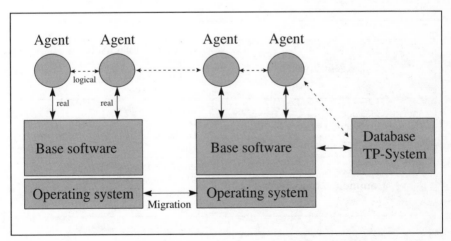

Figure 4.2/9: Software architecture of a mobile agent system

pability to communicate with each other. Such a communication can be made in two ways. In the first variant, two agents communicate directly with each other by sending each other messages or invoking their provided procedures. This is the more flexible method and provides the agents with the maximum freedom. However, the base software, and thus also the server, has little chance of following and controlling the actions of the agents. Consequently, many security aspects remain to be resolved. The base software is included in the communication between two agents in the second, more restrictive, variant. An agent can only communicate directly with the base software. The access to other agents is made in the same manner. If, for example, a mobile agent wants to communicate with another agent that is currently active on the server, it invokes one of the procedures provided by the base software for this purpose with the appropriate communications parameters. The base software passes the query to the other agent. Thus the logical communications connection between the two agents actually consists of two real connections between the associated agents and the base software.

The connection of traditional database and transaction systems provides a further communications interface. An agent must use a base software procedure, for example a search function, if it wishes to access information in an external database. The base software then extracts the required data from the database and returns them to the agent. A direct connection between agent and database is neither possible nor desired.

The base software of mobile agent systems is made up of three layers that build on each other (see Figure 4.2/10).

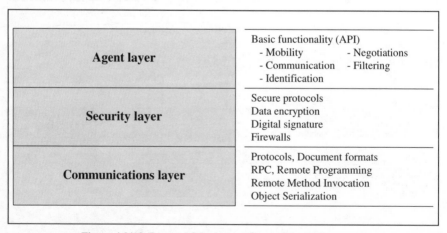

Figure 4.2/10: Layers of the base software for mobile agents

- **Agent layer**. The agent layer has the primary task of the execution and monitoring of all active agents on a computer. It is quite possible that several hundred agents are present at any one time on a computer in a large system. The agent layer must provide all these agents with a standard work environment and execute them independent of each other, that is, process their program code. Furthermore, it must provide them with basic functionality. Figure 4.2/11 shows the most important functions of the agent layer in tabular form.

  The agent uses the *move* command to go from one computer to another; the agent must provide the agent layer with its agent Id and the required target system address. The agent Id is a unique number that is created when the system creates the agent. The agent Id serves to uniquely identify the agent during its lifetime. The agent layer then transports the agent to the target address. The action is completely transparent for the agent, that is, it requires just a simple move command and then the next command is performed in the new system environment. The communications layer provides the basic functionality and methods used by the agent layer for the migration.

  The following section provides a detailed description of the fundamental communications model and the flow of a typical communication between mobile agents. An agent must first identify itself when it arrives at a new computer. It is also possible to make the identification before the arrival of the agent, for example, even before it leaves its original computer. The agent uses the *identify* command provided by the agent layer. The newly arrived agent has no rights on the system until a successful identification has been made and so cannot execute any other functions. The agent has relatively limited rights even after the identification. It can invoke the commands and the associated resources provided by the agent layer.

Command	Parameters	Function
move	agent-id, address	Movement
identify	agent-id, personal-key, agent-type	Identification
getAvailableAgent	agent-id, agent-type	Determine available agents
contact	agent-id, agent-id	Contact local agents
sendCommand	agent-id, agent-id, command	Invoke function of another agent
sendMessage	agent-id, agent-id/agent-type, [address], message	Send message to other agents

Figure 4.2/11: Central functions of the agent layer

The agent provides its agent Id, its agent type and its user's personal identification key (see Figure 4.2/12, step 1). Every system user has a personal identification key that his agents must keep with them (see Section 4.5). The agent layer uses this key to check the correct identification of the agent and enters it in a local agent list after it has been validated (see Section 4.5). The local agent list provides a directory of all agents currently active in the system. Every entry in the list contains the agent Id, the status of the agent, for example available or busy, and the agent type, for example information agent or transaction agent. The agent type serves as a resource for other agents, because the type can be used to determine the functions made available by an agent. A buying agent can use the agent type of its communications partner to determine whether it is involved with a selling agent that, for example, possesses a negotiating function, or with a pure information agent that does not provide any negotiation mechanisms. It must be noted that following the identification, only the agent layer knows the true identity of the new agent and consequently also that of its user. The agent remains anonymous to the applications that build on the agent layer. Other agents can identify a new agent only when it is prepared to provide its identity by transmitting an appropriate message.

If an agent does not know the exact agent Id of its communications partner, it can invoke the *getAvailableAgent* command and pass the agent type of the re-

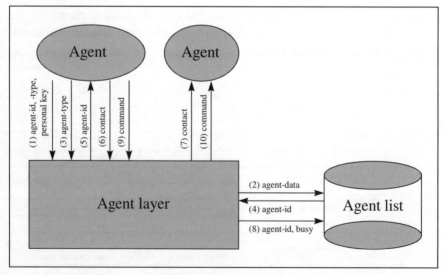

Figure 4.2/12: Communication flow between agent and agent layer

quired partner as parameter (step 3). The agent layer informs the communications partner with the agent-Id of an available agent (steps 4+5). The *contact* command is used to contact an available agent (steps 6-7). Once contact has been established, the communicating agents can set their status in the local agent list to busy and so inhibit further contact attempts (step 8). However, an agent can communicate in parallel with several agents. Once the contact has been established between two agents, they can use the *sendCommand* command to communicate with each other. The *command* parameter contains the required function call with parameters (steps 9+10). As mentioned previously, the commands that an agent understands depend on its type and not on the agent layer. The use of the *sendCommand* command means that the communication between two agents always takes place indirectly using the agent layer. A direct inter-agent communication is not possible.

The *sendMessage* command is the last basic command of the agent layer. An agent can use it to transfer a message to a local or remote agent. Together with the actual message, it must supply its Agent Id, the Id of the receiver, and possibly the system address of the remote computer. The agent receives an appropriate acknowledgment from the agent layer if the transfer to the agent was successful.

- **Security layer**. The security layer provides functions that permit the secure transfer of messages and objects within the network, such as mobile agents. Security in this context means that an object cannot be altered or read by unauthorized parties during its transmission, and also no unauthorized object can enter the system. The security layer is not responsible for security violations by agents already registered in the system; as mentioned previously, the agent layer has responsibility here. However, the agent layer can use the functions provided by the security layer, such as digital signatures or certificates. Section 4.5 provides a detailed introduction to the security topic.

- **Communications layer**. The communications layer contains the specifications of the transmission protocols and detailed document and object formats. The aim is the provision of base functions for the communication between remote computers and the transmission of documents or objects between these computers. The communications layer services are primarily used for the transfer of agents. In particular, services such as *Remote Procedure Call (RPC)*, *Remote Programming (RP)* or *Object Serialization* must be implemented. Functions for *object serialization* are of fundamental importance for the use of mobile agents.

Object serialization permits the conversion of an object into a serial data stream, the transfer to a remote computer, and the reconstruction there of the original object from the data stream. Not only the actual program code of the object but also its current state and its system environment must be expressed in serial form.

4.2.2.4 Migration

From a technical viewpoint, the migration process constitutes one of the most complex tasks in the use of mobile agents. The communication and agent layer must clarify two important questions to achieve an unrestricted migration capability. Firstly, a method must be provided to transport program objects, such as mobile agents, between two computers. Secondly, it must be determined which components are to be transferred during the migration of an agent, i.e., what constitutes an agent. Because mobile agent systems are almost always implemented with the use of an object-oriented development language, it is relatively easy to find an answer to the second question. The identity of a mobile agent is formed by its program code, which is present as agent-specific classes, and its current state, which is formed by the state of its instance variables. Both components must be transferred during migration, namely the classes that belong to the agent and the values of the instance variables. Care must also be taken that the agent's system environment is identical before and after the migration, or that the agent has been informed beforehand of any changes that have taken place. The environment variables used by an agent are the most important part of the system environment. For example, if an agent uses a number of system variables to store information, these must have the identical form and content after migration to the destination system. The agent cannot be resumed if this is not the case.

The actual migration process can be performed in two different ways. In the first variant, the migration is fully transparent for the agents involved. The agent invokes the move command provided by the agent layer and then does not need to concern itself with any other details of the transfer. The agent and communication layers of the base software perform the tasks involved with the migration. The agent's execution is stopped and all required components brought into a persistent form, for example by being converted into a serial data stream and then written into a file. The components are unpacked and reconstituted on the target system. The agent is started on the target system at the exact position where it was previously interrupted and it can resume its work. It does not receive any information on the migration operation and because of its passive behavior it does not even know that a migration has taken place. This methodology corresponds to the agent layer architecture described in the previous section. The advantages of this generally applicable, fully transparent procedure are counteracted by the disadvantage of requiring a more complex implementation and extensive changes to the runtime environment. However, only this concept provides support for the characteristic of proactivity for an agent.

The second, simpler to implement, concept uses a different methodology. Here the mobile agent to be transported is actively involved in the migration. It is fully responsible before and after the migration to transform any components it requires into a persistent form. It must possess two appropriately designed methods for this purpose with which it can explicitly invoke to perform the read or write operation. The increased effort for the development of such mobile agents is compensated by the significantly reduced effort for the implementation of the system environment, because no extensive changes to the runtime environment are required in this case. The agent has the task to choose an appropriate representation form for its internal state.

4.2.3 Existing Architectures

A wide range of system architectures exists for agent-based systems. Figure 4.2/13 provides an overview, classified into deliberative, reactive and hybrid systems [Müller 1996].

A representative of each category is introduced in the next section: the formal BDI architecture from Rao/Georgeff for deliberative agents, the 'subsumption architecture' from Brooks for reactive agents, and the Interrap architecture from Müller for the hybrid systems.

4.2.3.1 Rao/Georgeff: BDI Agents

Rao/Georgeff developed a model that can be used to implement BDI-based agents (see Section 4.2.1) [Rao/Georgeff 1991, 1995]. The model introduces both a theoretical foundation of the BDI concept, in particular definitions of the basic logic and an introduction of semantics, and also concepts for the practical realization of BDI systems, in particular the definition of a specific BDI interpreter.

	Existing System Architecture	
Deliberative Agents	IRMA (Bratman et al) BDI (Rao, Georgeff) Agent0 (Shoham)	GRATE (Jennings) COSY (Sundermeyer et al) MECCA (Steiner et al)
Reactive Agents	Subsumption Architecture (Brooks) Pengi (Agre, Chapman) Dynamic Action Selection (Maes)	Situated Automata (Kelbin, Rosenschein) AURA (Arkin)
Hybrid Agents	RAP (Firby) AIS (Hayes-Roth, Dabija) Sim_Agent (Sloman, Poli)	Interrap (Müller) Procedural Reasoning Systems (Georgeff, Lansky)

Figure 4.2/13: Agent Architectures (based on [Müller 1996])

Rao/Georgeff assume two properties of BDI-based agents and the environment [Rao/Georgeff 1995]: at any time there is a range of possibilities of how the environment of an agent can change and there is a range of possible actions that the agent itself can perform. For this reason, both the environment and the agent form a non-deterministic system. Decision trees are a suitable structure to describe such systems. Every branch of a tree represents a possible execution path, where the tree nodes represent an environmental state and the transitions between two nodes represent the primitive actions of the agent or events within the environment. Depending on the form of the transition, as agent action or environment event, two types of node can result, so-called choice nodes and chance nodes. The term choice makes clear that the agent has the choice between various actions, whereas chance nodes reflect the unforeseen nature of the environment and thus also indicate the inability to be influenced by the agent.

A specific path through a decision tree represents the agent's objective. The selection of the actions associated with a path provides the specific work steps to be performed by the agent. Because of the existence of chance nodes, problems arise during the practical use of this methodology. An agent does not have any influence which of the possible events associated with a chance node will occur, because this depends entirely on its environment. For this reason, Rao/Georgeff use a possible worlds semantic that is used to eliminate the chance nodes from the decision tree. Figure 4.2/14 illustrates the methodology.

All branches of the tree are processed starting with the root of the decision tree. A new decision tree is generated for every connection that leaves a chance node. Except that the corresponding node is removed and the connection path is connected with the father of the chance node, this new tree is identical to the original tree. This methodology is repeated until all chance nodes have been removed. This produces a series of individual decision trees, each of which reflects a potential state, that is, a "possible world".

Every possible world is connected with a concrete probability value, which reflects the probability of occurrence of the state represented by the decision tree, and result values that indicate the agent's profit for every path of the tree. If functions are formed from this information, an agent can use its reasoning components to make decisions. The probability linked with the possible world is then transformed into a belief-accessibility and the result values into a desire-accessibility function. The agent uses these functions to select the best possible action paths. The action paths are themselves used to form a third function, the intention-accessibility function.

To summarize, the possible worlds model developed by Rao/Georgeff consists of a number of individual possible worlds, each of which is represented by a decision tree. A specific index within a possible world is designated as being a situation

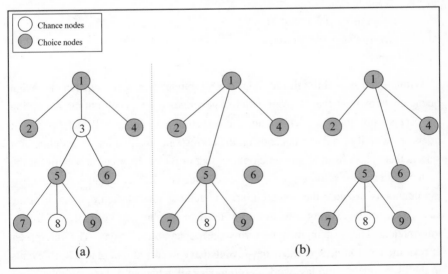

Figure 4.2/14: Possible worlds semantics

[Rao/Georgeff 1995]. A set of belief-accessible, desire-accessible and intention-accessible worlds is associated with every situation. They indicate the set of worlds that an agent considers to be possible (belief), to be desirable and to be invoked (intention).

Rao/Georgeff developed a formal logic based on this model that permits agents to perform reasoning and to form intentions. Because of the complexity of the model, this is not discussed further here. [Rao/Georgeff 1995] and [Müller 1996] contain a detailed discussion. The abstract architecture of a BDI interpreter introduced by Rao/Georgeff is much more relevant for the practical use of BDI agents. Rao/Georgeff thus refute the frequently voiced argument that BDI-based systems are largely unsuited for use in dynamic, realtime-oriented application fields because of their complex axioms and their non-deterministic runtime behavior.

The BDI interpreter uses three dynamic data structures (one each for beliefs, desires and intentions) and an event queue that maintains all events that occur. The interpreter has the following main loop [Rao/Georgeff 1995]:

> *initialize-state( );*
> *repeat*
> > *options:=option-generator(event-queue);*
> > *selected-options:=deliberate(options);*
> > *update-intentions(selected-options);*
> > *execute( );*
> > *get-new-external-events( );*
> > *drop-succesful-attitudes( );*
> > *drop-impossible-attitudes( );*
> *end repeat*

Within each pass through the loop, the interpreter first tests whether the event queue contains new events, from which it generates a series of options. An option represents a possible goal that the agent could attempt to achieve. Which options or goals are actually available depends on the corresponding situation. The deliberator selects that subset from all possible options that provides the greatest benefit for the system using those resources currently available. This subset is added to the existing intentions, because the system intends to achieve the selected options. In some cases a currently existing intention may need to be changed because of the new information. The system then performs the outstanding actions. The interpreter checks the environment whether new events have occurred and places such events in the event queue. The last work step removes all achieved desires and intentions as well as impossible desires and non-attainable intentions from the appropriate data structures.

Although the introduced BDI interpreter represents a distinctive step away from the formal BDI logic to a practice-related concept, a number of questions are deliberately left open. No decisions are made concerning the concrete form of the option generator and the deliberator. In particular, the use of object-oriented applications places high demands on the response time of the components and requires a correspondingly efficient architecture. Because of their complexity, the formal proof mechanisms required to satisfy the tasks of the BDI interpreter can be used only to a limited extent.

Rao/Georgeff are aware of these restrictions, and consequently suggest a number of simplifications that can be used to achieve a practical use of their model. For example, it is possible to consider only those beliefs that relate to the current state of the environment. Information on how an agent plans to satisfy certain desires and which options are available to it can be combined as plans. The plans to be performed are set into runtime stacks, which then implicitly form the intentions of an agent [Rao/Georgeff 1995]. The Procedural Reasoning System (PRS) [Rao/ Lansky 1986] and its further development dMARS (distributed MultiAgentReasoning System) are sample implementations of the mentioned concepts.

4.2.3.2 Brooks: Subsumption Architecture

The subsumption architecture from Brooks is the best known representative of the few reactive agent architectures that exist [Brooks 1986]. Brooks started with the basic assumptions of reactive systems [Woolridge/Jennings 1995]: intelligent behavior is possible even without explicit knowledge representations and abstract reasoning capabilities; and the intelligence is contained implicitly in complex systems, or first occurs with the interaction of the individual agents with their environment. Consequently, the subsumption architecture is characterized by a distributed behavior architecture, the omission of explicit representations and a reflex-like stimulus response reaction pattern, without being influenced by complex modules, such as reasoner, deliberator or planner.

An agent based on the principles of the subsumption architecture consists of a number of hierarchically arranged, task-oriented competence modules. In contrast to classical AI systems and deliberative agents, no functional decomposition takes place, but rather a pure activity-oriented task division. Every competence module of a subsumption architecture is responsible for a specific task, more correctly, for a concrete behavior pattern of the agent. The modules located at the lower end of the hierarchy are responsible for the basic, primitive tasks, whereas the higher modules reflect more complex behavior patterns. In addition, every competence module can operate autonomously and higher modules incorporate a subset of the tasks of the subordinate modules, hence the name subsumption architecture. Figure 4.2/15 illustrates this principle using one of the robots developed by Brooks as example.

The robot's competence module 0 at the lowest level has the capability of avoiding contact or interactions with other modules. The robot can use its sensors to recognize potential obstacles in advance and so initiate an appropriate response. A robot that possesses just this one module is fully functional and forms an autonomous unit. Competence module 1 extends the capabilities of the robot by enabling it to wander indiscriminately in the vicinity. What is important for the subsumptive architecture is that module 1 can monitor and influence the inputs and outputs of module 0. Only in this manner is it possible to achieve a sensible behavior of the robot, that is, wandering around without making contact with obstacles. Thus, module 1 incorporates the functionality of module 0. Similarly, module 2 is added on top of module 1 and permits the robot to explore its environment. Module 2 incorporates the capabilities of module 1, because to explore the environment the robot must look for distant objects that appear to be of interest and then wander over to them.

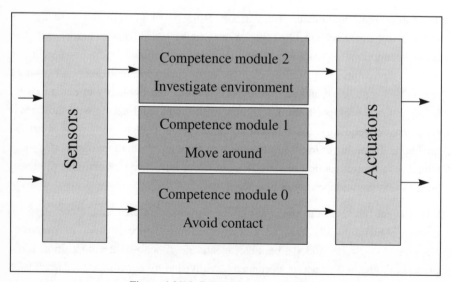

Figure 4.2/15: Subsumption architecture

Every competence module is described using a subsumption language that is based on the principles of Augmented Finite State Machines (AFSM). An AFSM initiates a response as soon as its input signal exceeds a specific threshold value. It should be noted that AFSMs are pure computing units that do not contain any symbolic representations or models. The task or the behavior of an AFSM is defined from the beginning and cannot be modified. Every AFSM operates independently and asynchronously from other AFSMs and is in continuous competition with other competence modules for the control of the agent.

The previously discussed incorporation of the functionality of a subordinate competence module by a higher module is performed using suppressor and inhibitor nodes as shown in Figure 4.2/16. A suppressor node that can be placed within every input signal of a module listens to the input signal, which it modifies if required. The same applies for output signals. An inhibitor node can inhibit the output of a specific signal for a certain period.

Brooks later extended this simple subsumption model to cope with the problems that eventuated with the cooperation and synchronization of a large number of competence modules. Brooks introduced a so-called Behavior Language [Brooks 1990]. This language that was specially developed for the development of complex AFSM structures modeled a concrete behavior pattern for an agent as a group of AFSM competence modules, where suppressor and inhibitor mechanisms also can be active within a group. Every group possesses so-called monostables, that is,

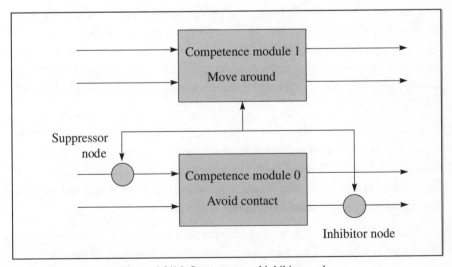

Figure 4.2/16: Suppressor and inhibitor nodes

variables that are active only for a specific period, and registers, that is, variables that can contain a set of values [o.V. 1997a]. Although the variables are visible only within the group, their values can be exchanged with messages between various behavior module groups.

Brooks specially developed the subsumption architecture for the use in dynamic, difficult to predict situations for which a quick response is essential. Although the behavior patterns of the agent or robot developed with its help are not particularly complex, they produce results of such a quality that can only be attained with difficulty using deliberative agents. The simple system structure permits the development of relatively inexpensive systems. However, subsumption architectures are subject to a number of limitations [o.V. 1997b]: the distributed control structure sets limits for the learning and planning capability, complex models cannot be represented in the simple layer structure, and the large number of modules required to create complex behaviors demand a high synchronization and management effort.

4.2.3.3 Müller: Interrap

The Interrap architecture from Müller is a typical example of a hybrid agent system [Müller 1996]. To combine the benefits of the deliberative and reactive concepts, hybrid agents usually possess a multi-layer architecture. Whereas the agent's basic behavior pattern is implemented in the lower layers, which corresponds to the reactive component, the deliberative processes of goal formation, reasoning and planning are performed in the higher layers. This principle is also present in the three layers of the Interrap architecture, the behavior-based layer, the local planning layer and the cooperative planning layer. The two first mentioned layers form the classical reactive and deliberative components of the agent, whereas layer 3 extends the agent's capabilities for communication and cooperation within multi-agent systems (see Section 4.3).

Although Interrap is based on a classical BDI concept, the architecture does not concentrate on the definition of a formal BDI model, as for example in the case with Rao/Georgeff (see Section 4.2.3.1), but rather on the dynamic control process of an agent [Müller 1996]. The fundamental conceptual agent model and the Interrap architecture provide a clear description of this process.

Figure 4.2/17 shows the conceptual Interrap agent model. As in many other BDI-based architectures, the facts that an agent determines through the use of sen-

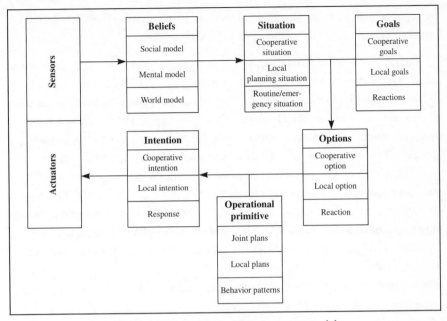

Figure 4.2/17: Conceptual Interrap agent model

sors form the basis for its beliefs. During an agent's runtime, new beliefs can be formed and the contents of existing beliefs revised or even completely deleted on the basis of new facts.

The beliefs received by an Interrap agent can be grouped within three separate models: the world model contains the fundamental beliefs relating to the agent's environment, the mental model consists of the beliefs that the agent has of itself, and the social model contains beliefs about other agents. From the viewpoint of their contents, these three models correspond to the three Interrap architectural layers previously described. The beliefs stored within the world model are mainly used for reactive behaviors, those of the mental model for deliberative purposes, and those of the social model for the cooperation with other agents.

To permit the practical use of the very general beliefs, an algorithm is used to derive so-called situations from the beliefs. Situations form a subset of the beliefs and represent those states that are of concrete interest for the agent. They also serve as basis for the goal determination process. The situations are divided into three layers: simple routine or emergency situations, situations that require a local planning, and situations in which a cooperative planning of several agents is required. Every situation is described by the appropriate belief models [Müller 1996]. For example, a local planning situation is based on the world model and mental model, whereas a cooperative situation also includes the social model.

The agent's goals are subdivided into reactions, local goals and cooperative goals. The interpretation of reactions as a type of goal is of particular interest here. With this regard, reactions represent very short-term goals that are initiated by events and which require a fast answer. This definition completes the link between reactive systems and the concept of goals normally present only in deliberative systems. The occurrence of a specific situation typically activates one or more goals of the agent. Options are designated as being the set of goals that satisfy a particular situation. The planner and the scheduler use so-called operational primitives provided by the system to derive intentions from the options, which then correspond to the actual reasoning process. Depending on the option or goal, these primitives can be very different. Whereas simple reactions are defined as behavior patterns, local and cooperative goals may require the explicit creation of special goal states before the planning process can use them. Any specific intentions that have been created will be executed.

Müller used the discussed agent model as basis for the Interrap architecture shown in Figure 4.2/18. The architecture is based on a number of design principles [Müller 1996]:

- The three-layer structure describes an agent using various degrees of abstraction and complexity

- Not only the control processes, but also the agent's knowledge base are multi-layered

- The control process is bottom-up, that is, a layer receives control over a process only when this exceeds the capabilities of the layer below.

- Every layer uses the operation primitives of the lower layer to achieve its objectives.

As the figure shows, the Interrap architecture consists of three major components: knowledge base, control unit and world interface. The agent uses the world interface to maintain contact with its environment. The knowledge base consists of the three previously described belief models. The control unit also consists of three layers that closely correspond to those of the knowledge base. The behavior-based layer describes the reactive capability of the agent. It is used when time-critical situations demand fast responses. The local and cooperative planning layers form the agent's deliberative components. They are used when a situation exceeds

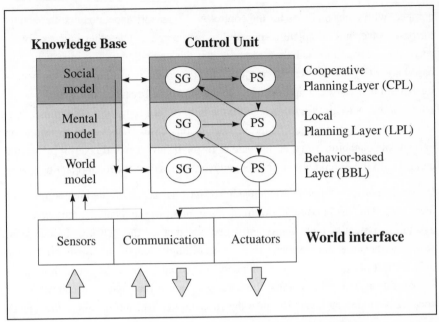

Figure 4.2/18: Interrap agent architecture [Müller 1996]

the capabilities of the behavior-based layer and demands longer term objective determination and planning.

Every control layer consists essentially of two modules: the situation recognition/goal activation (SG) module and the planning/scheduling (PS) module. The SG module performs all steps described as part of the conceptional model up to the option creation. The PS module then performs the planning process, the provision of intentions and the scheduling. A control layer can only use its assigned knowledge base layer and all lower layers to fulfill its tasks. Thus, the behavior-based layer can use only the knowledge of the world model, whereas the cooperative planning layer has access to the complete knowledge base. In this manner, every layer receives only that information (both in terms of content and degree of abstraction) that is suitable for it. For example, it would not be particularly useful for the behavior-based layer to have access to the negotiation knowledge stored in the social model, because it neither needs nor understands this knowledge.

The control process within Interrap flows from the lower layer to the higher layers. Only the behavior-based layer has direct access to the world interface. In contrast to Brooks' subsumption architecture in which every competence module must compete with other modules for the control of the sensors and actuators, the behavior-based layer has complete responsibility for this task. The other layers only receive the information that they require. If a new situation occurs, the behavior-based layer first recognizes the resulting changes to the world model. If the behavior-based layer can react appropriately to the situation, because, for example, it is a pure reactive activity, it will do so with the help of its PS module. The higher control layers are not informed of the activity in this case. However, if the situation exceeds the capabilities and competencies of the behavior-based layer, it passes the control onto the SG module of the above layer, in this case the local planning layer.

Because of its extended knowledge horizon (it has access to the mental model of the knowledge base) and longer term planning process, the local planning layer has a solution potential that significantly exceeds that of the behavior-based layer. However, because the response time is accordingly longer, many situations can only be usefully processed within the behavior-based layer. If the situation requires a cooperation with other agents, the local planning layer passes the control to the cooperative planning layer. Because the cooperative layer has access to the agent's complete knowledge, all occurring situations must be able to be processed at this highest level.

The execution process runs in the exact opposite direction to the activation process, that is, from top to bottom. Only the behavior-based layer can actually initiate a concrete action, because it alone has access to the agent's actuators. Even if a specific intention was created in the cooperative planning layer, it must be passed down to the lowest layer in order to be executed.

Müller tested the Interrap architecture in a simulated loading area [Müller 1996]. Within this scenario, a number of Interrap agents act as automatic fork-lifts that move in the loading area, remove and replace stock from various storage bays, and so compete with other agents for resources. This example makes clear the demands made on a hybrid agent structure. On the one hand, the agents move in a highly-dynamic environment that continuously demands fast responses. For example, if two fork-lifts block each other, an immediate response must result and not some long-term planning process. On the other hand, the scenario also requires a long-term complex planning, if, for example, a newly arriving truck is to be loaded in the most efficient manner. In addition, such a strategy cannot be created by an individual agent, but represents a cooperative planning process between a number of agents.

4.3 Communication and Cooperation in Multi-Agent Systems

4.3.1 Introduction

The previous considerations concentrated primarily on the architecture, namely, the internal structure of individual intelligent software agents. However, it has already been apparent in many places that the use of individual agents is not equally suitable for all problem situations that occur in practice. The central approach, to solve a problem using a single agent, can cause serious restrictions [Sycara et al. 1996, Nwana 1996]. An individual agent requires an enormous amount of knowledge to solve complex problem situations, if it is to be capable of developing goal-oriented solution strategies. In the worst case, the problem is so complex that the agent cannot by itself find a useful solution using the technologies currently available. Many problems because of their form are distributed and so for this reason alone require distributed problem solving units. The specialized knowledge is often not available at a single location, that is, within an agent, but distributed over various agents. Even if an individual agent is capable of solving a specific problem, it would always represent a bottleneck with regard to process speed, reliability, flexibility and modularity.

Multi-agent systems offer a concept to avoid the described problem situations. A number of independent, largely autonomous agents are active within a multi-agent system. Every agent of a multi-agent system can either follow its own objectives and only contact other agents to obtain information, or contribute to the coordinated solution of an overall problem. In both cases, every individual agent has a precisely defined task to which it is particularly suitable and whose solution does not exceed its capabilities. This permits the processing of even complex problem situations. Multi-agent systems provide a further advantage: they permit the integration of existing agents in a larger system. Thus, the solution of problems does not necessarily demand the design and development of a new, specialized agent, but instead the knowledge of existing agents can be used by combining them into a multi-agent system and then letting them work together to solve the problem. Section 4.3.2 introduces the fundamentals required for distributed problem solving.

Distributed problem solving with multi-agent systems is appropriate only when agents integrated in the system are capable of communicating and cooperating with each other. No common solution strategies can be developed without these capabilities and the specialized knowledge of an agent cannot be used by other agents. The communication forms the basis of the cooperation (see Figure 4.3/1) and is

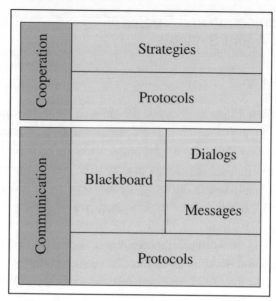

Figure 4.3/1: Communication and cooperation in multi-agent systems

formed from the communications protocols and the resulting communication methods.

The communications methods can be differentiated into blackboard systems and message/dialog-based systems. Both will be described together with the protocols in Section 4.3.3. The cooperation protocols and strategies build on the communications methods. In this context, both the selection of the cooperation strategy, which permits the knowledge of individual agents to be used in the most efficient manner, and the power of the cooperation protocol used as basis, are of paramount importance. Two important cooperation protocols, the contract net system and the partial global planning, are described in detail in Section 4.3.4. Cooperation strategies are composed of a wide range of modules. The negotiation strategies, described in Section 4.3.4.2, and the principles of matchmaking and brokering, described in Section 4.3.6, play a central role.

4.3.2 Distributed Problem Solving

If several distributed agents are to work on a problem within a multi-agent system, it is first necessary to choose the strategic methodology to be used for the problem solving process. Only then can concrete considerations be made on possible com-

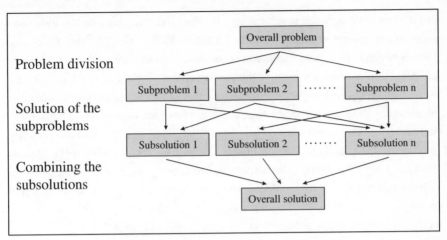

Figure 4.3/2: Process of distributed problem solving
(based on [Albayrak/Bussmann 1993])

munications and cooperation strategies. The methodology used with distributed problem solving can be divided into three sequential steps: division of the problem into subproblems, solution of the subproblems, and combination of the subsolutions (see Figure 4.3/2).

The division of the overall problem into a series of subproblems and the assignment of the subproblems to the associated agents takes highest priority in the phase of the problem division [Albayrak/Bussmann 1993]. Both aspects address different questions. It must be decided during the division of the total problem how the concrete division can be determined and from whom it will be performed. This task can be performed by a coordination agent that is given special rights or by all agents together. In every case, a methodology should be found that assigns a specific subproblem to the agent that is particularly suitable for solving the problem. This distribution or assignment problem is designated as the connection problem as part of the DAI [Albayrak/Bussmann 1993]. If there is only a single suitable agent for every subproblem, no connection problem exists, because the assignment is simple. Difficulties arise when several agents have a very similar knowledge. The contract net system and global planning strategies described later offer concepts that can be used to attempt to solve the connection problem in the most efficient manner (see Section 4.3.4).

Because each individual agent is primarily responsible for the solution of its subproblems, the second step of the distributed problem solution process, doesn´t necessarily require communication and cooperation procedures. On the other hand, direct interaction between several agents is often necessary because the individual subproblems cannot normally be solved autonomously. Consequently, direct conflicts between two or more agents can occur during the solution process, which then requires communication to resolve the conflict (for example, this is always the case when two agents each separate subsolutions that contradict each other). Similarly, resource conflicts can occur, for example caused by lack of computing capacity or storage space. The agents must contact each other in this case to arrive at a common solution to the problem. The subsolutions do not necessarily need to be directly associated with the subproblems. It is possible during the course of the problem solving process that a subproblem results in several subsolutions or several subproblems resolve to a single subsolution (see Figure 4.3/2). Consequently, the number of subproblems and subsolutions is not always identical.

The agents involved in the subproblem solving process can support each other in two different ways. These are called task sharing and result sharing. Task sharing means that an agent requests other agents for help in solving specific subtasks, because either it is overextended with the solution or it determines that other agents already have the knowledge required for the solution. The previously described connection problem also occurs here; to assign unsolved subproblems to other agents, an agent must find the agent that it considers to be most suitable to solve this problem. Only then can it be guaranteed that the subproblem can be solved in the shortest time with the lowest resource usage. Alternatively, the agent also has the possibility of publicly announcing to all other agents the subproblem in question, and then select the best candidate from the responses. This concept, for example, is used in the contract net system (see Section 4.3.4.1).

Result sharing is the method used above all within human groups. For example, in the development of software programs, the intermediate results of individual developers, such as completed software modules, are used by other developers. This is the same methodology as used in multi-agent systems. Once the connection problem has been solved, that is, the subproblems have been assigned to the individual agents, and any difficulties of the individual agents resolved through the use of task assignment, result sharing shares the individual results. Those subsolutions already determined can be made available to other agents and so help them with their work. This permits the faster recognition of conflicting or incorrect subsolutions. For example, if an agent receives a subsolution from another agent that contradicts its previously determined solutions or the subsolution can be definitely determined to be incorrect based on its knowledge, it is then possible to inform the other agents of this and solve the conflict together. The cooperation protocols and negotiating strategies described in Sections 4.3.4 and 4.3.4.2 can, for example, be used for this purpose.

The third step of the distributed problem solving process, the merging of subresults to form a complete solution, must consider similar questions as those raised during the problem division phase: who is responsible for the merging and which concrete methodology is selected. Difficulties occur if subsolutions cannot be uniquely assigned to a subproblem. In this case, a simple inversion of the problem division process does not necessarily lead to the complete solution. However, if a unique subsolution is assigned to every subproblem, then the merging of the subsolution to a complete solution is usually relatively straightforward.

4.3.3 Communication

4.3.3.1 Methods

There are a number of fundamentally different methods of communication. An invocation of an agent's procedure by another agent represents the simplest case. The invoking agent explicitly uses calling parameters to inform its communication partner of a specific wish and its intentions. The return values of the procedure represent the answer of the addressed agent. Depending on where the addressed partner is physically located within the network, the procedure invocation can take place either locally or as RPC. However, only very simple communication methods can be implemented using procedure calls. Extended communications processes can be used to cater for more complex cases which could not be realized with pure procedure calls. For this reason, the procedure call does not provide any communications method in the narrowest sense and is not further discussed here.

4.3.3.1.1 Blackboard systems

The second method of agent communication arises out of DAI and is designated as being the blackboard metaphor. The blackboard represents an extension to the agenda of traditional AI systems and rule-based expert systems and makes the first attempt to support the process of distributed problem solving through the use of suitable structures [Kirn 1996]. A blackboard provides all agents within a multi-agent system with a common work area in which they can exchange information, data, and knowledge (see Figure 4.3/3).

An agent initiates a communication action by writing an information item on the blackboard. This is then available for all other agents of the system. Every agent

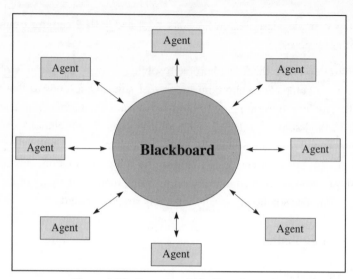

Figure 4.3/3: Structure of blackboard systems

can at any time access the blackboard to determine whether new information has
arrived since its last access. If yes, it can read this information. However, in practice an agent seldom reads all new information, but rather only that information of
interest. For example, it can use a filter to extract that information that affects its
current area of work or originates from agents with which it is currently in contact.
An agent must register with a central site to receive an access authorization to a
specific blackboard. This site administers all agents assigned to a blackboard and
blocks unauthorized accesses. A multi-agent system can have several blackboards
on each of which different agents are registered. No direct communication between
agents takes place in the blackboard system. Every agent is obliged to solve its
subproblems independently and under its own responsibility.

The blackboard can be used both for the task sharing and result sharing described
in the previous section. An active, event-based problem solution strategy is also possible. If an agent tests the blackboard for new information in regular intervals, it obtains information on the progress of other agents in obtaining the solution. It can use
this knowledge for its own tasks, and it has the possibility to recognize conflict situations and incorrect solutions, and then communication this knowledge appropriately.

No private areas exist within simple blackboards. All agents have access to
every information item and they have the complete responsibility in deciding which
actual information they access. If the number of agents is large, the amount of data

associated with the blackboard grows exponentially. Similarly, the individual agents must search through a large amount of information on every access blackboard to determine what is of interest. To optimize this process, the more advanced blackboard concepts provide different regions within a blackboard to which individual agents are assigned. In this case, an agent only needs to observe those regions to which it is assigned.

Although the actual data structures placed on the blackboard are not subject to any fixed definition, it must be ensured that every agent registered on the blackboard is capable of understanding the information stored by other agents. General information on the current solution state, the next subproblems to be performed and the current tasks of the individual agents is required in addition to the actual task-specific content to permit the logging of the complete problem solving process using the blackboard.

The validation of the quality of the individual contributions on the blackboard represents a general problem. Every agent has the right to write any information on the blackboard. The original blackboard concept did not have any instance to check the contributions or to stop agents from storing information for subproblems that were not part of their area of responsibility. More recent concepts have introduced a central management component or agent for this function. This is also called the moderator. The moderator publicizes on the blackboard the next subproblems to be solved and checks which agents apply for the solution of the associated tasks. It even performs the assignment of the subproblem to an agent. Figure 4.3/4 illustrates such a structure. Any agent can use the blackboard to read the open subproblems. If it has particular interest in specific subproblems, it reports this using a database by creating a so-called Knowledge Source Activation Record (KSAR) in the database [Kirn 1996]. The moderator uses its control and evaluation knowledge in the knowledge base to select the most appropriate agent and uses the blackboard to inform it that it has received the task of solving the subproblem. In particular in combination with the contract net system introduced later, this concept is very efficient.

The introduction of a so-called dispatcher represents a second innovation. A dispatcher has the task to inform those agents registered on a blackboard of changes made to the blackboard. For example, if new messages arrive and have new subproblems are offered, the dispatcher can contact those agents that it considers could have an interest in the new information. The affected agents in this approach are not

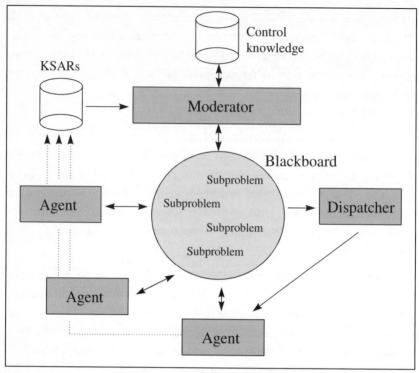

Figure 4.3/4: Extended blackboard structure

required to actively search the blackboard for new messages at regular intervals, but are supplied automatically with the information of interest.

The BBI model developed by Hayes-Roth and illustrated in Figure 4.3/5 goes one step further [Hayes-Roth 1971].

BBI architectures contain two blackboards that are provided for various tasks. The domain blackboard is comparable with the previously discussed concepts and is used for the solution of the actual problems. Information pertaining to the control processes derived from the contents of the problems is stored in the control blackboard. This control information covers all data required for the control of the complete system and the progress of the problem solution. The structure of the control blackboard does not depend on the domain blackboard but is determined exclusively by the coordination and control strategy selected by the system. Agents use both the domain and the control blackboard to satisfy the problem solution or control tasks. As previously, the application for the pending tasks takes place using the KSARs, with the difference that separate databases are maintained for the content

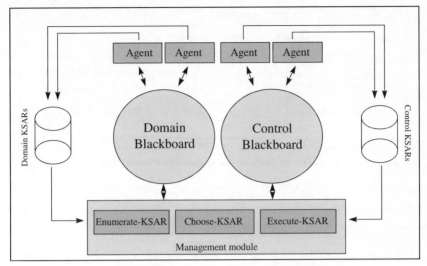

Figure 4.3/5: BBI blackboard model (based on [Kirn 1996])

and the control data. The management module for the BBI architecture comprises of three independent components: the enumerate KSAR module lists KSARs currently present, the choose KSAR module selects a KSAR from the applications, and the execute KSAR module performs the action of the selected KSAR.

Blackboards provide a very flexible concept for the cooperation and communication of distributed problem solving units. They are independent of the selected cooperation strategy and provide only minimum demands on the architecture of the associated agents. However, the central structure of a blackboard is developing into an increasing obstacle to the continuing expansion of network-centric applications. All agents registered on the blackboard are forced to place their information directly on the blackboard, irrespective of their current position in the network. The reading of the blackboard information also causes a high network load. For these reasons, the importance of the message-based systems described in the following section is continually increasing.

4.3.3.1.2 Message passing

The communication using messages forms a flexible basis for the implementation of complex coordination strategies. In message-based concepts, the messages that agents exchange with each other can be used to establish communications and cooperation mechanisms using defined protocols. The free format of the message

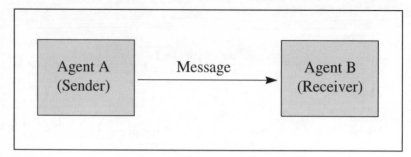

Figure 4.3/6: Principle of message transmission

contents provides very versatile communications capabilities that are not restricted to simple command and response structures.

Figure 4.3/6 illustrates the basic principle of message-oriented agent systems. An agent, also called the sender, transfers a specific message to another agent, the receiver. In contrast to blackboard systems, messages are directly exchanged between two agents. No buffering is performed and other agents are not capable of reading a message that is not addressed to them. The so-called "broadcasting" represents an exception, in which a message is sent to all agents of a system or to an exactly specified group. However, in normal cases, the sender assigns a unique address to a message, which then can be read only by the agent with this address. Two questions must be clarified to permit messages to be used to implement cooperation strategies. Firstly, a communications protocol must be defined that specifies the exact communication process, the format of the messages, and the chosen communications language. Secondly, and this is of particular importance for the exchange of knowledge, all associated agents must know the semantics of the communications language. The first question is of little interest to agents, because it is primarily concerned with the technical parameters of the communication. In contrast, the knowledge of the semantic content of a message is a central component of all distributed problem solving systems. Consequently, this aspect takes priority in the following considerations.

If human communication is analyzed, one determines that not only simple statements, true or false, can be exchanged through the transfer of messages, but rather messages can implicitly start single actions or even complete action chains. For example, if you ask the question "Can you give me the book?", you do not normally expect a simple yes or no, but rather you implicitly request to be given the book. Thus, a concrete action is initiated. The intentions of the sender's message are not always so obvious as in this example. The question "Can you tell me where I can find a book on intelligent agents?" combines several possible intentions. The questioner may only want to know generally whether his partner can answer the question, however, he could just as easily expect a detailed description where such a book can be found. Thus, the content of a message also always depends on the corresponding mental state of the sender. The same applies for the receiver. A simple request can cause completely different responses, depending on the mental state of the receiver and his current relationship with the sender.

The above described problem results in the following situation for an agent: it should not treat a received message just as a fact and, for example, store it in its knowledge base, but rather analyze the message for implicitly associated actions and intentions. The situation is made more difficult through lack of knowledge of the sender's current mental state, which, as we have seen, can play a significant role in the analysis. The speech act theory developed by the English philosopher and linguist Austin attempts to cater for these demands [Austin 1962]. A speech act designates a message that contains not only a true or false statement but also exercises a direct influence on its environment by causing changes within its environment. The changes initially affect only the mental state of the receiver of the message from where they continue. For example, if an agent receives the speech act "Can you give me certain information", this initially changes only its own mental state. Only through the execution of the implicit handling request, namely, the transfer of the information, does the speech act exhibit its full effect. Every speech act contains three different components, which Austin described as locutionary, illocutionary, and perlocutionary acts. Whereas the locutionary act describes the expression of the message, namely, the pure transfer operation, the illocutionary act contains the sender's intentions implicitly associated with the message. These can be, for example, a request, a command or a question. The perlocutionary act describes the effects of the speech act on the environment, namely the changes caused by the locutionary and illocutionary action.

A speech act can have several intentions (illocutionary actions) associated with it, which themselves depend on the mental state of the sender. To simplify recognizing the intentions for the receiver of a speech act, it can be desirable to categorize these into so-called speech act types. The selection of the speech act types is not subject to any fixed rules and can be made as part of the development of a communication protocol. For example, the Knowledge and Query Manipulation Language (KQML), described in detail later, defines speech act types such as *ask-about* (request information), *tell* (transfer information), *achieve* (the receiver should perform a certain task), or *reply* (answer to a speech act). If the involved agents know the associated speech acts, they normally know the intention associated with the speech act and can respond accordingly.

The previously described message-based concept cannot be used to solve most communication problems. The communication within a multi-agent system, for example, does not usually consist just of sending unrelated messages. Normally dialogs take place, in which an exchange of several related messages takes place between two or more conversation partners. Figure 4.3/7 shows a simple dialog process.

Agent A sends a speech act to agent B in which it requests specific information. Agent B itself requires information from agent C, because it does not itself possess the required information. It sends an appropriate speech act to agent C from which it receives a reply. If the reply from C contains the requested information, agent B can send this as a speech act to agent A. It is also possible that an action consists of several consecutive and interrelated message transmissions between two agents. More complex dialog structures can have a dramatic influence on the effects of speech acts, because the mental states of the associated agents change continually during the dialog process, which in turn have direct consequences for the interpretation of the speech act. The classification of speech acts into speech act types does not solve this problem, because it is determined a priori and makes no allowance for the changing mental states or of the effects of dialog processes.

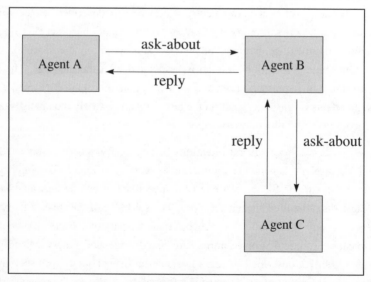

Figure 4.3/7: Sample dialog structure

4.3.3.2 Protocols

The Knowledge and Query Manipulation Language (KQML) represents the most widely used protocol for communication in multi-agent systems. KQML was developed as part of the American Knowledge Sharing Efforts (KSE) project at the University of Maryland [Finin 1993, Labrou/Finin 1997].

KQML defines both a message format and a message transmission system that provides a general frame for the communication and cooperation in multi-agent systems. In particular, KQML provides a group of protocols for identification, connection establishment, and message exchange. The semantic content of a message is not specified in more detail in KQML. Because the standard is open, various languages can be used to exchange knowledge and can be integrated in a KQML message.

KQML differentiates between the three layers: communication, messages and content. Whereas protocols for all technical communications parameters are defined at the communications layer, the message layer defines the speech act type associated with a message. The content layer specifies the contents of the message, although, as mentioned previously, KQML is limited to specifying only a general frame in which the actual contents can be embedded in some arbitrary language. Every KQML message has the following basic structure:

> *(<Performative>*
> *:content<statement/speechact>*
> *:sender<name>*
> *:receiver<name>*
> *:language<text>*
> *:ontology<text>*
> *)*

The performative corresponds to the speech act types introduced in the previous section. To ensure a general usability, KQML defines a wide range of speech act types that can be used for almost all application purposes; Figure 4.3/8 shows the most important speech act types.

The actual message contents, such as a specific speech act, are inserted in the Content field. The language used is not defined, and for this reason it is specified in the Language field. The receiver can use the Language field to determine the language used to code the message contents and then read the Content field. Obviously, for this purpose, it must be capable of understanding and interpreting the

Speech act type/ Performative	Meaning
achieve	S wants E to make true some statement in his environment
advertise	S is particularly suitable to perform some particular speech act type
ask-all	S wants all answers in E´s knowledge base
ask-one	S wants an answer in E´s knowledge base
broker-one	S wants E to find help for the answering of his speech act
deny	The speech act no longer applies for S
delete	S wants E to remove specific facts from his knowledge base
recommend-one	S wants the name of an agent that can answer a speech act
recruit-one	S wants E to request an agent to perform a speech act
sorry	S does not possess the required knowledge or information
subscribe	S wants continuously information of E´s answers for a speech act
tell	S transfers an information item

Figure 4.3/8: Important KQML speech act types [Finin 1993]

language used. The Ontology field defines the special dictionary or vocabulary used for the message contents. An example KQML command could have the following form (see [Finin et al. 1994]):

> *(ask-one*
> *:content(PRICE IBM ?price)*
> *:receiver stock-server*
> *:language LPROLOG*
> *:ontology NYSE-TICKS*
> *)*

The sender uses the *ask-one* speech act type to inform the receiver of its wish to receive an answer to the asked question. The actual content of the message in this example is formulated in the LPROLOG language and asks the question what is the price of an IBM share. The fact that the required price concerns a share price results from the ontology used, in this case New York Stock Exchange (NYSE) ticker symbols. If, for example, the receiver was a computer dealer and the ontology computer systems, the contents of the message could be interpreted differently, for example, as a question asking the price of an IBM computer system.

Not every dialog in KQML must be modeled in the form of simple question/answer processes. KQML introduces the function of a facilitator [Finin et al. 1994] to also permit the use of more complex data structures. The main task of a

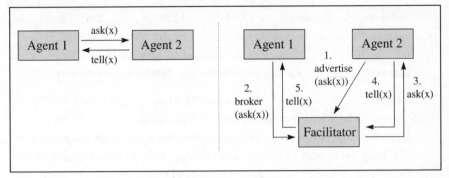

Figure 4.3/9: Use of a facilitator

facilitator is to bring together those agents who are searching for information and those providing information. Figure 4.3/9 shows such a scenario.

Whereas the classical question/answer structure, with the corresponding language types, is expressed in the left half of the diagram, the right half shows the tasks of the facilitator. If an agent searches for specific information but does not know which other agents can provide the sought information, it can use the *broker* speech act type to make use of facilitator services. The facilitator accepts the query and attempts to find an agent with the appropriate knowledge. Every agent can use an *advertise* speech act to register its knowledge with the facilitator.

Figure 4.3/10 shows two other possible variations. The left of the figure shows a similar process to that of the previous example, but with the difference that a *recommend* speech act is used in place of the *broker* speech act. In this case, the facilitator supplies only the address of a suitable agent. The knowledge transfer takes place directly between the two agents and not, as in the previous example, also by means of

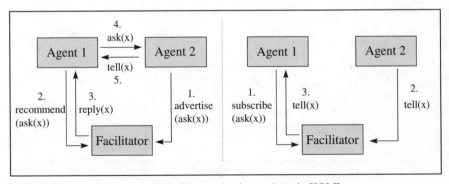

Figure 4.3/10: Communication variants in KQML

a facilitator. A *subscribe* speech act (right half of Figure 4.3/10) informs the facilitator to continually search through its knowledge base for a specific change. If such a change takes place, it is forwarded to the questioning agent. Section 4.3.6 contains a detailed introduction to the various principles of matchmaking and brokering.

There are two possible concepts to integrate existing agents in a multi-agent system based on KQML: every agent could be extended with the capability to process KQML messages, or an additional component could undertake this task for the agent. To keep the system as flexible and open as possible, it is desirable to consider the second variant in more detail. Figure 4.3/11 shows a possible architecture that was tested as part of several systems [Finin et al. 1994]. Every agent is given two additional modules, a KQML router and the KQML router interface library (KRIL). The KQML router manages and controls all messages that are sent from its associated agents or are addressed to it. Every agent of a multi-agent system possesses its own KQML router, which are identical copies. The router has no interest in the actual content of the message and performs no further processing on it. Its only task is to forward outgoing messages to the required receiver and to accept incoming messages. If for an outgoing message a service is specified instead of a receiver, the router must be capable of finding an appropriate service provider, possibly with the help of a facilitator.

The KRIL represents the interface between KQML router and agent. It must analyze the content of the agent's query and convert these into KQML messages. The KRIL transfers incoming KQML messages into a form that agents can understand. Because of the strong emphasis of the KRIL on the contents, it may be necessary to use different KRILs for different application fields, that is, assign several

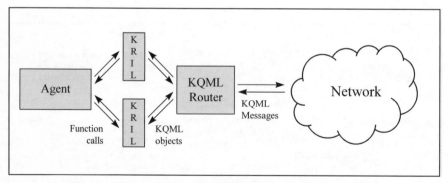

Figure 4.3/11: Architecture of a KQML-based multi-agent system
(based on [Finin et al. 1994])

KRILs to an agent. For example, if an agent makes a request in the LISP language, the corresponding KRIL accepts it, packs it into a KQML message and forwards the message to the KQML router. The router's answer is again transferred into a LISP expression and passed to the agent.

4.3.4 Cooperation Protocols

Before starting the discussion of specific cooperation protocols and strategies, it is appropriate to define a cooperation topology in order to obtain an overview of the various categories and forms of cooperation. Figure 4.3/12 shows a possible typology developed by Franklin [Doran et al. 1997].

Franklin differentiates at the top layer between independent and cooperative agents. If the individual agents of a multi-agent system are completely independent of each other and follow their own goals, this is described as an independent system. If the independently acting agents also have non-correlated goals, Franklin describes the system as being discrete. Discrete systems in which, for example, one agent searches for information and another supports the user in the purchase of products, do not possess any explicit cooperation. Systems with emergent cooperation develop when agents independent of each other follow their goals and so from the outside give the appearance of a cooperation. For example, if several agents independently of each other follow an identical goal, a non-participating observer can have the impression of a cooperative methodology.

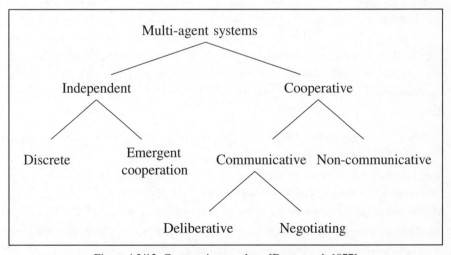

Figure 4.3/12: Cooperation typology [Doran et al. 1977]

Cooperative systems have explicit cooperative mechanisms. The agents are constructed in a way that they can cooperate with other agents to achieve their goals; such agents make intentional use of this capability. Franklin considers that the cooperation can proceed either communicatively or non-communicatively. Communicative cooperation agents use communications protocols and procedures to cooperate with other agents. For example, they send messages or dispatch KQML performatives. The non-communicative cooperation takes place indirectly using the environment. An agent observes its environment and in this manner notices changes caused by other agents. Its response to these changes in turn causes a response from other agents observing the environment. An indirect cooperation occurs.

Communicative cooperation agents can be divided into deliberative and negotiating systems. A common planning and agreement of the methodology of all agents occurs in deliberative systems. The partial global planning discussed in Section 4.3.4.2 provides an example of a deliberative protocol. Negotiation-oriented methodologies, such as the contract net system (see Section 4.3.4.1), have a competitive component in addition to the mechanisms of deliberative systems. The negotiations can resolve conflicts and assign tasks.

4.3.4.1 Contract Net Systems

Contract net systems represent a concept that can be used to establish efficient coordination mechanisms between the agents integrated in a multi-agent system. A contract net consists of a number of nodes that are formed by the individual agents in the multi-agent system. In a methodology similar to that of a market-place, the pending subtasks are openly offered for bids, to which every node can apply for those tasks of interest. The task assignment represents an interactive process in which all nodes (agents) are involved. The aim is to use the available resources and the currently existing knowledge of the agents as efficiently as possible; this is done by assigning subtasks to that agent which is best suited for the processing at this time.

The contract net protocol that forms the basis of the contract net systems defines a common internode language that must be understood by all agents [Smith 1980]. The communication between the agents is always performed on the basis of the agreed message format. The actual contract net system provides a contract protocol that is based on the contract net protocol. This specifies the exact process of the task assignment and defines the roles of the associated agents. The nodes of a contract net system have the structure shown in Figure 4.3/13.

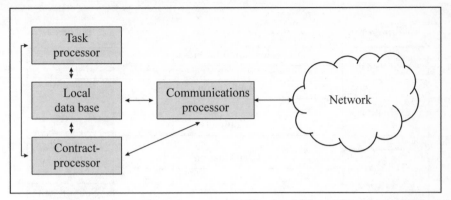

Figure 4.3/13: Structure of a contract net node (based on [Albayrak/Bussmann 1993])

The local data base contains the knowledge base of the associated node and also information on the current status of the cooperation negotiations and the problem solving process. The three other components use the local knowledge base to perform their tasks. The communications processor is given the task of performing the communication with other nodes. It is the only component of the node that has a direct connection to the network. In particular, the communications processor undertakes the sending and receiving of messages.

The contract processor has the task of observing the tasks offered for bids, the sending of applications and the finalizing of contracts. It also analyzes and interprets incoming messages. Finally, the contract processor performs the coordination of all the nodes. The task processor is responsible for the actual processing and solution of the task assigned to a node. It receives the problems to be solved from the contract processor, makes use of the local data base to determine a solution, and passes this to the contract processor.

The work of a contract net system begins after the problem division phase, namely after the complete problem that is to be solved has been divided into a series of subproblems. A special node, called the manager in the following section, undertakes the task of the assignment of the subproblems. Figure 4.3/14 shows an example of a typical contract negotiation process.

The manager makes a public offer for bids as a so-called contract for every pending subproblem that is to be solved. For this purpose it uses the message structure defined by the contract protocol; the following example shows how it could look ([Albayrak/Bussmann 1993]):

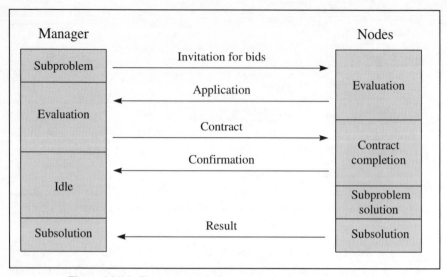

Figure 4.3/14: Contract negotiation process in contract net systems

TO:	*all nodes*
FROM:	*manager*
TYPE:	*task bid announcement*
ContractID:	*xx-yy-zz*
Task Abstraction:	*<description of the subproblem>*
Eligibility Specification:	*<list of the minimum requirements>*
Bid Specification:	*<description of the required application information>*
Expiration time:	*<latest possible application time>*

The offer for bids is open to all agents and is evaluated by their associated contract processor. This makes use of the local data base to evaluate the currently available resources and the agent's knowledge. The contract processor decides whether an application should be made for the announced task. If it arrives at a positive result, it can inform the manager accordingly:

TO:	*manager*
FROM:	*node X*
TYPE:	*application*
ContractID:	*xx-yy-zz*
Node Abstraction:	*<description of the node's capabilities >*

The manager must select the node it considers most suitable from all received applications for a specific contract. It has access to special evaluation knowledge and methods with which it can evaluate every application. It selects the application with the highest evaluation and it is given the task to solve the subproblem associated with the contract. The manager assigns the contract in the form of a contract message:

TO:	*node X*
FROM:	*manager*
TYPE:	*contract*
ContractID:	*xx-yy-zz*
Task Specification:	*<description of the subproblem >*

The commissioned node sends a confirmation to the manager indicating the acceptance of the contract in the specified form. On completion of the problem solving phase, the solved problem is transferred to the manager. The commissioned node has full responsibility for the solution of the subproblem, namely the completion of the contract. The contract net systems are a pure task distribution. A node does not receive any information on the current state of the other nodes. If a node later determines that the task assigned to it exceeds its capabilities or resources, it is permitted to further subdivide the problem and then assign the subcontracts to other nodes. In this case it adopts the role of the manager and offers the subproblems for bids. The result is a consequent hierarchical task structure in which a node can be manager, bidding applicant and contracting party all at the same time.

There are several extensions to the original contract net systems that affect different factors of the negotiating process. The public offer for bids is one affected point. Although this action may be appropriate for lightly loaded systems, because all nodes can participate in the bidding, it requires high communications and resource capacity. The affected manager must evaluate a large number of bids, which uses up a large part of its resource capacity. For this reason, heavily loaded managers can deviate from the principle of the public request for bids. Firstly, they have the capability of informing only a small group of nodes about the public request for bids. This is always conceivable when the manager already has concrete knowledge of the capability of individual nodes and a rough estimate which nodes are possible candidates for the processing of the subproblem. Secondly, the public request for bids can be completely renunciated. If a pending subproblem is constructed in a similar manner as a previously solved problem, the manager can directly contact the node that solved the problem in the past, and, if it has resources available, assign it the contract. In an other variant, nodes themselves can submit bids even without a request for bids being received. In this case the manager has a number of open bids that it can investigate for new tasks. A request for bids is required only when it does not find a match. In certain cases it can be useful or even necessary to commission complete groups of subproblems as a common packet. For example, if there are dependencies between subproblems, a separate commissioning may not be appropriate, because this would not lead to an efficient solution.

The second starting point for extensions to contract net systems affects the actual contract assignment. In the original protocol, the manager after assigning a contract must wait for the acceptance from the associated node. Until this confirmation arrives, the manager does not know whether the node is prepared to accept the contract. No contact has taken place since the node's bidding and a bid does not constitute a binding acceptance. The suggested extensions address this point by moving the binding acceptance into an earlier negotiation phase. For example, a node when it places its bid can also provide a fixed statement for the acceptance of a possible later commissioning. Similarly, the acceptance possibilities are not restricted to just an acceptance or rejection, but can be linked to parameters or conditions [Sandholm et al. 1995]. The maximum duration of the contract confirmation represents a further extension concept. If a node does not confirm a contract assigned to it within a specific time interval, the manager can itself terminate the contract. The contract processor can also be built so that the manager is always sent an answer to the assigned contract (positive or negative). This has the advantage that the manager does not need to wait until the end of the agreed maximum time interval before it can reassign the contract.

4.3.4.2 Partial Global Planning

The most significant feature of the Partial Global Planning (PGP) methodology is that every agent of a multi-agent system is given the capability during its work to gather information on the current state and achieved goals of the other agents. The agent can use this knowledge to optimize its own tasks. The PGP thus provides a flexible concept for the coordination of distributed problem solving units [Durfee/Lesser 1991].

The basic condition for the use of PGP is the requirement that several distributed agents work on the solution of an overall problem. If this is the case, an agent as part of the PGP can observe the actions and relationships between a group of other agents and then form conclusions for its own work. This knowledge is called the

Partial Global Plan because it reflects the partial knowledge of the plan determined by an agent to solve a global problem. Figure 4.3/15 uses an example to illustrate the basic working of a PGP-based system. Two agents work on two subproblems (A and B) of a problem. The subproblems themselves consist of a series of subproblems (A1 to A3; B1 and B2). Every agent passes information on its current state to its opposite partner. In the example, agent 1 informs agent 2 that it is currently working on subproblem A. Similarly, agent 2 communicates the work on subproblem B. Every agent can use this information concerning the situation of the partner for its own work. For example, if agent 1 recognizes that its subproblem A2 is dependent on the subproblem B of agent 2, it can inform agent 2 appropriately. In some cases this can have the result that the subproblem A2 is transferred completely to agent 2, because it would have to process the subproblem anyway as part of the solution of B.

The process of the PGP is subdivided into four consecutive steps [Durfee/Lesser 1991]:

1. Creation of the local plans for every agent
2. Communication and exchange of plans between the agents
3. Creation of the PGPs
4. Modification and optimization of the PGPs

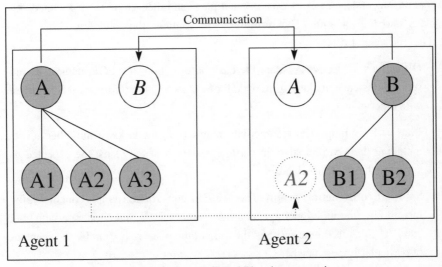

Figure 4.3/15: Partial Global Planning processing

Before the start of the coordination process, every agent must create local plans to be used for the solution of the tasks assigned. Although the strategy selected to be used here is not defined as part of the PGP, it is assumed that an agent is capable of dynamically adapting its original plans if the newly won knowledge makes this necessary. Furthermore, every local plan should have at least two different levels of detail: a general structure that contains the most important steps to solve the problem and which reflects the agent's long-term problem-solving planning, and a detailed structure that contains the detailed information for every specific subproblem.

Once the local planning has been completed, the second step exchanges the knowledge between the agents. Every agent must possess a certain amount of organization-specific knowledge in order that it can decide what role the other agents play in the problem solving process and for which agents what information could be of interest. Furthermore, this so-called meta level organization determines the hierarchy of the agents. Higher placed agents receive plans from subordinate agents, improve these and return the modified plans. If the agents have the same authorization, any party can make modifications. The question what information does an agent forward still needs to be answered. It is not usually appropriate that every agent always communicates all its plans to all other agents, because this behavior does not permit an efficient cooperation. Thus, an agent must decide which parts of its information it passes to which agents.

Once an agent has received information on the plans of other agents, it must combine these in the form of a PGP. It must check whether the new information contains dependencies to its own internal plans and then group the associated subplans into logical units. The resulting PGP contains the following components [Durfee/Lesser 1991]:

- **Objectives**. Objectives contain the basic information of a PGP, namely its reason for existence, its long-term overall objective and the priorities in comparison with other plans.

- **Plan activity map**. The plan activity map covers the tasks of the other agents, including their current state, in particular, details of the plans, the expected results and the effort involved.

- **Solution construction graph**. The solution construction graph contains information how the individual agents are to communicate and cooperate with each other. The details on the size and the time of the plans to be sent by the agent are of particular importance here.

- **Status**. The status contains a report of all important information for the PGP, for example references to the plans received by other agents and an indication on the time of receipt.

A central PGP-planner developed especially for this task analyzes the incoming information from the other agents and determines whether several agents are working on the same overall objective. The PGP-planner integrates this knowledge in the plan activity map. It also makes forecasts concerning the further behavior and the results expected from the other agents. The plan activity map forms the basis for the agent's further work. The map is used to compare the local plans with the new knowledge and so create a modified local plan. The solution construction graph is also created at this time. The PGP planner produces as end result a modified local plan, which has been optimized using the current knowledge of the overall system, and also precise details when specific plans are to be sent to specific agents.

The use of PGP provides a number of advantages. The most important benefit is the highly dynamic behavior of the system. All plans can be adapted at any time to the new environmental situation, which produces a high flexibility and efficiency of the overall system. The PGP goes as far as recognizing that changes to the original plans can be unavoidable. However, it must be ensured here that the modifications made to a plan are passed in time to the other agents, because the changes could affect their work. For example, if an agent itself changes one of its plans, then the achieved result will very probably be different to that originally expected. If the agent had assured other agents that it would supply the originally planned result, it must now inform them that the data it supplies will be different. If the other agents are informed of even the most minor modifications, a very high communications and cooperation requirement occurs, which places unnecessary load on the complete system. For this reason, it is often appropriate to accept small inconsistencies and only communicate the important modifications. The system developer is responsible for the development of such tolerant systems and the specification of a threshold value that indicates when a modification can be considered to be important.

The second benefit of PGP systems lies in their efficiency and the almost complete avoidance of redundancy. If two or more agents are working on similar or even identical problems, sooner or later they will register this through their PGPs, and then reassign and restructure their tasks amongst themselves. The work assignment is also very efficient. If an agent's resources are not being used fully, it only needs to offer an empty plan to make the other agents aware of its free capacity. The mechanism operates similarly in the reverse direction. If an agent with free capacity receives plans from other agents, it can use its own local knowledge to create a PGP and then pass this to other agents. In this way it indirectly provides assistance for the solution of the task.

In addition to the undisputed advantages, the original PGP model has a number of restrictions, in particular with regard to use in multi-agent systems [Decker/ Lesser 1992]. How can heterogeneous agents with different problem solution strategies be integrated? How do you treat dynamic agents whose solution strategies are subject to repeated changes? How could possible real-time requirements be handled that demand fixed deadlines for the completion of specific tasks? And how can negotiations between agents be implemented on the basis of a PGP? Extensions to the PGP model, such as the General Partial Global Planning (GPGP), attempt to cater for these requirements by adding new components to the original algorithm [Decker/Lesser 1992, 1994].

4.3.5 Negotiations

The existing multi-agent systems handle the meaning of negotiations in various ways. Whereas one way describes the assignment of subproblems and resources as negotiation, another way relates to the direct one-to-one negotiation between two agents. The overall aim of all negotiation activities is to permit a constructive cooperation from within the group of independently operating agents that have their own goals. Whereas the negotiation protocol provides the basic rules for the possible forms of the negotiation, the form of the negotiation process and the communications basis, the negotiation strategy depends on the specific implementation of each agent. Although the developer of an agent can provide different degrees of complexity of the negotiation capabilities, care should be taken to ensure the protocol and strategy match, that is, the selected strategy can be performed with the available protocol.

Three different situations can arise when two agents negotiate with each other:

- **No synergy effects**. Neither of the agents can achieve an advantage as the result of the negotiation. Each agent follows its own specific goal, and there are no direct dependencies between the two goals. This has the consequence that although both agents can achieve their own goal, neither agent has any improvement to their goals compared with their opposite party as a result of the negotiation.

- **Positive synergy effects**. At least one of the two agents achieves its goal faster or with less effort. A qualitative improvement of the goal is also possible. For example, if the negotiation determines that the goal of one agent is contained in the goal of the other agent or this goal has been attained already, this produces a positive synergy effect.

- **Negative synergy effects**. This is actually the most interesting case. A negotiation is only really appropriate when there are conflicting goals. The negotiation is very short in the first two situations because neither of the agents had anything to lose. Functioning negotiations and negotiation strategies are demanded only in situations of conflict. Negative synergy effects can appear in different ways: the goals of the two agents are in direct conflict, which has the effect that only one can achieve its goal; although an goal acceptable for both sides is theoretically possible, it cannot be achieved with the available operations; or the agents' resources would be exceeded to achieve a common goal.

Depending on the situation, there may be other interaction schemes for the agents involved in the negotiation. From the individual agent's viewpoint, the objective of the negotiation can be an improvement of its own state, the support for other agents without degrading its own situation or requesting a result. Although the agent must make compromises, the capability of the overall system must be maintained. Zlotkin/Rosenschein with this knowledge identified four forms of interaction in negotiations [Zlotkin/Rosenschein 1996]:

- **Symmetric cooperation**. The negotiation can produce a result that is better for both agents than each could achieve by itself. The work of the other agent has a positive effect on each agent's work.

- **Symmetric compromise**. Both agents would prefer to achieve their goals independently. The negotiation means a compromise for both parties and causes a degradation of their results. However, because the existence of the other agent cannot be ignored, a compromise is essential, and both parties, from a rational viewpoint, can accept the result of the negotiation.

- **Non-symmetric cooperation/compromise**. In this case the situation appears as a cooperation for one agent, namely the negotiation for it is linked with a positive result, whereas the other agent must make a compromise.

- **Conflict**. The agents cannot agree on a rationally acceptable solution because their goals conflict with each other. The negotiation must be ended without a result being achieved.

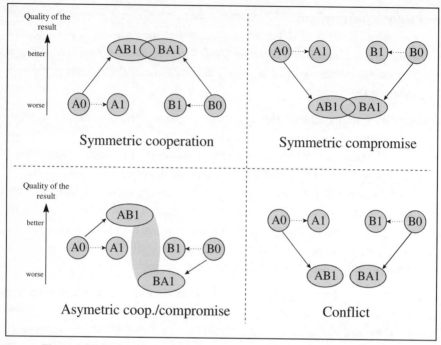

Figure 4.3/16: Negotiation situations (based on [Zlotkin/Rosenschein 1996])

Figure 4.3/16 illustrates the described effects. The two agents in the symmetrical cooperation are in state A0 and B0, respectively, prior to the start of the negotiation. The states A1 and B1 would be attained if no negotiation takes place. The two are in states AB1 and BA1, respectively, after a successful negotiation. The diagram indicates that a common negotiation result was attained (union of AB1 and BA1) and the quality of the result is higher than that attained as each individual result. The same applies for the other three situations.

If the figure is analyzed, it becomes apparent that no common solution set exists in a conflict situation, that is, the negotiation leads to a result that is unsatisfactory to one of the two parties. One of the negotiating parties must yield and abandon achieving its goal. The question which agent leaves the negotiations as winner is now of interest. A simple decision process selects an agent at random, and then permits this agent to achieve its goal, whereas the other agent fails. This methodology causes problems, in particular, when the goals of the agents have different importance for the overall system.

For example, if two agents follow two conflicting goals but achieving the goal for agent 1 is significantly more important for the system, then a decision based on the pure random principle is not appropriate. Rather, the probability that agent 1 is selected as winner of the random decision must be increased in accordance with its importance. An instance is required here to make an appropriate judgment and whose decision is binding for all agents. Such an instance is often not present. The negotiating agents themselves in this case must possess some method other than pure random decision. For example, the agent that is prepared to pay the largest amount (for example, as points, tokens or financial units) could win the decision. This would also reflect the agent's importance, because normally larger amounts would be paid for more important goals. An other possibility is the consideration of the time and resources required by the two agents to solve their task. If an agent can attain its goal in proportion to its importance significantly faster and with fewer resources, then it should have preference. Combinations of the two concepts are also possible.

The previously described variants all assume that one agent renounces. In practice, however, problem situations often arise in which two agents can achieve a common subgoal despite an existing conflict situation. In these cases it is appropriate to divide the negotiation into two successive additive steps. In the first step, the two agents negotiate about the common subgoal to be attained. Only when one of the agents achieves this, does the second negotiation level begin in which the actual conflict must be considered. In some circumstance a third level may be required. Previously only the agent that leaves the conflict situation as winner follows its goal at the end of the negotiations. Alternatively it is possible that the agents agree in advance to continue to work together even after the conflict situation decision and attempt to achieve their common goals. This produces completely new negotiation situations and patterns.

The use of genetic algorithms provides an interesting variant for the design of negotiation strategies. Genetic algorithms are based on the knowledge of the Darwinian evolution theory and attempt to transfer this to the area of computer systems. A negotiation strategy developed under the aspect of genetic algorithms could have the following appearance [Bean/Segev 1996]: every agent involved in the negotiation process possesses before the start of the actual negotiation a number of different negotiation strategies that were selected randomly. It uses these strategies as part of a defined scenario against the strategies of the other agents. The agent evaluates the results of every used strategy after the end of the first negotiation round. A new generation of strategies is derived from the current strategies, where the successful strategies have a larger effect on the inheritance process than the less successful variants. The agent uses the second generation of negotiation strategies produced in this way to begin a new negotiation round with the other agents. A new generation of strategies using the described algorithm is created after every round.

Because of the large influence of the successful strategies on the inheritance process, the agent possesses a series of very efficient, success-oriented negotiation strategies after a certain number of generations. However, the effort required to create them is extremely high; it can be expected that between 20 and 400 generations are required for the development [Bean/Segev 1996]. This means the processing of an identical number of negotiation rounds between two or more agents that should take place under conditions that are as realistic as possible.

The previously described scenarios and examples assumed that the agents involved with a negotiation possess all required information before the start of negotiations, that an agent does not knowingly issue incorrect information, and that the goals of each negotiating partner are known in advance. It is usually the case that an agent does not have in advance all information for the pending negotiation. In particular, it does not normally know the intentions of its opposing partner. For this reason the agent cannot make any decision concerning how important it is to achieve a particular goal for its negotiation partner and what costs the negotiation partner is prepared to bear to achieve a successful negotiation from its viewpoint. However, this information, in particular, can have a significant effect on the negotiation strategy. The negotiation strategy of an agent must be able to vary so that it leads to sensible results even when the information is incomplete and when there is uncertainty.

Agents can intentionally issue incorrect information. This can relate both to their own intentions and also to general problem information. For example, an agent can incorrectly state the negotiation goal it follows. It can specify the importance of the negotiation from its viewpoint as being very low, even though it is actually very high. It can also specify the goals it follows in such a form that its opponent draws the wrong conclusions. The extent to which negotiations are possible and useful in an atmosphere of intentionally incorrect information is questionable. Consequently, the currently available systems use almost exclusively agents that truthfully inform the other agents in the system.

4.3.6 Matchmaking and Brokering

A question that occurs very frequently in multi-agent systems concerns the efficient search for suitable agents to solve a specific problem. Because an agent may not have the necessary knowledge or the necessary resources, the situation can arise for both the problem division and the solution of subproblems that an agent would like to delegate a task to another agent. Provided the agent knows a suitable partner, it does not require any external assistance. It can itself contact the appropriate agent and then negotiate with it the transfer of the task. However, if the agent does not know any contact partner, it is dependent on external support. This can be provided in the form of matchmakers or brokers. Although both variants have a similar structure, they differ in a number of details.

A matchmaker is an agent with special capabilities that has the task to match information-searching and information-providing agents. Figure 4.3/17 shows such a scenario in which the messages are KQML performatives (see Section 4.3.3.2). An agent, a so-called requester, searches for a contractor to process a task, but does not itself know any suitable agents. The requestor asks the matchmaker to provide the names of one or more agents capable of solving its tasks. The matchmaker possesses a database with information on the information-providing agents. Every agent can report its services with a matchmaker and is then accepted in this data storage. The service-providing agent is called a server. When a requester makes an inquiry, the matchmaker searches its database for suitable servers and passes their

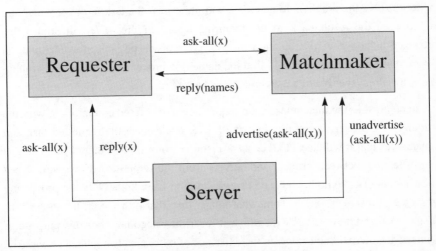

Figure 4.3/17: Operation of a matchmaker

names to the requester. This then can directly contact the servers and negotiate on the acceptance of tasks. The inquiry by the matchmaker does not represent a binding commitment for a requester. The requester can, once it has obtained the name of a server, decide not to pass the corresponding problem to a server, but instead search for some other solution. The situation for the server is different. When it reports the availability of its services to the matchmaker, it also makes the binding commitment to perform the corresponding tasks. Depending on the form of the system specification, it may be possible to change the duration of this commitment. In general, the matchmaker must assume that the reported server service remains valid until it is explicitly withdrawn.

The fact that the name or the address of a matchmaker is known to all agents of the multi-agent system is of decisive importance. Furthermore, every agent must have the authorization to contact the matchmaker irrespective of whether this is to make an inquiry or to provide its services. Although the specific contents of a matchmaker's database are not generally fixed, every matchmaker should at least store information on the name of the offering agent, the type of the offered service (namely the problem or subproblem to be solved), the costs or resources required to solve the problem, the reliability of the agent, and a certain amount of information on the agent. These data normally suffice to supply a satisfactory answer to the requester inquiries.

A broker's task differs from those of a matchmaker. If an agent makes an inquiry to the broker, it expects as answer not only the name of a suitable contact partner, but also the direct solution of the problem. It is the task of the broker to find a provider to solve the problem, to negotiate with it, to pass the task to the provider and to forward the result back to the inquiring agent. Figure 4.3/18 illustrates this changed behavior. A combination of both concepts is possible, for example, an agent that uses a matchmaker to find the name of a broker or an agent that simultaneously adopts the role of a matchmaker and a broker.

In contrast to the matchmaker, the requester enters a fixed commitment with the inquiry to a broker. It commissions the broker to delegate the requested task and guarantees that it will accept all costs or resource consumption that occur. There is no difference between brokers and servers from the requester's viewpoint. It can pass its inquiries to both, and it receives a solution from both. Only the processing duration of a broker may be somewhat longer than that of a server, because a broker must first find a server with which it must then negotiate. For this purpose, it can use its internal knowledge on the existence of other agents it gained previously,

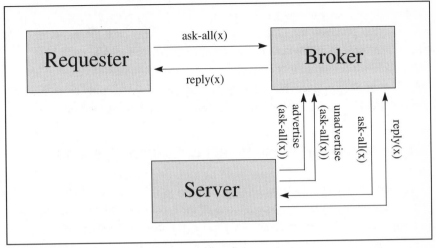

Figure 4.3/18: Operation of a broker

or it can make use of existing directory services. An advantage of the use of a broker is the better resource distribution. Because a requester does not normally have
an overview of the current load of other agents, it must get this information by
direct contact. If, however, it makes its inquiries through a broker, it profits from
the broker's total knowledge. The reportings from agents permit a broker to judge
which agents are currently overloaded or underloaded. This places the broker in the
position to guarantee an efficient load of all agents provided that the types of the
outstanding tasks permit this.

As is apparent from the figures, the KQML communications protocol provides a
number of speech act types and performative types for the realization of matchmakers and brokers. An agent uses the *advertise* performative to register its services with a matchmaker or broker. The contents of an *advertise* message themselves
form a KQML performative. The requester informs the broker/matchmaker in this
manner that it is able to process performatives contained in the Content field of the
advertise message. The degree of detail of the performative can have several levels.
An agent that provides a very general content in which several performative parameters are missing, offers its help for a wide class of problems. If, however, the
statement is specified exactly, the offer applies just to this single problem field.

The requester can use either the basic *ask* performative, or the *recommend, broker* and *recruit* performatives that are specially created for this purpose. *Recommend* corresponds to the previously discussed inquiry to a matchmaker, that is,

the answer to a *recommend* inquiry consists just of the agent's name. The *broker* performative provides the broker's functionality. In this case the inquiring agent receives the solved problem as reply. *Recruit* represents a middle case. If an agent sends a *recruit* command to a broker, the broker then commissions another agent to solve the supplied problem but requests the result to be sent directly to the requester and not first to the broker. This reduces the communications and resource load.

4.4 Learning and Planning in Multi-Agent Systems

Independent of the architectonic form of an agent as deliberative, reactive or hybrid system, the ability to learn represents one of the most important criteria for intelligent operation. The intelligence of an agent for the user makes itself apparent mainly through its ability to learn. If an agent repeats the same error a number of times, its user will hardly describe it as being intelligent. Specifically, the ability to learn means that an agent in the course of time can achieve its object with a continuously decreasing use of resources. Resources here refer to all measurable values, such as time, computer capacity, memory use, communications effort or financial costs.

With regard to the ability to learn, reactive agents possess advantages compared with deliberative systems. They can adapt themselves much better to dynamic environment situations and receive, through their intensive interaction with other objects, a range of information from which they can draw conclusions. Four subquestions must be answered in the design of reactive agents that have the ability to learn [Maes 1994b]:

- What mechanism is used to select the actions to be performed? At any one time an agent has a range of actions, the execution of which brings it a step closer to its goals. Because usually not all possible actions can be performed concurrently, priorities must be set (a task that the scheduler performs for deliberative systems).

- Which principle is used for the actual learning activity? How does the agent decide which information or facts it saves (that is, learns) and which it does not save?

- In what situations does the agent use its previously gained knowledge and when does it attempt to learn? Although an agent will normally perform the optimum action for a particular situation, it is of large importance for the learning process

in some situations also to select non-optimum actions and so learn from their results.

- Which method is used to evaluate the results of an action? Only when a discrete
  value can be assigned to each result, is the agent capable of making conclusions
  on the success of its action and to use these for its learning process. The main
  problem is not in the quantitative evaluation but in the decision which of the actions performed in the past are responsible for a specific result and how high are
  their respective shares.

A number of different concepts exist that can be used to design the learning
process. The selection process should take into consideration that both the architecture used for the agents and the given problem situation affects the efficiency of
the learning algorithm. If, for example, an agent already possesses comprehensive
knowledge when it is created or if it remains in a relatively static environment, the
importance of the learning activity is less than in highly dynamic situations. The
existing concepts can be grouped into three large categories [Maes 1994b]:

- Reinforcement learning

- Classifier systems

- Model builder

The reinforcement learning has the objective to make increased use of those actions that achieved good results in the past and similarly make reduced use of those
actions that achieved poor results in the past. Specifically, this means that an agent
attempts to select those actions in a particular situation that promise it the maximum benefits. A situation/action pair is formed for this purpose from a situation
and an action possible in this situation. A unique value (benefit) is assigned to
every situation/action pair as second step. If a situation arises, the situation/action
pair that currently has the highest value will be performed. If the agent receives a
feedback on the success or lack of success of the action, it must modify the value of
the corresponding situation/action pair. If the same situation occurs in the future,
the agent can make a better selection of an action, because the modified values of
the pairs reflect the past experience. The learning process can be further enhanced
when actions are performed at random intervals that do not have the maximum
value in a particular situation. This permits alternative action-paths to be followed
and their consequences tested. Furthermore, it prevents actions that for some reason
produced several poor results from never being performed, even though in some
circumstances they provide interesting capabilities.

Classifier systems represent a special case of reinforcement learning. Every agent in this concept possesses a number of rules, also known as classifications, that are to be used in specific situations and have been assigned a performance value. The performance value in the simplest case consists of just a single value, the so-called rule strength. As with the classical reinforcement learning, the rule with the largest strength is chosen from all possible rules. However, the learning process itself has a different form. If the actions specified in a rule are performed and the agent has recorded the effects of the actions, the performed action relinquishes part of its strength to the previous rules. This ensures those rules that provided the pre-requisites for a subsequent success or failure are also affected. The agent sometimes removes rules with a very low strength and replaces them with combinations of more successful rules. This uses an algorithm comparable to the scientific selection and mutation mechanism with the aim of detecting new types of processing alter-natives and forms.

The execution process in model builder systems is clearly separated from the actual learning activity. The agent possesses a probabilistic model of the effects of a specific action at a specific time. Situations, actions and the expected results (including their probability) are combined and stored in the form of so-called schemes. When a situation occurs, the scheme with the highest relevance is selected from all those available. The agent observes changes within the environment as part of the learning process and forms correlations between individual situation/action pairs and specific results. It uses these to update the results (and probabilities) of all suitable schemes. The major advantage of the model builder systems is that they can transfer the behavior pattern from one context, such as a goal, to another [Maes 1994b]. However, their complexity, in particular in the action selection phase, is higher than that of other learning algorithms.

One source of a more detailed introduction in the topic of learning in multi-agent systems is contained in [Weiß/Sandip 1996, Weiß 1997].

In addition to the type of the learning algorithm used, the capability to plan is a further important criterion for evaluating the intelligence of an agent. The term planning is considered to mean the considerations an agent makes to use actions from those available to achieve one or more goals. A plan consists of a series of actions that change the agent's environment into the state it requires (its goal). Two basic planning categories must be differentiated in the AI (see Figure 4.4/1). [Martial 1993]: the classical single-agent planning and the multi-agent planning of distributed AI. The term single-agent planning makes apparent that the complete

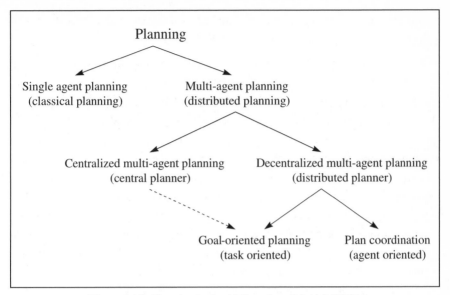

Figure 4.4/1: Planning in the AI (based on [Martial 1993])

planning process in this concept takes place within one agent. This agent adopts the role of both the planner and the executor, because it also performs the plans it creates. Classical planning systems, such as STRIPS [Fikes et al. 1971], belong to the single-agent planners.

The prerequisite for a successful use of the classical planner is firstly a static environment that changes only as the result of the actions performed by the agent, and, secondly, complete information on the side of the planning agent. However, in many scenarios these particular conditions are not met, which forces the creation of new planning concepts. Similarly, the realization that an individual agent is over-extended (from both the resource viewpoint and from content) with the planning and execution of complete actions also plays a role in this context.

Multi-agent planning provides a solution concept for the described problems. As part of multi-agent planning, several agents work together in a coordinated manner. Every agent has a number of plans for whose execution it is responsible and which it uses to achieve the system's overall goal. In contrast to single-agent planning, multi-agent planning can also be used in dynamic environment situations. The integration of communication and cooperative component forms another important aspect in the actual planning process. Whereas the communication on the one hand

and planning on the other hand were treated as separate areas in traditional research, multi-agent planning represents integrating concepts.

As can be seen from Figure 4.4/1, the distributed planning is divided into the central and distributed planner categories. The actual planning process for the central multi-agent planning is performed by a central agent, the planner. This knows the system's central goals from which it derives a series of subplans, which then can be used to achieve the overall goal. The central planner must be informed about the capabilities and available resources of all active agents in the system. It requires this knowledge to be able to assign the subplans to the individual agents in the most efficient manner. The central planners first create a multi-agent plan in which they divide the problem to be solved into subproblems and then create a subplan for each of these subproblems. The second step assigns the subplans to the individual agents after agreement with them. For example, it is possible that the subplan assigned by the central planner to a specific agent exceeds its capabilities or that the agent, for reason of its specialized knowledge, detects an inconsistency in the subplan. The agent in such a case can inform the central planner, which then makes a modification to the original subplans.

No central planner with global knowledge is provided when decentral multi-agent planners are used. In addition to the execution of the subplans, even the planning process is performed by several agents in this concept. The decentral multi-agent planning is always appropriate when the problem to be solved has such a form that the creation of a global knowledge base for the central planner would require excessive effort or is not possible. Distributed planners differentiate between goal-based planning and plan coordination. The overall goal of the planning is known in advance for the goal-based planning, also known as task-oriented planning. The individual subplans are then developed using this overall goal as basis. This methodology is also used by the central planning. A number of agents each with their own plans exist in advance for the plan coordination, which is also known as agent-oriented planning. The task of the distributed planner in this case is to match the existing plans, resolve conflicts and to optimize the results. The task-oriented planners from their nature correspond to the DAI subarea of the distributed problem solving, whereas agent-oriented planners are assigned to the area of the multi-agent systems (see Section 4.1.2).

There are significant differences between the single-agent and the multi-agent planning if the quality of a planning process is to be evaluated. Whereas factors such as correctness, completeness, optimality or efficiency are used for the evaluation criteria for classical single-agent evaluation criteria, because their realization in central environments is difficult, they are not particularly suitable for judging the distributed planning processes [Martial 1993]. For example, a formal proof of the correctness and completeness as frequently implemented for classical planners, is hardly possible in distributed environments. Even terms such as optimality are difficult to quantify and evaluate in decentral structures. Together with the classical evaluation criterion of efficiency, factors such as lack of conflicts, response capability, consistency or fault tolerance are more suitable for the judgment of the quality of a distributed planning process. Only when such criteria are used, is it possible to measure and evaluate the real problem of the distributed planning, namely the division, coordination and synchronization of subplans.

There are a number of central and distributed multi-agent planning concepts. Some have been introduced already in other parts of this book, for example the principle of partial global planning in Section 4.3.4.2. [Martial 1993] provides a good overview of the most important planning methods from a research point of view.

4.5 Security

The commercial success of intelligent agents is largely linked with the solution of the security problems associated with the use of agents. A user will give an agent important tasks or trust it with confidential data only when he is sure that the agent will treat his data confidentially and there are no possibilities that other persons or objects can affect the agent's work, for example by illegally accessing the agent's confidential data. The concrete questions in the security area depend very heavily on the design of an agent as stationary or mobile system. Whereas stationary agents are confronted with the general security risks of network-based applications, the use of mobile agents introduces a new dimension. Their capability to move freely within a network means they possess a danger and damage potential that raises completely new security questions and need to be carefully analyzed.

Intelligent agents, whether stationary or mobile, are almost always associated with electronic networks that they use to perform their tasks and for communication with other agents. Information is transmitted over the network for this purpose, for example as messages or RPCs. When information is sent over the network, the potential danger arises that information is read or changed, or illegal information is introduced by unauthorized persons. This situation is further exacerbated because the exact transmission route used is not normally known in advance. Worldwide networks in particular, such as the Internet, provide countless opportunities and ways in which a message can be transported from the sender to the receiver. Consequently, it does not suffice to protect a specific transmission route. In general, the following security risks can be recognized for the use of electronic networks [Nickisch 1997]:

- Unauthorized reading, copying or modifying of information

- Publicize confidential information (such as credit card numbers)

- Deny the sending or receiving of information

- Masquerade (adopt the identity of another person)

- Repeated input of information (such as repetition of financial bookings or transactions)

- User identification

The use of coding methods, such as encryption, attempts to largely remove a number of the indicated risks. The information to be transmitted is coded using a key and cannot be decoded without knowledge of a suitable corresponding key. This can avoid the unauthorized reading and thus the associated loss of trust. A special check-sum created to avoid the modification of information can be used to detect a change to the information content. Figure 4.5/1 illustrates the basic principle of encryption.

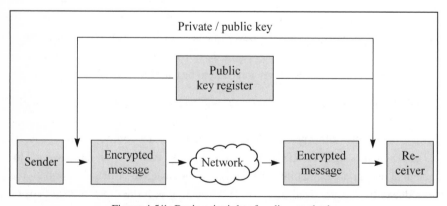

Figure 4.5/1: Basic principle of coding methods

A person or unit trusted with this task creates the key to be used for the coding. There are two possible methods: the private key method uses the same key for both coding and decoding. This key is called a private key, because it is known only to the two parties but not to any other persons. Public key methods use a key-pair, one half of which is publicly known. The public key-half is used by all users of the coding. The decoding requires the other half of the key, which is only known to the receiver. Private key methods have the major disadvantage that both parties must possess the private key before the coding can be made and the key's transmission over the network is not possible because of lack of security. Consequently, sophisticated key transmission procedures must be defined, possibly using non-electronic communications paths. If a third party is commissioned with the administration and provision of the keys (public key register), the key transmission problem may be solved, but not without major security deficits. The third-party in this case is the owner of the private key and so capable at any time of using this key to access coded information. The key administration position must also create and administer an individual key for every communications pair, which results in an exponential growth of keys.

Public-key methods avoid many of the mentioned problems. The receiver of information publicizes a public key that can be used by all senders. Only the receiver is capable of decoding information coded with the public key, because only it knows the private key-half. As for the private-key method, the sender has the security that no unauthorized person can decode the information addressed to the receiver. The assignment and publicizing of the public key are significantly simpler than that of a private key. The receiver makes its public key directly known to either the receiver or the public key register. This publicizing can take place over an unsecured network, because the unauthorized listening to the public key does not have any direct use for a third-party (it can be used only to code but not decode information). The transmission of the public key to an administration instance does not produce problems, because this also does not have any capability of decoding information. If a sender wants to send an information item to a receiver, it requests its public key and uses it for the coding. The coded information is sent to the receiver, which then uses its private key to decode the information. The obvious advantages of the public-key methods are counteracted by the higher (sometimes much higher) computational effort required to create the appropriate key halves.

Although the described coding methods inhibit an unauthorized reading of confidential information, they cannot protect against its falsification. A third-party can change encrypted information, even when it is not able to understand its content.

There are two methods that can be used to protect the authenticity of information: Message Authorization Codes (MAC) and digital signatures. A MAC is added to the coded information to be sent and is derived directly from its content. Only the original content of the information yields the supplied MAC. This agreement is lost if a third-party changes either the information content or the MAC, and the receiver can detect that the information has been changed. Together with the previously discussed problems with the key transmission, the use of MACs has a significant disadvantage. A receiver cannot prove to a third-party that the received information actually originated from the specified sender [Nickisch 1997]. Because the receiver possesses the required key, it could theoretically create the information itself and provide a matching MAC. Such a deception attempt is not possible if digital signatures are used.

As with a MAC, a digital signature is a data block appended to an information item. In contrast to the MAC, a digital signature confirms the origin of the information. Because a valid signature is created with the sender's private key, a signature is always uniquely associated with a sender. The receiver thus has the guarantee that the information actually originates from the apparent sender. It also has the proof that the sender sent the information. The receiver has a legal proof for third parties, such as a bank or a court. In particular, the integration of a system for digital signature is of fundamental importance for the introduction of electronic payment systems and contract acceptances.

The importance of the public key register has been mentioned already in several places. It would not be possible to realize the administrative-intensive coding methods for a large user base without such a register. Because the trustworthiness of a public register is of decisive importance for its function, it is designated as trusted third parties or trust center. If a sender or receiver trusts a public register with its private or public key, it must be sure that it is treated confidentially. On the other hand, and this is the main danger, the user of a key from a public register must be able to assume that the received key originates from the specified person. For example, if agent 2 obtains the public key for agent 1 from a trust center and uses this to code a message, there is the danger that the received key does not actually originate from agent 2 but from agent 3. Because agent 3 possesses the appropriate private key, agent 3 in such a case would have the possibility to read the message actually sent to agent 1. It is clear that agent 2 must be absolutely sure that the received key comes from the register site and this guarantees the correctness of the key. For this reason, the transmission of the key from the public register to the receiving agent must be given a digital signature of the register. Such a construction of public key and signature of a register is also known as a certificate. The prerequisite for the practical usage of this method is the basic assumption that the receiver trusts the register's signature.

Stationary agents do not place any higher demands on security than traditional network-based systems. Only the fact that an agent often represents a user raises the question for this user as to the extent to which it can trust its agent. In contrast, mobile agents represent a different situation. For reason of their special capabilities, mobile agents have a significantly greater danger potential and raise security questions for which significant points have not yet been solved satisfactorily. The risks in the use of mobile agents make themselves apparent in a number of new problems: the unique identification (authentication) and authorization of mobile agents, the protection against mobile agents with similarity to viruses in that they have malicious and disruptive program functions, the protection of mobile agents against malicious computer systems, and the guaranteeing the agent's capability and willingness to pay. All these subareas are discussed in the following section.

Various identification and authentication processes are required, some of which have been described already in Section 4.2.2.3, if a mobile agent wishes to migrate from one computer to another. The destination computer must receive assurance who owns the incoming agent; it must be able to uniquely identify both the agent and its user. Only when both checks are performed successfully, does the mobile agent receive the authorization to enter the destination computer. The information required for the authentication can be exchanged directly with the agent or in separate form, for example between two security modules at the sender and receiver. Various methods can be used for the identification of the user. The server is normally requested to uniquely identify the user of the incoming mobile agent. However, for some application scenarios it is possible that the server accepts that the user belongs to a specific user group [Harrison et al. 1996]. The exact identity does not need to be determined in this case.

Not only the identification of the agent and its user, but also that of the receiving server, are required for the complete authentication process. The user or its mobile agent must know which servers the agent uses in the course of its work. This is essential in some situations, such as for financial transactions. If, for example, a mobile agent makes a payment at its user's bank, it must be able to uniquely determine whether the addressed server is actually the required bank. Otherwise the situation can occur that an appropriately programmed server acts to the agent like the bank and so causes the agent to make the payment to it. The agent has no possibility to determine the correct identification of the destination server if identification mechanisms do not exist.

The next subproblem arises after the identity validation has been performed satisfactorily for both parties. Although the server accepts the mobile agent, it does not have any information on its intended processing or its internal structure. These questions must be answered before the execution of the agent commences. The exact access authorizations of the agent (or of its user) must first be obtained from the server. How much computer capacity can the mobile agent use? Does it have write authorization, and, if yes, how much storage space can it use for its own purpose? Does the agent have the authorization to make financial transactions and what is its maximum money limit? Because all these questions primarily depend on the user's authorization, the server must know these in advance. Given this information, the server can determine the agent's processing limits appropriately, for example, by assigning it only read rights, which result in an error message if a write attempt is made, or all financial transactions can be blocked.

The knowledge about the agent's theoretical authorization does not release the server from the task of also making a detailed analysis of the agent's program code. The server must ensure that the agent does not plan any illegal accesses, which, for example, would be the case of a virus disguised as a mobile agent. This problem has particular importance because, unfortunately, the advantages of mobile agents make them ideal for use as viruses. The validation of the internal program structure of an agent proves to be extremely difficult, if not practically impossible. A preliminary control is useless in some circumstances, in particular for the case of self-modifying agents that dynamically change their program logic during the execution. For example, although a mobile agent could have a harmless program structure when it arrives at a server, it could itself generate malicious procedures during the course of execution.

The executing server has two possibilities for the active monitoring of an agent. It can either explicitly determine the agent's access authorization before its start or it could continually monitor the agent's task during execution. Access lists are normally maintained in the first case in which every agent (or every user) is allowed certain access rights. The agent must identify itself before the start of work and the server uses the agent's identity to determine its access rights. The agent executes within a secure environment (such as the Java Virtual Machine presented in Section 5.2.2) and cannot make any access to resources that lie outside the environment. A special security module of the server used in the second case continually receives information on the agent's requested work steps with which it decides whether the agent's activity is expected or whether the agent wishes to perform some unplanned action. Figure 4.5/2 illustrates such an architecture [Rasmusson/ Jansson 1996].

If an active agent attempts to use certain resources on a server, the system creates control data that contain precise details for the requested actions of the agent, which it then saves in a database. Control modules extract the information from the database and produce an analysis of the agent's behavior. Every control module is responsible for a specific analysis or resource area. The analysis contains a comparison of the agent's expected behavior with its actual behavior and is used by the server's security module to monitor the agent. The task of the agent being monitored plays a decisive role. If, for example, the analysis of the agent for a specific user indicates that this attempts to read confidential data of another user or a purchasing agent tries to read the order data of another customer, these attempts deviate without doubt from the agent's expected activities. The security module can respond and reset the agent's access rights or completely prohibit its further execu-

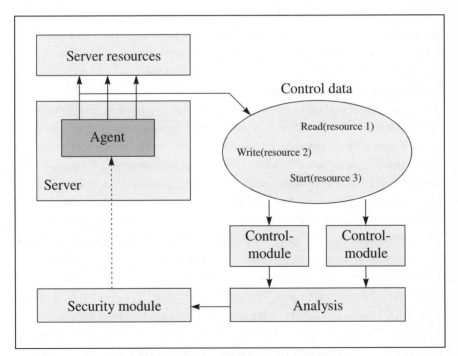

Figure 4.5/2: Monitoring mechanism for mobile agents
(based on [Rasmusson/Jansson 1996])

tion. If, however, the agent's work corresponds to the expectations of the security module, this does not have any reason to intervene. The determination of the agent's expected tasks and the specification of the threshold when the control module starts to become active remain a problem here. A server can only obtain this information empirically provided it does not want to be dependent on details supplied by the agent's user.

The guarantee of the mobile agent's capability and willingness to pay forms the next important question. Generally, the financial value of the resources or information used by an agent should be presented to it as an invoice. Because the agent normally acts on behalf of its user, the service provider must determine in advance whether the user is capable of paying. In the optimum situation, the agent will be requested to transfer the appropriate money amount to the server before a resource is used. However, this is possible only when electronic cash and a complete payment cycle exist. If an agent's cash reserves are exhausted or it is unwilling to pay the demanded price for a service, all further actions of the agent on the server are terminated immediately.

This makes apparent the range of information a server must have on the intentions and internal structures of the mobile agent executing on it. This raises as question the extent to which it is practical to protect confidential information an agent received from its user. If, for example, an agent possesses credit card numbers or account information of its user, this information must not under any circumstances be read by other objects. There are several conceivable possibilities for the loss of confidential information: other agents can specialize in spying out confidential information, which they then use for their own purposes. Servers can come in possession of confidential data while they are monitoring mobile agents; this is a danger that occurs in particular while checking the internal program structure of an agent. Servers can intentionally cause agents to crash and then read their data. Finally, agents themselves can betray confidential data. The last reason makes apparent how much trust a user must have in its agent before he entrusts it with personal information. Only mobile agents for providers with absolute integrity provide sufficient trust with the user to be entrusted with important financial or legal tasks. Together with the agent itself, the servers that a mobile agent enters in the course of its activities must also appear as trustworthy to the user. If, for example, a mobile agent buys specific products from the electronic marketplace for its user, the user of the agent will only provide his credit card number when he is sure that the marketplace is run by a serious provider and the agent can operate on the target computer in a protected environment. Although both stationary agents and mobile agents are confronted with this problem, mobile agents, in particular, provide a particularly large attack surface and for this reason must adopt significantly higher protective measures than stationary agents.

4.6 Demands Made on the Base Systems[1]

4.6.1 Introduction

The central modules for intelligent software agents were described and discussed in the previous sections. The need for a more intensive consideration of the overall system in which an agent is embedded has arisen already a number of times. It has been noted during the discussion of the effects of networks and communications systems in the area of intelligent agents (see Section 4.1.3) that agents normally occur within the application layer of the OSI reference model. Also during the introduction of mobile agents (see Section 4.2), a detailed discussion was given on the layers and functionalities of the basis software for a mobile agent system.

The following section presents and discusses the demands made on a general base system for intelligent software agents. It should be noted that the base system should not be seen as a contradiction to existing layer models (such as the OSI model), but rather a provider of that functionality that is of special interest for the previously introduced basis software for mobile agents. The concepts and functions discussed there are part of the general base system and form exactly that subset required for the development of mobile agents.

The base system forms a standardized environment that serves as basis for the development and execution of intelligent software agents, and provides basic functionality. Because the base system provides services for the agents, the specific functionality components are called services in the following section. An agent can use those services that of interest to it and ignore the less relevant services. It is more difficult to answer the question which services should be provided by the base system and which functions are more appropriately placed in the agent. On one hand, it is conceivable to realize as wide a range of services as possible within the base system. Although this would provide the agent with a wide range of services for its use, this concept significantly increases the complexity of the base system, which causes problems in the practical realization. The methodology where the

---

[1] The authors thank Prof. Steinmetz and Prof. Kalfa for the interesting exchange of ideas while writing Sections 4.6 and 4.7.

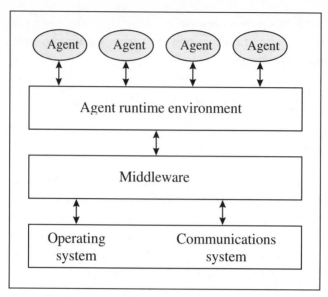

Figure 4.6/1: The base system layer model

base system provides only general services, and the agent itself realizes the special functionality that is of limited interest to most other agents, appears to be the most appropriate solution.

Figure 4.6/1 illustrates the layers of the general base system. A general differentiation is made between different degrees of abstraction, from which the type and range of the provided services can be derived.

- **Agent runtime environment**. The intelligent agent's runtime environment is characterized by the provision of a number of powerful universal services for use by the intelligent agents.

- **Middleware**. The middleware contains powerful services for the administration of distributed environments and has the specific task of providing consistent interfaces.

- **Computer operating system/communications system**. This layer contains all services required for the operation of the computer and communications system.

As with the traditional layer models, the services are characterized by service access points. To describe the available services, it is important that these are treated in detail together with the corresponding layer assignment.

If one attempts to differentiate precisely between the services and properties of the agent runtime services, a strong intermixing of the functionality is apparent in some cases. It is also apparent that no standardized agent runtime environment exists, as is the case for the operating system or middleware.

4.6.2 Agent Runtime Environment

The range of services provided by the agent runtime environment ranges from simple administrative services through to complex services for cluster analysis and rule-based system support. The runtime environment of the intelligent agent itself makes use of services provided by the middleware layer, and the operating system and communications system. The use of the latter can create system dependencies.

The activity of the intelligent agents frequently requires data that relate to the descriptions of the working environment. For example, an agent is given the task of producing suggestions for a specific recreational program. In this case it is important to know which areas of interest are relevant for the user and which recreational activities belong to the user's areas of interest, such as the Berlin marathon for sport. These data are designated as meta data, because they provide information about other data, which they assess or classify. The areas of processing meta data and user details, in particular, require a comprehensive range of modules, whose use and central implementation within the runtime environment is of particular relevance for agents. A profile provides a collection of selected meta data. Media profiles are a range of data that characterize the media.

It is usual to administer profiles and meta data in the agents or their runtime environment. Methods based on user details are available to start filtering processes for comparisons. The comparison of profiles is called "matching operation" or just "matching". The common features can be extracted from a range of profiles. This is called "clustering". For example, if empirical values are analyzed, it is useful to provide the appropriate algorithms, such as cluster analysis, within the intelligent agent's runtime environment.

Because of the common usage of the methodology in various applications and destination systems, the runtime environment services can be used rationally, which means that intelligent agents and applications can be developed in a highly productive environment. Several examples are provided to show which service types may be available for the development of intelligent agents within the agent runtime environment.

4.6.2.1 Administration of Meta Data

The administration of meta data has particular importance especially for intelligent agents, because these modules, and others, have information-compression tasks.

It can be assumed that different types and instances of meta data are necessary depending on the application domain. This requires that the administration of the meta data is flexible with regard to their contents. Figure 4.6/2 shows an example of a category scheme. Meta data are used in an intelligent television program magazine to describe program categories [Wittig/Griwodz 1995]. The general categories, such as films, news, sport, and music are divided into subcategories. For example, the fighting sports form a subgroup of the sport types. The types of fighting sports themselves can be divided into boxing, fencing and in the subgroup of the Asian martial arts, where this subdivision is arbitrarily selected based on a basic knowledge of this category. Judo, Karate and Sumo, for example, belong to the Asian martial arts. These data are used in two ways. Television programs are classified based on the meta data. Users can express their wishes and interests, where the degree of abstraction actually depends on the agent application.

Other examples for meta data and their representation within the base system exist as part of the Internet. A standard has been agreed within Internet that provides the outline for the formulation of the meta data, the so-called meta tag. Consult the server for the World Wide Web Consortium if further information is required [W3 1997].

For the viewpoint of the development of intelligent agents, there is a close connection between categorization by meta data and the evaluation of content.

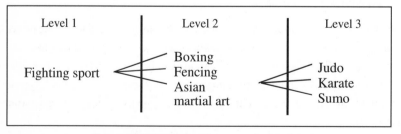

Figure 4.6/2: Example of structured meta data

4.6.2.2 Fuzzy Logic

One of the most important advantages of intelligent agents is the ability to recognize situations, to deduce the appropriate action, and to put this knowledge into practice. It is important to be able to evaluate the success of each action. Developers of intelligent agents would make a mistake if they formulated and digitized the environment conditions and inputs as precisely as possible. If one considers the behavior of an intelligent agent in reality, it soon becomes apparent that is not normally possible to describe an environment situation precisely and comprehensively. Furthermore, user instructions are imprecise when they make statements such as wishes, suppositions, and intentions (see Section 4.2.3).

If, for example, an intelligent agent has to produce a personal music program, it is important to know the user's musical preferences. The agent has the task to select and play the most suitable items from a database of music titles. The artist or the type of music is often important for the user. Assume that a user is interested in music from the rock-and-roll era. It is difficult for the agent to recognize this wish, because this is a colloquial and imprecise description. The agent is not capable at first of finding music titles from the database on the basis of this wish. It requires a means of changing the imprecise description into a form it can use to find the suitable titles from the music database. Figure 4.6/3 shows the transformation using the description of the rock-and-roll period as example. A function is shown that deduces the relationship of a corresponding time period to the rock-and-roll era. This relationship was selected arbitrarily in the example, although a high percentage value means that the period has a higher weighting for belonging to the rock-and-roll era. This function then transforms the imprecision in the specification into

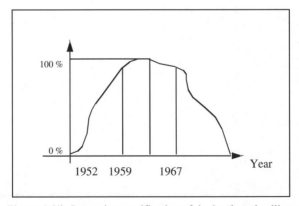

Figure 4.6/3: Imprecise specification of the 'rock-and-roll' era

discrete values, which the agent can use to control intelligent processing logic. This processing method is known as "fuzzy logic".

4.6.2.3 Filtering Services

One of the most important subtasks in the implementation of intelligent agents is to investigate a quantity of information for information that is of interest to the user and extract only the relevant information. The filtering services perform this task and are used by agents in particular for those applications for which a reduction of the quantity of information is necessary. The filtering services help in individual information systems from a general range of messages to select those that best meet the user's particular information requirements. Filtering services are generally used when a subset is to be obtained from a quantity of information. The required filter criteria are specified at the start of the filtering process.

Figure 4.6/4 uses an example of a personalized television magazine to show what results the filtering process can produce. The German television program on a weekday served as basis for the filtering; the user preference was largely news

Figure 4.6/4: Results of the television program filtering

broadcasts and action programs. The comparison of the television programs from 10 o'clock to 12 o'clock and the individual user profile produced the shown program.

4.6.2.4 Services for Cluster Analysis

Agents capable of learning can draw conclusions from their own actions, which they can use in their subsequent behavior. Special procedures provided in the agent runtime environment are required to process the conclusions and the capabilities already described in Section 4.4.

An analytical consideration of the learning process can generally assume that the performed handling steps are recorded and the handling results used to evaluate their success. The singular behavior pattern is not of primary importance. Rather, agents should be capable of converting individual behaviors into general behavior patterns or character properties. The cluster analysis is a basic procedure for the structured, weighted aggregation of information. It serves to recognize related information from a quantity of information and to structure these relationships. Two basic forms of cluster analysis can be differentiated:

- Hierarchical procedures

- Non-hierarchical procedures

Hierarchy as used here means that the result of the cluster analysis represents a hierarchical structure. Non-hierarchical methods are not subject to any hierarchical order and possess relatively limited complexity and provide imprecise results [El-Hamdouchi/Willet 1989].

Figure 4.6/5 shows an example of the basic principle of the cluster analysis. A similarity function that forms the basis specifies the position of the individual elements in the shown point cloud. The arrows indicate the most similar element. Thus, element A is the most similar element to element F in the set, whereas the element C is the element most similar to element A. This permits the determination of which elements belong together with regard to the similarity relation and so form a cluster. The points can are determined by forming the middle points of the individual chains of elements. These are designated as c_1, c_2, c_3 and c_4 in the figure. This operation is repeated until a single element set results.

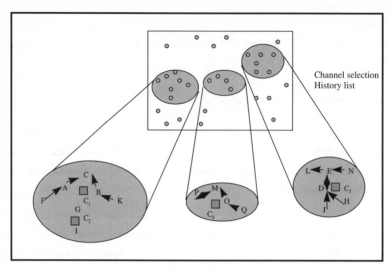

Figure 4.6/5: Principle of the cluster analysis

When we consider the application cases for clustering methods, two primary application areas occur more often:

- The self-learning capability of the intelligent agent is used for the optimization of its own actions.

- Learning at the interactions with the human-machine interface permits intelligent agents to draw conclusions for its own objective-oriented actions and so optimize the user acceptance.

4.6.2.5 Initialization of User Profiles

If the agent-based application requires that a model of the users is to be maintained as user profiles, this raises the question how these profiles are to be initialized. From the agent's viewpoint, it would be desirable to know as much as possible must about the user so that it can provide useful results from the start of its action as agent. On the other hand, the user is prepared only to a limited extent to provide time for the specification of his user profile. For this reason, the method of the initialization of user profiles represents a non-trivial aspect of the planning and development of intelligent agents.

The agent's runtime environment has the task of providing a number of initialization functions. These must cover a spectrum that ranges from the manual input of user profiles, through a semi-automatic procedure, to the automatic recognition of

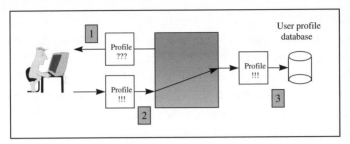

Figure 4.6/6: Explicit installation of the user profile

user profiles by the intelligent agents themselves. Using a personalized television magazine as example, the basic characteristics are evaluated and weighted. The installation modes can be characterized as follows:

- **Explicit installation of the user profile** (see Figure 4.6/6). Menus prompt the user in this installation mode to explicitly enter his preferences, wishes and intentions in the form of attributes or rules (phases 1 and 2 in Figure 4.6/6). For example, in the case of the personalized television magazine, this means that the user specifies his favorite films, artists, and types of film, as well as all other attributes. The agent directly places the specified profile data in the internal user profile. Although this action provides a very precise result when performed correctly, it demands a detailed basic knowledge of the actions and can easily result in errors. The manual updating turns out to be difficult when the requirements change. In particular, this mode cannot be recommended for those users without detailed basic knowledge. The threshold for the use is extremely high. Thus, this mode is more appropriate for very advanced users who can tune their own user profiles.

- **Initialization using user characteristics** (see Figure 4.6/7). This method makes use of the concept that selected characteristics of the user permit an assignment

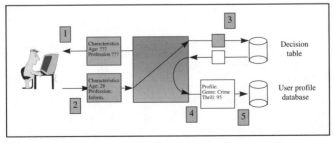

Figure 4.6/7: Initialization using user characteristics

into user classes. The user is requested to specify personal data (phase 1 and 2). For example, the layout of a personalized television magazine using demographic data determines that user characteristics such as age, sex, education and profession have a significant effect on the viewed program. An individual profile for every user class is created based on these accumulated statistics, and is stored in a table. The initial user profiles are then determined from a table in which the corresponding user class is used as access key (phases 3, 4 and 5).

This mode has the advantage of simplicity. However, the precision largely depends on how many user classes have been defined and the degree to which personal characteristics can be represented in the initial user profiles. Although more classes mean higher precision, they make more demands on the determination of the data base.

- **Initialization using examples** (see Figure 4.6/8): The background of this initialization method is the fact that it is easier to supply examples or to complete a questionnaire than to specify concrete objectives. The creation of the initial user profile in this mode requires that the agent requests the user to specify examples for the required results of the agent's task or to answer the specified questions (phase 1). Once the user has made the appropriate answers (phase 2), the agent can evaluate these answers. This evaluation requires that the agent classifies and weights the answers using its internal weighting scale, and so produces complete information for the user profile. In the example of the personalized television magazine, the meta-information for the favored example programs are determined from a supplied database (phases 3 and 4). These individual information items then must be combined as a user profile. The cluster analysis has the task of recognizing preferred use patterns, from which it produces a compressed user profile.

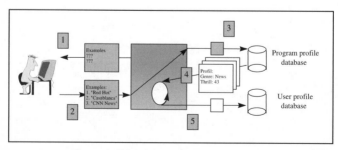

Figure 4.6/8: Initialization using examples

This mode has the advantage of simplified handling. It has the disadvantage of the danger that the selected examples for the wishes and intentions of the user are not representative, and so the results are less precise. Furthermore, an increased computer load results from the intelligent processing logic.

- **Initialization by observing the user's behavior** (see Figure 4.6/9). If a very simple operation of the user interface is the highest priority, it is advisable that the agents automatically create the user profile. This action is based on the initial observation of the user's behavior (phase 1) with the aim of being able to draw conclusions with regard to his wishes and expectations. This observation phase ends when the agent considers that it has obtained sufficient information to make conclusions with regard to the general behavior pattern. Finally, in phase 2, an evaluation of the observed behavior is made with the aim of combining its wishes as they affect the agent's objective. Cluster analysis methods can be used in phase 2. Using our example of the personalized television magazine, this means that the agent determines the usage of the television set over an adequate time period and so deduces the personal preferences of the user or user group.

Because the user is completely relieved of having to make any input, this mode has the advantage of a very simple operation. The observation method

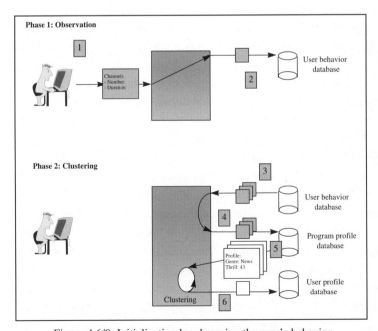

Figure 4.6/9: Initialization by observing the user's behavior

provides a further advantage of determining changes in the user's preferences over the complete period of use and then adapting itself appropriately. However, the disadvantage should be noted that the agent is operational only after a learning phase and so requires an introductory phase before it can start work, that is, an agent cannot be immediately operational.

4.6.2.6 Rule-based Systems

The described principles of matching and clustering cover only a limited range of agent-based applications. Deliberative agents with a high degree of intelligence, in particular, require knowledge of the agent's objectives and environment that far exceeds the recording and evaluation of meta data. Agents with learning ability require strategies and tactics for knowledge acquisition.

Rule-based systems are a further possibility the intelligent agents can use to perform tasks. Such systems consist of a knowledge base that contains a number of rules and facts. The knowledge base describes the reality section in which the intelligent agent operates. The reality section can also be used to cover only part of the agent's activity while the previously described runtime modules cover other elementary parts.

The example of the personalized television magazine is used to illustrate the use of a rule-based system. The agent has the task during the automatic initialization mode to create a user profile from the watched programs. Although the assumption is made here that the view duration of a program is directly related to the user's interest in this broadcast, there are a number of cases where such a conclusion is incorrect. For example, it is possible that the user has gone to sleep while watching television. Although the program hat not changed, this cannot be evaluated as interest in the corresponding program. Thus, it is also necessary that such cases are treated and evaluated separately. The use of a rule-based system helps to describe, recognize, and react appropriately to exceptional situations. Figure 4.6/10 uses a model to illustrate the special case of going to sleep while watching television over the course of time. The user frequently changes between television channels in the phase t1 to t2, and finally finds a program to his liking. The channel remains unchanged between times t2 and t5 even though the program has changed several times. This is a strong indication that the user has gone to sleep or has left the room. Sensors can be used in rule-based systems to determine this. If a user stays longer than usual on a television channel or if he watches programs that do not usually interest him during this time, it can be assumed that he is absent. The rule-based

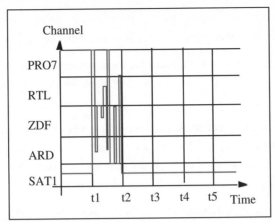

Figure 4.6/10: Intelligent recognition of behavior patterns while watching television

system uses these indicators to recognize that an exceptional situation exists. The intelligent agent either totally ignores this special case or deduces that this program was only of limited interest. Zapping, where channels are frequently changed, or vacation times, when the television is not switched on at all, are similar situations.

Rule-based systems largely depend on formalized knowledge and a so-called inference machine. The knowledge is stored as rules and facts in a knowledge base. The inference machine has the task of searching the knowledge base when queries are issued and then providing an answer for the query. It is also possible to return imprecise answers.

Using the example of the personalized television magazine, a rule-based system would be used to handle the special cases. Agent developers frequently use rule-based systems to model their environment, that is, to define facts and to create a control mechanism for the agent's behavior.

4.6.3 Middleware

The middleware layer is primarily concerned with the infrastructure services that are based on the basic services of the computer operating system and the network operating system. The supporting services for the mobile agents are a first example in which the attempt is made to achieve both the ability for the agent to move within a heterogeneous usage environment and the platform independence of the agent. The provision of a "virtual machine" within the intelligent agent's middle-

ware permits programs, modules and agents to operate on all computers. The Java
Virtual Machine, described in Section 5.2.2, is one of the best-known examples.

The provision of supporting services for the administration of an object-oriented,
distributed infrastructure is also an important middleware task. Such services include:

- **Information and object brokers**. Information and object brokers provide in a
  distributed middleware services for access, invocation and forwarding of information queries and method calls. A broker makes extensive use of directory and
  distribution services here.

- **Replication services**. Objects and services can be queried at various locations
  within a distributed environment. The service user and the service provider enter
  into communication with each other. Delays arise here, for example, as a result
  of the separation of the two communication partners in the network. Replication
  services have the task of duplicating information and services with the aim of

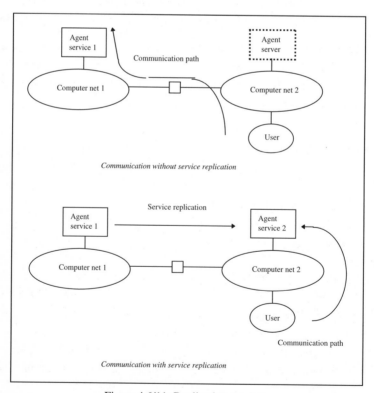

Figure 4.6/11: Replication services

reducing delays in the communication and in the communication volume in the networks. Figure 4.6/11 shows an example of intelligent agents in which a replication reduces the communication paths.

- **Distribution services**. Three main scenarios can be envisaged for the communication. In addition to the traditional scenario that provides a duplex communication between agents, agents can also send information to a group of agents ("multicasting") or, as part of general distribution services, provide the information in the complete information region ("broadcasting").

- **Directory services**. Several, often obscure, services and service providers exist within an agent-based complete system. Directory services are provided to locate these services and their providers. The most important task of the directory services is to provide categories of services, to administer services and providers, and to give information on the available services.

- **Billing services**. Section 4.5 provided an introduction how intelligent agents can maintain confidential information and so, for example, carry electronic money or initiate effective transactions. The middleware should be assigned the functionality of the billing services.

Section 5.1.1 and [Vogel 1996] contain further discussions of middleware, in particular object-oriented concepts.

4.6.4 Computer Operating System and Communications System

As is the case in all other software, the agent runtime environment and the middleware require an operating system that provides basic services for the control and the management of the local runtime environment in the computer. The operating system provides application interfaces (graphic or command line-oriented) and programming interfaces. The programming interfaces are of particular interest for the intelligent agent. The provided services are independent of the hardware and firmware. The computer operating system provides the following important service classes:

- **File and directory management**. The data of the system and the user are stored in the computer as directories and files. The basic services that exist as part of the directory and file management are responsible for the creation, opening, closing reading, writing, updating and deletion of directories and files.

- **Process control.** Most current computer systems possess a main processor. If several tasks (so-called processes) need to be performed concurrently, the processes compete for access to the main processor. One of the process control's tasks within the operating system is to control access to the processor and thus control the processing of a process executing in the operating system. It is possible to follow various goals as part of the process control: to process the processes as fast as possible or to maximize the load on the processor.

- **Memory management.** The memory management has the task of organizing access to the computer's main memory. Such tasks include the release of main memory for use in application programs, such as the agent runtime environment, control of the access to areas of main memory, or writing to hard disk those memory contents that are no longer required.

Further service groups are access controls to the operating system, devices and files, programming help, and the device control. [Kalf 1988] contains a conceptual introduction to the terms and the architecture as well as details of the services within the operating system.

The communications system is responsible for the provision of basic services and service primitives for the communication of the local computer with other computers of the network complex.

4.7 Development Tendencies

4.7.1 Introduction

Both intelligent agents and multimedia systems have the goal of making use of new principles to provide an improved information transfer at the human-machine interface. Multimedia attempts this through the use of new and attractive media forms. Intelligent agents have the responsibility of using a more intelligent type of the information processing to reduce the flood of information to an acceptable amount.

The current development of intelligent systems shows that future systems will be characterized by intelligent extensions or an increasingly intelligent nucleus. The combination of multimedia and intelligent agent technologies appears to be coming nearer. This means for the current multimedia systems:

- Responsive and intelligent form for multimedia applications

- Situation-dependent control of multimedia use in accordance with the available environment conditions (for example, end unit, user characteristics)

- Adaptation of the complete system and the information processing with regard to the multimedia input and output units.

Figure 4.7/1 shows the historical development of the traditional computer systems, through multimedia systems, ending with agent-based and intelligent systems. The original human-machine interface was text based, namely, text command sequences initiated processing operations that produced output in text form.

The development and introduction of graphical user interfaces and windowing in the 1970s permitted the progression to the graphic-oriented operation of the computer using a mouse. The introduction of multimedia systems was particularly characterized by the integration of new media, such as video or audio in the user interface of computers. The next development step, that of intelligent multimedia agents, has already begun. Instead of attempting to make all functional characteristics visible on the user interface, intelligent agents help in the following ways:

- Extension of context-sensitive assistants to support the user in the operation

- Format the user interface and the contents in a form appropriate for the user's level of knowledge

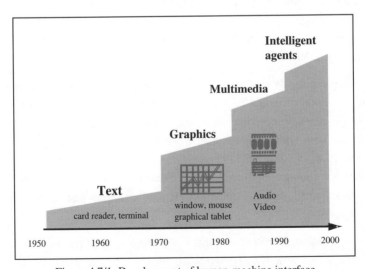

Figure 4.7/1: Development of human-machine interface

- Utilize general layout principles of the human-machine interface and rules for individual layout principles

- Signal to the user that monotonous processing operations could be performed faster and better by the agent.

The term user-friendliness adopts a central role in this connection. Some of the objectives of the more user-friendly human-machine interface include:

- Ease of being remembered and of being recognized again

- Usability

- Adaptivity

- Effectiveness in the operation

- Ease of being learnt

- Aesthetics

If we consider in detail the development of intelligent agents with regard to multimedia systems, two main development tendencies become apparent:

- **Intelligent agents in multimedia environments**. Multimedia specialists have increasingly recognized that the mixture of the established multimedia application area and intelligent concepts, for example in the form of intelligent agents, provide new multimedia application areas and customer potentials.

- **Multimedia in intelligent agents**. Another group has previously concentrated on intelligent agent technologies and applications. It has been recognized that the increasing integration of multimedia concepts into intelligent systems can provide benefits.

The process of the development of multimedia systems was and is accompanied by a large volume of media formats and processing standards. New information media for the user have been developed and increasingly standardized for this process. Two directions are forcing the standardization: the de facto standards set by the market monopoly of a few software companies and standards set by the established standardization committees. Standards for multimedia in WWW, such as HTML, and in interactive television, such as DAVIC, are examples that serve to illustrate the developments.

It can be increasingly recognized that multimedia systems and intelligent agents currently provide a wide-ranging symbiosis for the solution of specific tasks. The process of increasing integration of both concepts ending with intelligent media agents is already active. The following section uses the WWW and an interactive television system to show how multimedia services and intelligent agents can be combined.

4.7.2 Intelligent Agents in Multimedia Environments

Intelligent agents and their runtime environments cover services that multimedia applications can use. This permits the development of a more intelligent form of application control as an extension of the multimedia presentation of information. All application areas of multimedia systems are suitable candidates.

Navigation in the WWW is based in the assumption that providers make information available on their computers for downloading. On request from the user, these provided data are transferred from the provider's computer over the Internet to the user's computer. These actions take time, which, because of network bottlenecks, are often unacceptably long. Long load times significantly hinder the Internet user in interactively requested large volumes of content. On the other hand, there are times during an online session in which the user observes and absorbs the information. Although the customer is online and also paying accordingly during this time, he is not making use of the available network capacity. To make optimum use of this time, it is conceivable that previously subscribed content is transferred to the user's computer with the content not being transferred from the provider but more quickly from the local user computer. If the transfer of the information blocks is controlled from the service provider's computer, this is called "push", and push technologies are used for the implementation. This permits a temporal decoupling between the observation of WWW contents and their delivery, and provides the user of push-based systems the capability of subscribing to WWW contents. Figure 4.7/2 shows a navigation interface for the push methodology. The hierarchically arranged items that can be seen on the left-hand side of the figure each represent a subscribed topic area. The information is shown within the navigation user interface if such a topic area is selected. If the service user's computer initiates the supply of the content, this is called "smart pull".

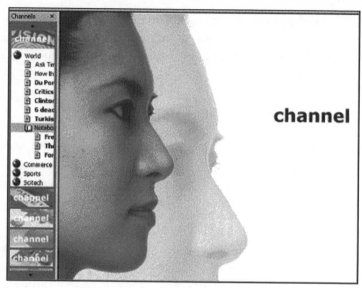

Figure 4.7/2: Navigator with push channels

In combination with intelligent agents, push technologies provide a number of new capabilities:

- **Coupling of push technologies with intelligent filtering**. The success of the push technologies depends on the degree to which the supplied content matches the user's information requirements. In the simplest case, the user is permitted to subscribe to individual WWW pages. Subscriptions to topic areas (such as sport or politics) are permitted as extended selection, which then represents the filter criteria. Intelligent agents then have particular importance when the user requires support in the definition of the filter. An intelligent agent then can make a recommendation based on the pages request from the WWW as to which specific information filters would be appropriate for the user.

- **Intelligent agents as push objects**. Push methods also can be used to transfer intelligent agents if an information channel for intelligent agents is created. This then provides an information channel for agent-based markets. This concept also can be transferred to advertising agents. A particular use of this linkage results from the combination of multimedia information in the navigation user interface with the agent-based markets, because the user communication with the WWW and the agents takes place in a standardized navigation user interface.

- **Intelligent push agents**. Users make use of intelligent push agents to detect new information sources in their areas of interest, to subscribe to offers or to perform price negotiations. Additional application areas can be found in Section 6.3.

4.7.3 Multimedia and Intelligent Agents

The integration of multimedia in intelligent agents initially means that the application areas of intelligent agents have different relevance. For example, a personalized television magazine is particularly suitable to combine agent functionality with the multimedia user interface of the television system and thus simplify the navigation. On the other hand, intelligent control systems are initially little affected by the multimedia integration.

The WWW currently embodies a number of standards that represent the foundation for the representation, presentation and transfer of multimedia. For example, the Hypertext Markup Language (HTML), as basic language for the description of multimedia information, and the Hypertext Transport Protocol (HTTP), as communications protocol, belong to the basic standards of the WWW. These standards are agreed and ratified within the WWW Consortium (W3C). Furthermore, a number of de facto standards that have established themselves complement and extend these basic standards. Java, which extends the HTML clients and servers with local processing capabilities, is an example.

Developments and standardization efforts are taking place within the W3C that will have a significant effect on the development of intelligent agents in the Internet.

4.7.3.1 Multimedia Extensions

The extension of the existing HTML description language introduces new multimedia characteristics that also provide the intelligent agents with an improved programmability for applications and presentations. Examples are window-based user interfaces or the synchronization of various monomedia. Figure 4.7/3 shows an example of the cascadable user interface layout within a WWW navigator, where the term cascading can apply to both the stepped and overlapped windows within the navigator and the text representation using different sized fonts.

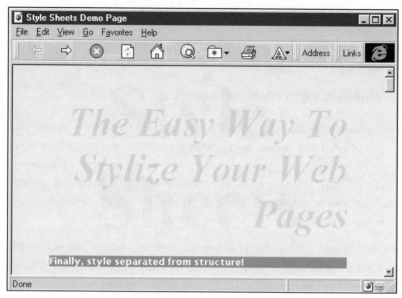

Figure 4.7/3: WWW demonstration page for cascade style sheets

4.7.3.2 Platform for Internet Content Selection (PICS)

Rating systems are used to provide the infrastructure prerequisites for the standard-ized evaluation of information. An individual agreement is made within the rating system which evaluation criteria are to be used for the specific Internet application. PICS (Platform for Internet Content Selection) provides the basis for the rating system in the Internet. PICS is an infrastructure that permits the linking of the de-scription of the meta data for the media. Although PICS was originally developed to give parents and teachers the capability to restrict the Internet access of children, it can be used for other types of rating systems.

The following example uses a PICS label for a WWW page to illustrate how the attributes can be specified as part of PICS.

> *<head>*
> *<META http-equiv='PICS-Label' content='*
> *(PICS-1.1 'http://www.gcf.org/v2.5'*
> *labels on '1994.11.05T08:15-0500'*
> *until '1995.12.31T23:59-0000'*
> *for 'http://w3.org/PICS/Overview.html'*

ratings (crime 0.5 sex 0))

>

</head>

... contents of documents here ...

The attributes (crime, sex) of a WWW page are evaluated in this example and are identified with the agreed *ratings* keyword within the PICS specification. The rating information is contained in the WWW page header.

Users of the rating system can use these descriptive rules to define their wishes and requirements for the usage of the online and Internet access. Attributes are generally formed that contain meta data. Figure 4.7/4 illustrates the use of a PICS client.

This example shows a selection page in which the user can specify the extent to which content with violence can be transferred within his or her Internet access. The shown example permits the transfer of contents that show simple violence, such as damage to objects. This selection explicitly prohibits the showing of violence to people.

PICS is also suitable for use with intelligent agents to form the basis for the evaluation of agents and the extraction of meta data for the associated application context. The value of PICS is in the rigorous structuring rule that results from the defined standard. This, however, has the disadvantage that the specification of the attributes is performed on an individual basis. If, for example, an application with

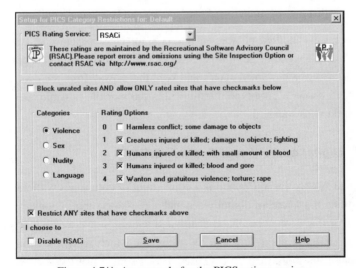

Figure 4.7/4: An example for the PICS rating service

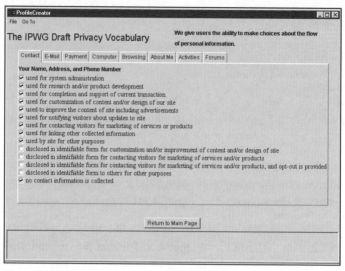

Figure 4.7/5: User interface for the specification of personal preferences

distributed intelligent agents is being developed, a standardized scheme for the attributes must be defined.

4.7.3.3 Platform for Privacy Preferences (P3)

It is necessary that the intelligent agent knows its user's wishes and intentions. The provision of a platform for user preferences, the Platform for Privacy Preferences (P3), means that the specification of user wishes can be standardized.

Intelligent agents then possess an interface for the acceptance of requests that apply to the adherence of general parameters. On the other hand, this platform can be used to describe unwanted agents and keep these away from the own computer. Figure 4.7/5 shows a prototype that illustrates parts of the possible considerations with regard to this standard.

4.7.3.4 Digital Audio Visual Council (DAVIC)

The Digital Audio Visual Council is a consortium of companies with the objective of expediting the spread of digital video and audio-based applications and services, in particular that of the broadband distributed television and interactive television. DAVIC consists of approximately 200 members, which represent companies and institutions from more than 20 countries. It is assumed that the success of multi-

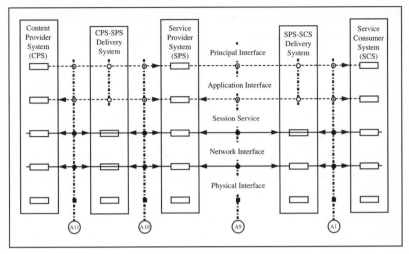

Figure 4.7/6: Reference model of the DAVIC system

media systems depends among other things on the use and integration of open standards for content providers, service providers, network providers, and hardware and software providers. DAVIC has the aim of identifying, selecting, evaluating and incorporating formal standardizing committees, such as International Standardization Organization (ISO) and Digital Video Broadcasting (DVB), and existing standards for interfaces, systems, protocols and architectures. The essential basis for the work of DAVIC is a reference model that describes the architecture of the system addressed in DAVIC (see Figure 4.7/6). The five elements of the DAVIC reference model are apparent in the figure:

- **Content Provider System**. The Content Provider System is used to provide information and content. It can be assumed that the content is available in various media formats and the corresponding infrastructure is made available.

- **Service Provider System**. The Service Provider System bundles the offers of several content providers and serves a primary contact point for the Service Consumer System. The Service Provider System frequently serves as central component to provide access to the services and to manage these.

- **Service Consumer System**. The Service Consumer System describes the properties and interfaces of the user systems to achieve access to the available services and content.

- **Delivery Systems, CPS-SPS Delivery System and SPS-SCS Delivery System**. Both distribution systems in this connection serve to link the subsystems with each other.

The specifications of DAVIC refer to the represented subsystems, modules and their interfaces. Furthermore, the model provides for the separation of communications layers (= service layers). The service layers provide abstract views of the DAVIC system. Thus, for example, the various applications of the DAVIC system are defined by the "Application Interface", whereas definitions are made in the physical layer which interfaces are to be provided by the hardware of the DAVIC-conforming computer and communications systems.

There are many possibilities to use intelligent agents in the context of DAVIC. The agent-based concepts introduced in the "Application Technical Committees" represent a framework on which applications such as "Personalized Video on Demand" and a personalized television magazine can build [Wittig 1995].

Various general parameters can be found if one considers the development tendencies of television systems: increasingly digital transmissions and media are used instead of analog transmissions and media, for example, Digital Video Broadcasting (DVB). The media here are heavily compressed before the transmission in order to make better use of the communications channel. Television in the current sense is distributed television. A return channel to the program provider or to the transmitter does not exist. Systems that give the users interactive communications capabilities through the provision of a return channel are currently being evaluated in field test (for example, broadband telephone network in Nuremberg). This interaction permits the provision of new services, such as shopping, online games, video on demand (VoD) or news on demand. Video on demand is a request service in which video films are shown on remote request in a similar manner as being played on a video recorder. If one considers the action that takes place within films, the current films exhibit a linear storyline. As part of interactive capabilities it is conceivable that programs will offer several alternatives that the user can individually select. Other possibilities are offered by cyberspace. The described scenarios and resulting usage perspectives into digital and interactive television systems are classified in Figure 4.7/7. In particular for the personalization of interactive and nonlinear films, and in the area of virtual reality films, the specific use of intelligent agents is to be expected.

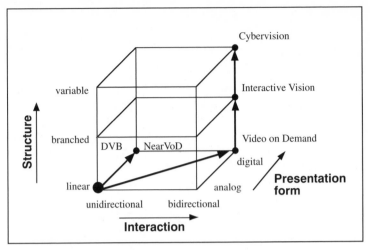

Figure 4.7/7: Development tendencies for television systems

4.8 Summary

Building on the basic areas of influence for intelligent agents (in particular, AI, DAI and network communications systems), the internal structure of an agent and the cooperation of agents within a multi-agent system has been introduced in detail. The internal structure is primarily determined by two different design characteristics: firstly, the design as deliberative or reactive system, and, secondly, with the differentiation between stationary and mobile agents. Each of these individual concepts is based on a number of fundamental theories, each of which has been discussed in detail. The communications and cooperation protocols/strategies form the central aspect during the cooperation of several agents. There are a number of methodologies that support the efficient design of a multi-agent system and the distributed solution of problems in the areas of communication and in cooperation. The most important concepts (KQML, contract nets system, Partial Global Planning) have been introduced and evaluated. Short introductions to a number of central topic areas for the design of agent-based systems formed the conclusion. This section has been primarily concerned with learning, planning, security, and consideration of the demands made on the multimedia system.

5 Development Methods and Tools[1]

The design and development of complex application systems requires the use of phase-oriented design methods and the use of development tools. This does not only apply for traditional software systems, but also for agent-based architectures, because they also represent complex application systems. This chapter discusses central development methods and tools with specific regard to agent-oriented systems. The aims are to investigate currently existing methods and tools with regard to their suitability for the development of agent systems, and to identify the specific requirements of agent-oriented systems. Figure 5.1/1 provides an overview of the central tool categories for the application development and shows the associated development cycle phases.

This chapter discusses three tool categories we consider to be important: Section 5.1 investigates the use of object-oriented design methods for agent-oriented systems, Section 5.2 presents three programming languages for agent systems, and Section 5.3 discusses the principles of component-based software development.

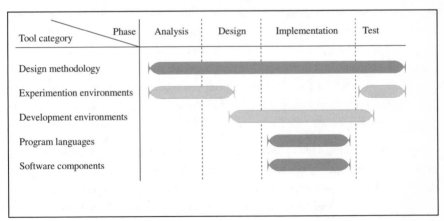

Figure 5.1/1: Development methods and tools (based on [Kraetzschmar/Reinema 1993])

---

[1] This chapter was written by Rüdiger Zarnekow.

Because the currently existing agent-oriented environments are mainly research-oriented or prototype realizations with limited value for commercial application development, the development and experimental environments are not considered in detail here. The developers of agent systems are still dependent on the use of general object-oriented or AI/DAI-oriented environments.

5.1 Agent-Oriented Analysis and Design

5.1.1 Object-Oriented Analysis

The classical models and methods of software development cannot be transferred without modification to agent-oriented systems because these exhibit various basic differences to traditional software systems and require extended concepts or objectives within the used development methodology. This section investigates the extent to which existing methods and models satisfy the particular requirements made by the development of agent systems and which characteristics an agent-oriented development model needs to exhibit.

Figure 5.1/2 illustrates the traditional phase model of software development. A general specification of the problem to be modeled is made in the analysis phase. The aim is the creation of an analysis model that precisely defines the tasks to be performed by the new system and what it intends to do to achieve this goal. The analysis does not consider in detail how the task is to be specifically solved. The design phase follows the analysis phase. The analysis model is used to complete the actual system design. The basic architecture of the system and the function units, data structures and algorithms are defined. As part of the implementation, a programming language and other development tools are used to convert the developed concept into a practical form. A comprehensive and full system test completes the process. The following section discusses just the analysis and the design. The programming languages used for the implementation are described in the next chapter.

Agent systems, from their nature, can be assigned to the object-oriented systems. Their objects, the agents, consist of attributes and methods, and communicate with each other by invoking methods or by sending messages, and use classical OO concepts, such as inheritance, data encapsulation or aggregation. Consequently, object-oriented development methods have particular relevance for the development of agent-based applications. Traditional, non-object-oriented development models, such as structured analysis/design (SA/DS) or the models of [Yourdon

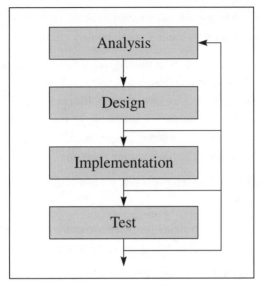

Figure 5.1/2: Software development cycle

1991] and [DeMarco 1985], have only limited relevance for the modeling of agent systems. They are based on functional program logic and cannot represent many aspects of an agent. In contrast, object-oriented methods build on the concepts of object-orientation and attempt to supply problem-free and complete support for the development of object-oriented systems. There currently exist a number of different methods, such as the Object Modeling Technique (OMT) [Rumbaugh 1993], Fusion [Coleman et al. 1994] or the methods of [Booch 1991] and [Coad/Yourdon 1991a, 1991b].

All these methods support the analysis and design process with a range of graphical models that attempt to simplify the system designer's difficult task of the conception and structuring of the system. OMT, for example, uses three models: the object model, the dynamic model, and the functional model [Rumbaugh 1993]. The object model represents the static structure of all objects contained in the system and their static interrelationships (for example, inheritances or aggregations). The object model is represented graphically as one or more object diagrams. The dynamic model contains all the dynamic processes of the system, namely, those processes that change during the course of time. Potential events and transitions of the systems are shown within one or more status diagrams. The third OMT model, called the functional model, uses data flow diagrams to describe the functional flows within the system and thus its internal structure. [Rumbaugh 1993] contains more extensive information on the individual models and their application.

Although other methods use other models and diagrams to some extent, the general procedure of object-oriented design methods can be divided into four processing steps, which are supported by three models [Burmeister 1996]: the identification of the objects and classes, the identification of the static relationships of the objects, the specification of the dynamic processes, and the description of the internal structures of the objects. The three models concern:

- The **base model**, which contains the actual objects including their attributes and methods (see Figure 5.1/3).

- The **static model** that represents the static structure of the system objects (for example, the object hierarchy and the grouping in subsystems)

- The **dynamic model** that models the control flow of the system by representing the dynamic relationships between objects (dynamics in the large), the processes within individual objects (dynamics in the small), and the internal structure.

Each of the three basic models is continuously developed during the course of the development process. Thus, for example, the very general model at the start of the analysis is extended during the design phase with the objects of the target area,

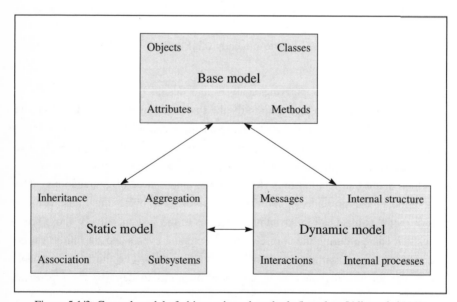

Figure 5.1/3: General model of object-oriented methods (based on [Albayrak 1996])

and the objects of the application domains and the target area coded as part of the implementation [Rumbaugh 1993]. The interaction of the individual models is also apparent. No one model can be considered independently of the other two models, but only in the complete system context. However, it is the aim of every design methodology to provide explicitly visible linkages and interfaces and so decouple to the maximum extent the various aspects and views of the system.

5.1.2 Agent-Oriented Methods

Although agents are normally represented as objects, they possess a range of properties that distinguish them from the classical object-oriented systems. Consequently, the described, purely object-oriented design methods have only limited suitability for use in agent-oriented environments. Various authors have investigated the particular modeling requirements of agent-based systems [Burmeister 1996, Kinny et al. 1995, Sundermeyer 1993, Iglesias et al. 1996]. The most important results of their work can be summarized as: agents have a significantly more complex internal structure than traditional objects. They do not consist just of attributes and methods, but also have mental states (BDI agents) and concepts, such as plans or goals [Burmeister 1996].

The internal structure of an agent thus consists of a functional component and also a number of behavior patterns. Both aspects must be taken into consideration in the modeling. An agent has more similarity with a subsystem of object-oriented methods than a single object. However, it is only of limited use to structure agent-oriented systems in the form of classical subsystems. Rather, the modeling should be performed taking into consideration the role of the agent within the complete organization, because this structuring can be used directly in the analysis, design and implementation [Albayrak 1996]. In contrast to the classical passive objects, agents are active units. They can be independently active (proactivity) and follow their own plans and objectives. Whereas objects are activated by the sending of messages or the invocation of methods, an agent can at any time decide whether and in which form it will respond to a specific message. An agent-oriented methodology must provide models to represent such behavior patterns.

The type of the communication is another significant differentiation factor between object-oriented and agent-oriented architectures. A communication is performed in object-oriented systems only at a fairly low language level; the exchange of messages forms the basis. An object makes use of the functionality provided by the other object by sending it an appropriate message. This procedure corresponds to the classical client/server principle. Agents possess a significantly more powerful communications level (see Section 4.3). They use complex communications protocols and dialog structures, which although based on the principle of message exchange, have far more content. For example, agents must be capable of informing other agents of their intentions and goals and provide them with knowledge. The cooperation protocols and strategies built onto the communications protocols must be taken into consideration. The dynamic models of traditional object-oriented methods offer only insufficient constructs to model such mechanisms.

In addition to the described content extensions of agent-oriented systems, there are also other factors that have significantly less importance compared with object-oriented systems. These include, for example, the principle of inheritance, which plays a central role in the object-oriented system development but is only a subordinate factor in agent systems [Albayrak 1996]. This is because an agent normally has a very special form and also the existence of knowledge based components. Both these criteria oppose a wide use of the inheritance mechanism.

The following section introduces two agent-oriented development methods: the concepts of [Burmeister 1996] and [Kinny et al. 1995]. Both authors define as part of their work a range of models and a step-by-step approach for their creation.

Burmeister supports the analysis phase of agent-oriented systems with three models: the agent model, the organizational model, and the cooperation model (see Figure 5.1/4):

- **Agent model**. The agent model contains the actual agents (including their internal structure). These consist of both the classical components of attributes and methods, and also the behavior patterns and intentions of the agents. Consequently, the agent model corresponds to a base model extended with behavior and intentions. The first steps in the creation of the agent model start with a base model. The agents and their environment objects must be identified, the motivation and the behavior of every agent must be defined, and the agent's knowledge must be described. Burmeister suggests organizing the information required for the creation of the agent model in the form of CRC (classes-responsibilities-collaborations) cards, as used, for example, in Responsible Driven Design [Wirfs-Rock et al. 1990].

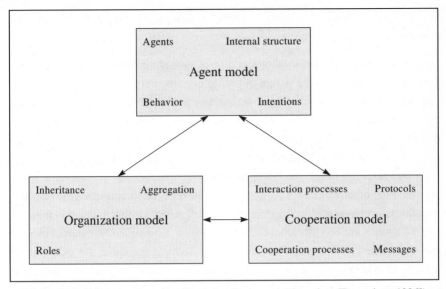

Figure 5.1/4: Burmeister's agent-oriented analysis model(based on [Burmeister 1996])

- **Organizational model**. The static relationships between agents and agent categories are shown in the organizational model. Relationships can consist of classical object-oriented principles, such as inheritance or aggregation, or be based on the associated role of the agent within the complete organization. Although agents are associated amongst themselves through their specific roles, such associations are not as close as with traditional classes [Albayrak 1996]. An aggregation also can be modeled using organization forms. Overall, the organizational model is similar to the static model of the object-oriented methods. Burmeister suggests three steps to create the organizational model: the identification of individual roles within the complete system, the creation of an inheritance hierarchy, and the combination of the identified roles as organizational units.

- **Cooperation model**. The cooperation model consists of the interaction and cooperation processes between the agents. Simple messages and the communications and cooperation processes built on these messages form the basis for such processes. The cooperation model corresponds to the dynamic model of classical methods, however with the difference that the dynamic processes within an agent (also known as the agent life-cycle) are not contained in the cooperation model but are part of the agent model. Burmeister also defines specific processing steps for the creation of the cooperation model. The cooperation objectives (including the associated partners) must be identified, the message types must be determined (for example, KQML messages), and the protocols used for the cooperation defined.

Although the methodology developed by Kinny is similar to Burmeister's concepts, it concentrates on the design of the agent's internal structures and processes, whereas Burmeister assigned more importance to the interaction and cooperation processes. Kinny distinguishes between two degrees of abstraction: the external and the internal view [Kinny et al. 1995]. Consequently, the models he developed are divided into external and internal models. External models model the agents, their tasks and responsibilities, the information required by the agents, and their interactions with other objects. The agent's architecture (including its behavior and intentions) is represented in the internal model. The aim of this division is to separate the agent's architecture from that of the system. Consequently, external models can be completely separated from the specific form of the agent, for example, as reactive or deliberative systems. Similarly, the internal models are not dependent on the structure of the complete system, for example, on the communications mechanisms and cooperation protocols used there.

Kinny defines two external models: the agent model and the interactive model.

- **Agent model**. The agent model describes the static relationships between the agents in the form of agent hierarchies. Thus, it fulfills the same tasks as the organization model from Burmeister. The agent model in complex systems consists of two components: the agent class model that consists of a number of class diagrams and which define the abstract and specific agent classes and represent their static relationships between each other; and the agent instance model that consists of a range of instance models which identify every instance of an agent.

- **Interaction model**. An interaction model represents graphically the responsibilities, services, communications and cooperation processes, and control relationships between agents. The information structure and protocols used are part of the interaction model. Thus, it largely corresponds to Burmeister's cooperation model.

The internal models of the Kinny methodology are the belief model, the goal model and the plan model. The use of these models is particularly suitable for the analysis and design of agent systems, for which BDI agents form their basic units. The extent to which other agent architectures, such as reactive agents, can be usefully modeled remains open. The three internal models have the following tasks:

- **Belief model**. The beliefs that an agent has of itself and its environment are structured as belief sets. The derivation of so-called belief states that represent specific instances of the belief sets can be used to model an agent's behavior states. Belief sets are graphically represented as object diagrams and belief states.

- **Goal model**. The goal model describes both the goals that an agent follows and the events to which it can respond. As with the belief model, the goal model consists of a goal set and the derived goal states.

- **Plan model**. The plans that an agent provides to achieve its goal are modeled in the plan model. A plan set describes the properties and control structures of the plans. Every plan is represented as a plan diagram. Figure 5.1/5 shows such a generic plan diagram that is based on the 'state transition diagrams' principle of traditional object-oriented methods.

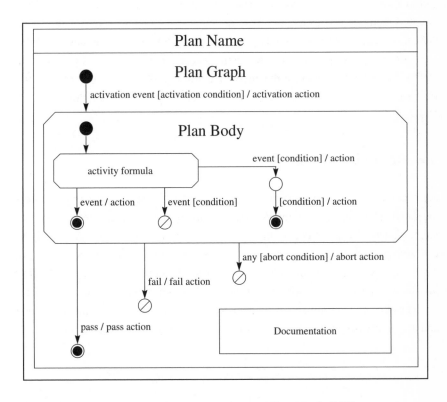

Figure 5.1/5: Generic plan diagram [Kinny et al. 1995]

Initially there is a description of the event or status that initiates the plan. These can be either external events or internal status changes, such as the change of the agent's belief. There are three types of states within a plan diagram: initial states (●), final states (successful: ⊙, unsuccessful ∅) and internal intermediate states (O). Internal intermediate states can be either active or passive. Whereas passive intermediate states do not have any substructure, active states are associated with a specific activity, such as an objective, and possible iteration operations (loops, conditions). Transitions between active states can be either successful or unsuccessful depending on the outcome of the associated activity.

The concepts of both Burmeister and Kinny represent a first step in the direction of a general methodology in the development of complex, distributed agent systems. Despite their sometimes different models and emphasis, both concepts are based on the same principles and attempt to solve similar problem situations. Neither concept has the aim to develop a completely new design methodology, but rather build on the knowledge and models of existing object-oriented methods. This methodology permits the use of existing practical experience gained with object-oriented methods and to use the new modeling constructions only for the special demands made by agent-oriented systems. Both authors have used and tested their methods in the design of practical agent systems. For example, Kinny used his methods to provide support in the analysis and design phases of a complex air traffic management system that was based on agent-oriented technologies [Kinny 1995].

5.2 Agent Languages

An agent language is a programming or development language that can be used in the practical realization of intelligent software agents. The choice of a suitable language has a large effect on the agent architecture that is to be produced. Not every programming language provides an adequate functionality to permit an efficient implementation of intelligent agents. Also the concepts of a language affect the suitability for the development of agents. The aim of this section is to define a number of basic requirements that agent systems make on a programming language and also to investigate the suitability of existing languages in practical use.

5.2.1 Requirements

Various authors have attempted to formulate useful criteria for an agent-oriented programming language (see [Hohl 1995], [Knabe 1996]). A number of central requirements result if their conclusions are combined. These requirements are briefly:

- **Object-orientedness**. Because agents are objects, an agent language should support the object-oriented program model. An agent possesses data and methods. The communication between agents normally occurs through the invocation of a method where every agent makes a subset of its methods public. This subset constitutes its public interface. The agent's data are manipulated only by the provided methods. A direct access to internal data structures is not possible.

- **Platform independence**. Agents are used within various hardware and software environments. This applies in particular for mobile agents that work in various heterogeneous computers of a network and for distributed agent systems. Also the access to an agent in heterogeneous networks can take place from different platforms. For these reasons, the agent language used for the development should possess a high degree of platform independence and support a wide range of heterogeneous systems.

- **Communications capability**. An agent language must provide constructs that can be used to implement communication-oriented components. Communication-oriented components here refer to both the communication of several agents amongst themselves and to the capability of an agent to operate in a network-oriented environment.

- **Security**. As mentioned many times previously, the security problem plays a central role in the practical design of an agent system. In particular for the use of mobile agents, a very high degree of security must be ensured. The agent language that is used must provide an adequate degree of functionality. This can be provided through the use of a language-specific security model or through the integration of external security models (such as firewalls or encryption protocols).

- **Code manipulation**. Many applications require that the program code of an agent is manipulated at runtime. The agent language must provide, for example, mechanisms to identify an agent's code from other objects and to differentiate it from other agents [Knabe 1996]. Also the transfer of program code over the network is often necessary. In addition, mobile agents require the agent language to provide the capability to receive and execute code from an agent.

Together with these central requirements, an agent language has other additional desirable properties, such as reactivity, multitasking, persistent data storage, and extensibility. The following section investigates various programming languages with regard to their suitability for the development of intelligent agents. Specifically, these languages are Java (which has gained popularity because of the Internet, which is also an area of increasing importance for agents), Telescript (a language designed especially for the development of mobile agents), and Tcl (an excellent script language from the UNIX world that has also become interesting for agent systems through various language extensions). Other agent languages are summarized in Figure 5.2/1. The figure provides references to explanatory literature.

Agent category	Language category	Example	Literature reference
Cooperation languages	Actor languages	Actors	[Agha 1986]
	Agent-oriented languages	Agent-0	[Shoham 1993]
		Placa	[Thomas 1995]
Information agents	Script languages	Tcl/Tk	[Oustershout 1994]
Mobile agents		Safe-Tcl	www.smli.com/research/tct/
		Agent-Tcl	www.cs.dartmouth,edu/~agent/agenttcl.htm
		Java	java.sun.com
		Telescript	www.genmagic.com
		Active Web Tools	
		Python	www.python.org
		Obliq	http://www.research.digital.com/SRC/personal/L uca_Cardelli/Obliq/Obliq.html
		April	[McCabe 1995]
			[McCabe/Clark 1995]
		Scheme-48	photo.net/~jar/s48.html
Reactive agents	Reactive languages	RTA/ABLE	[Wavish/Graham 1996]

Figure 5.2/1: Overview of agent languages [Nwana/Woolridge 1997]

5.2.2 Java

The Java programming language developed by SUN Microsystems is based on two concepts that would appear to make it particularly suitable for the development of intelligent agents: a network-based concept and a platform-independent development language. The architecture illustrated in Figure 5.2/2 shows how both these characteristics are achieved.

In traditional programming languages, a compiler or a runtime interpreter is used to convert the program source code into system-specific binary code. Java adopts another route here. The Java compiler does not directly translate the Java source code into binary code but into a so-called Java byte-code. This byte-code is platform-independent and can be executed without modification on all platforms that support Java. A Java interpreter developed for a particular platform is used to execute the byte-code on the target platform. That is, Java uses both a compiler (to create the byte-code) and an interpreter (to execute the byte-code). A so-called Java Virtual Machine is used to execute the Java byte-code on the target platform.

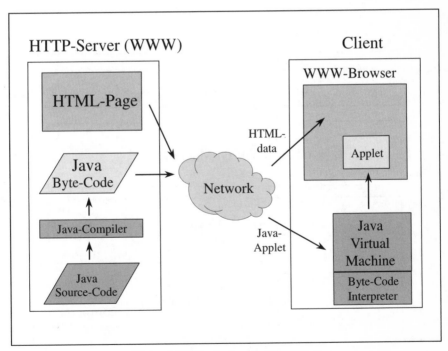

Figure 5.2/2 The basic principle of Java

The virtual machine is added to the existing operating system of the target computer and provides a simulated, consistent runtime environment (see Figure 5.2/3). Irrespective of the actual system platform (for example, UNIX, Windows or Mac-OS), the Java Virtual Machine always provides a Java program with a standardized runtime environment.

The byte-code can be either executed locally (as Java applications) or transferred over the network to a remote computer where it is executed as a so-called Java applet (see Figure 5.2/2). In the WWW, for example, the Java applet is embedded in the HTML page, transferred together with the HTML page, and executed on the target computer in a browser. The browser must provide the required Java runtime environment, that is, a Java Virtual Machine and a Java interpreter.

Java is based on the syntax of the C++ programming language. However, experience gained with C++ resulted in a number of simplifications and various extensions to the content. For example, Java has no pointer architectures, no overloading of operators, no direct access to memory, no multiple inheritance and no extended constructors, such as *structs*, *typedefs* or *unions*. However, in contrast to C++, Java provides exception handling, automatic garbage collection, multithreading, and validation of field accesses and non-initialized variables.

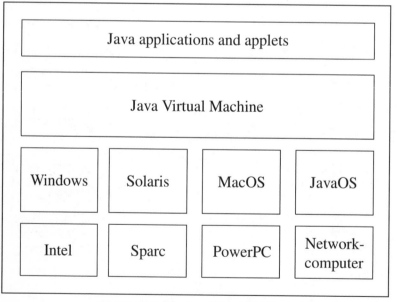

Figure 5.2/3: The Java Virtual Machine

The following section is not intended to provide a general introduction to the Java language, but rather it considers several fundamental Java principles as seen by intelligent software agents. In particular, these include the Java security model, the support of distributed Java architectures using remote method invocation/object serialization, and the Java Beans architecture.

The network-based concept of Java and, in particular, the principle of applets, place demands on the Java security model that far exceed those provided by conventional programming languages. If a user loads an existing applet from the network and executes it on his computer, he permits a program object that he does not know to execute on his local system. Although the task of the applet may provide the user with a general idea of the concrete actions that the applet performs, he can never be sure whether the applet behaves as expected or whether under certain circumstances it performs some unwanted actions. In addition, applets are well suited to implement computer viruses.

As seen from the security model, the execution of an applet can be considered from two directions. In one case, an applet could have full access to the execution system. This corresponds to the traditional model in which an operating system permits the executing software programs to have access to all important system functions. This concept requires the user to have complete trust in the executing program and the operating system to perform preliminary checks on the program. Both aspects are difficult to realize for Java applets. The actions of an applet can be restricted to a specified space within the system (see Section 4.5). SUN refers to this as the applet's 'sandbox' [Fritzinger/Mueller 1966]. Although an applet can perform any actions it wishes within its sandbox, it has no access capabilities to resources that lie outside the sandbox. The Java Virtual Machine provides the sandbox in practice.

The security concept of Java consists of various components, some of which are positioned in the Java language itself whereas other parts are in the applet executing application. The Java Class Loader represents the first security element. The class loader receives an applet sent over the network on the executing system and assigns it a so-called name space. The name space defines which parts of the Java Virtual Machine can be used by an applet. This means that applets can be assigned different rights depending on their origin. The class loader itself is protected from being accessed by applets. Applets are not able to modify the existing class loader nor create their own class loader.

The class loader invokes the so-called Verifier before the actual execution of an applet begins. The verifier checks whether the applet meets the specifications of the Java language or whether the language rules have been violated. The verifier also detects typical programming errors, such as errors in the memory management, stack underflows or overflows, or illegal data type assignments [Fritzinger/Mueller 1996]. This permits the suppression of many actions and language constructions that an applet could use to damage the target system.

The Java Security Manager continually monitors the applet during its execution. The security manager has the task of limiting the applet's actions to those provided by the sandbox. If an applet attempts to perform actions that directly affect the local system, the virtual machine activates the security manager and requests permission for the planned action. The specific actions the security manager permits the Java program to perform depend mainly on whether this is to be executed as a Java application or as a Java applet. A Java application is permitted to read, write and delete local files, and also establish any network connections to other computers. These comprehensive rights are justified because a Java application, as with all traditional software programs, must be explicitly installed and executed by the user on his system. The situation is different for applets. Certain WWW pages, for example, automatically load and execute applets on the local system. For this reason, applets have fewer rights. Because an applet does not have any access to the local file system, it is not allowed to read, write or delete local files. The establishing of network connections is also subject to strict control. An applet can establish a connection only to the originating computer, namely the computer from where it was loaded from. Connections to other external computers are not permitted. For example, if an applet was loaded from a SUN Microsystems server, this applet can only communicate with this one server. If the applet user trusts the SUN server, he can be sure that no contacts are made with other systems, for example the transferring or spying of information.

The sandbox cannot address a number of important security mechanisms. Above all, these include capabilities for the authentication and signature of applets, and the use of encryption mechanisms (see Section 4.5). For this reason SUN has developed extensions to the original Java security model. These include for example, the use of JAR (Java archive) files, auditing mechanisms and encryption algorithms. All the program code associated with an applet is contained in a JAR file. A Message Authentication Code (see Section 4.5) can be used to protect the JAR file against unauthorized modification and so significantly increase a user's trust in the applet. At the least, this permits the subsequent unique identification of the perpetrator of certain actions. The integration of various encryption standards in the Java architecture currently being worked on will stop unauthorized access to applets being transferred over the network.

From an intelligent agent's viewpoint, a second important functionality of Java concerns the development of distributed Java systems. Java supplies two interfaces for this purpose: Remote Method Invocation (RMI) and Object Serialization. RMI permits developers to invoke methods from remote Java objects on other Java Virtual Machines. For example, an active Java object on computer A can invoke the methods of a remote object on computer B even though both objects have no common shared memory and are separated from another by a network. Computer A in this example is the client whereas computer B operates as server. However, computer B can also contain objects that invoke a remote object C. Computer B is then both client and server.

The invoking object must obtain a reference to the target object to be able to use the methods of a remote object. This reference can be obtained either by a search for the remote object using the name service provided by RMI or by receiving the reference as argument or return value [SUN 1997a]. The complete architecture of the RMI system is shown in Figure 5.2/4.

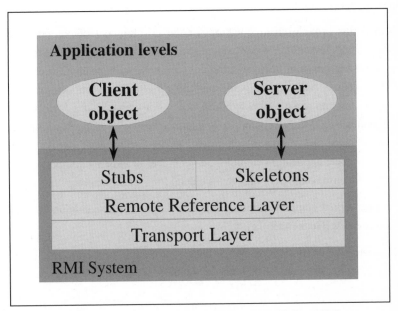

Figure 5.2/4: Architecture of the RMI system [Fielder 1996]

An object that wishes to make its methods available with RMI must first use a Java stub compiler to create the so-called stub code. The stub code of an object serves as representative for the server object at the client's remote object. If an object uses RMI to invoke the method of a remote object, this invocation actually refers to the methods of the locally available stub code. The operation is completely transparent for the invoking component. The stub code uses the lower layers to forward the method calls to the remote object. The skeleton code on the server forms the remote station for the communication. The remote reference layer is responsible for the semantics of the RMI calls being invoked, such as the determination of the referencing semantics (single/multiple server object) [Fielder 1996]. The transport layer forms the interface to the actual network layer.

Object serialization extends the central input/output classes of Java and permits sending a Java object over a network connection. This extension plays an important role in the implementation of mobile agents under Java. The functionality of the object serialization packet is concerned with the packaging of the classes that belong to a Java object (including the classes that the object can access) into a serial data stream, the transfer of this data stream over a network, and to reconstitute it to the original object at the target computer. Object serialization thus supports the creation of persistent objects. An object can be interrupted at any point in its execution, packaged and transferred, reconstituted at the target computer and continued at the original program location.

Java Beans provide an architecture for the development of component-based software using Java. Such a component model permits the developer to build an application from existing software modules (components or beans); see Section 5.3. The developer is not required to design and develop every application from the beginning, but can reuse available components. For example, if a Java Bean exists that provides a KQML communications interface, the developer of an agent can use this bean and so avoid new development. This principle is of particular interest when a complete application is built from a number of existing components, and in the optimum case completely obviates the need for specific development.

An operational component model makes a number of demands on the constituent components [Hughes 1997b]:

- The components must make public their configurable properties and the results they generate; this permits their use by developers and other components.

- It must be possible to modify the properties using a graphical editor (this is important for the developer) or directly from a programming language (this variant is used for the direct communication between components).

- The components must provide a mechanism that permits the combination of several objects.

In addition to the requirements made on the components themselves, the component model must also possess so-called containers (i.e., objects in which the components are embedded) and script support for the direct interaction between components, for example through the use of traditional program languages such as Java or C++.

The Java Beans model addresses all mentioned modules and concepts. Every bean has a so-called Introspector class that it uses to make public the component properties provided by the methods. Other components or developers can use this Introspector class to obtain information on the properties and events of the beans. SUN calls this an introspection mechanism. If a bean is added to a container, the developer is provided with a property sheet that permits the modification of all properties of the bean (customization mechanism). The properties themselves are provided by the introspection mechanism, whereas the customization mechanism provides the property sheet.

An event model permits the communication between distributed dynamic components. Every bean uses the introspection mechanism to provide a list of the events it can initiate. If other beans are interested in one of the events, the developer must implement a so-called listener that monitors a bean for the initiation of a specific event by another bean. If, for example, the previously described KQML-bean initiates a *KQMLMessageNotify* event when a new KQML message arrives and there is another bean within the agent that needs to interpret the new KQML message, this second bean can implement a *KQMLMessageNotifyListener* and register this with the KQML-bean. Each occurrence of a KQML message causes the KQML-bean to inform appropriately all beans registered by *KQMLMessageNotifyListener*.

If the reader wishes a more detailed analysis of the Java Beans model, in particular aspects such as security, interoperability and cross-platform development, he should consult the appropriate specialized literature [SUN 1997b, Hughes 1997a, 1997b, Shoffner 1997].

5.2.3 Telescript

The Telescript technology developed by General Magic represents one of the first commercial platforms that has been designed for the development of mobile agent systems. Although the original development background represented the structure of agent-based electronic malls, Telescript is generally usable for the widest range of scenarios. A number of general concepts provide its universal usability. In particular, these are locations, agents, travel, meeting, connections, authorities and permits [White 1996]. Figure 5.2/5 shows the overall architecture and interaction of the individual components within Telescript.

- **Places**. Telescript uses the concept of places to logically structure the distributed architecture of a network. Every computer of a network can have one or more places. In particular, a place is a unit that provides a specific service. For example, every trader has its own place on a computer that provides an electronic mall. Central services, such as directories or databases, also provide their services in the form of places. Not only central network servers, such as the described mall server, have places, but also the client computers of the associated users. In this case the place is primarily used for sending and receiving the user's agents.

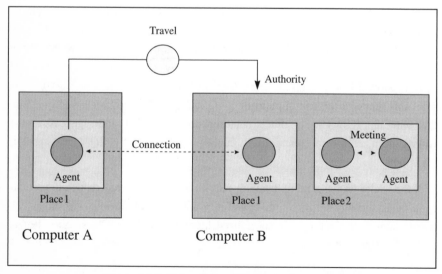

Figure 5.2/5: **Telescript** architecture and concepts

- **Agents**. The actual functionality of an application in Telescript is provided exclusively by agents. Although an agent is at every point in time assigned to a specific place, it has the capability to migrate from one place to another place. Typically, an agent visits various places during its work. An agent at every place can make use of the services provided by this place. In addition to the described mobile agents, Telescript systems often possess agents that are assigned stationary to a specific place which they never leave. If an agent visits a place, a stationary agent positioned there normally serves as its contact partner.

- **Travel**. As indicated previously, Telescript agents can travel between places. Every agent can itself determine when and in which order it visits which places. To make such a travel, the mobile agent uses the *Go* command provided by Telescript. In addition, it must have a so-called ticket that contains its travel route and the travel parameters (for example, maximum duration or cost). The Telescript Engine that performs the technical implementation of the travel and is fully transparent to the agent is described in detail below. In particular, this means that an agent does not concern itself with the need to pack and send itself and its environment over the network, to obtain access to the target system and to recreate itself at the target place. Instead, it uses the *Go* command and can perform its next command at the required target place.

- **Meetings**. If two agents contained within the same place make contact with each other, this is designated as a meeting. Usually, a mobile agent meets the stationary agent of a place in order to make use of the services provided at the place. If, for example, a mobile buying agent travels to a specific place within an electronic mall, it can meet the stationary sales agents located there, who represent the merchant in this case, to discuss his purchasing requirements with them. An agent can use the *Meet* command to arrange the meeting. It must pass a so-called petition, which contains all details of the required meeting (for example, start time or maximum duration). A specific contact takes place if the addressed agent agrees to the meeting.

- **Connections**. A connection is designated as being the communication between two agents that are not both part of the same place. For example, the mobile agent of a user could assume contact with the user from its current place to inform him about the initial results of its work. Instead of itself returning to the user's computer, it is more appropriate for the mobile agent to establish connection with one of the stationary agents waiting at the user's computer. A special Telescript command with the name *Connect* is available for establishing the connection. A *Connect* requires as additional parameters, in particular, exact details on the name and place of the remote agent. Only then is the system able to identify the required negotiating partner.

- **Authorities**. Telescript designates authority as the identity of the user/owner of an agent/place proved by a signature or certificate. Every agent or place of a Telescript system is capable of making its authority known and to obtain the authorities of other objects. Consequently, there is no anonymity within Telescript. The system is capable at any time of obtaining the authorities of all agents/places. This is essential to achieve an adequate security. Depending on the authority, the system can assign an agent/place specific rights or prohibit them from performing actions. The authority of an agent is always checked when it travels from one region of a system to another. A region is designated as being a set of places operated by the same authority (for example, an electronic mall). A travel is prohibited if the original region cannot prove to the destination region the authority of an agent who wishes to travel there. The Telescript *Name* command is used for the authority validation. An agent/place uses the *Name* command to obtain the authority of another agent/place. A so-called Telename is returned as answer. A Telename is a data structure that contains the exact identity and authority of the addressed agent/place. The *Name* command can be used for various purposes. A place can use the *Name* command to identify an arriving agent and so, for example, allow only agents with specific authorities. Similarly, an agent can determine the Telename of a place and only travel to places with specific authorities (to those which it has sufficient level of trust). In the same way, an agent can identify another agent and meet or establish a connection only with those agents having specific authorities.

- **Permits**. Authorities use permits to assign specific rights to their agents/place. This can be the right to execute specific commands or the right to use specific resources. For example, a user can assign his agents the permit to visit a specific marketplace, spend not more than one hour there searching for a product, and spend a maximum amount x. The system destroys an agent that exceeds his assigned rights. Not only authorities, but also places and regions, can assign permits. In practice, an agent has three sets of permits at any one time (authority, place, region) that are checked prior to every action of the agent. The agent can permit a planned action only when it is contained in all three permit sets. The agent must renegotiate its permits if it travels to another place or region. In this case, the permit for the new destination is used instead of the permits for the old place/region.

The Telescript language and its concepts are realized by the Telescript Engine (see Figure 5.2/6). Because the Telescript Engine forms the base software and provides the fundamental functionality (see Section 4.2.2.3 and 4.6), every computer that belongs to the Telescript system must possess such an engine. The Telescript Engine capability can be freely scaled. Depending on the function of the computer, it can support several hundred agents and places (for example with a mall server) or only a single agent/place at a user computer. Three APIs provide the interface to the actual computer system. The storage API permits the Telescript Engine to use the computer's storage media, for example, to provide the persistent storage of the places or agents. The transport API performs the access to the computer's communications subsystem. It can be used to realize all network-oriented concepts in Telescript, such as travel or connections. The transport API is also used for the communication between several Telescript Engines.

The API for external applications permits those parts of a Telescript system that were developed using the Telescript programming language to communicate with components that were written in another programming language, such as C/C++ or Java. Although Telescript provides a complete development system, typically a number of components are developed using traditional languages. This is particularly the case for stationary software components in user computers and servers

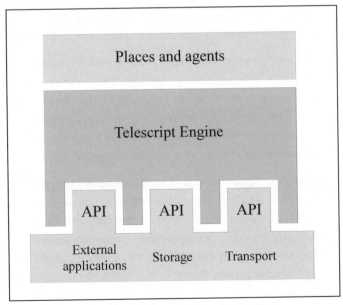

Figure 5.2/6: Telescript Engine [White 1996]

that, for example, realize the basic communications mechanisms between places or the connections to existing databases. Telescript itself provides a language that satisfies many of the requirements for an agent language formulated at the start of this section. Criteria such as object-orientation, persistence, portability and communication are realized as part of Telescript. [White 1996] provides a more extensive introduction into the functionality and syntax of Telescript.

As with other agent languages, Telescript must provide special security concepts and models to satisfy the high security demands of agent-oriented systems. This is achieved using four distinct security levels [Tardo/Valente 1996, GeneralMagic 1996]:

- **Object runtime safety**. This is primarily achieved through the use of the Telescript Engine and the characteristics of the Telescript language. Telescript, for example, does not use pointer constructions, is strictly object-oriented, and provides runtime type checking, automatic memory management including garbage collection as well as exception handling [Tardo/Valente 1996]. The Telescript interpreter serves both as security monitor (to monitor the object actions) and forces a strict observance of the object encapsulation.

- **Process safety and security**. This, the second major component, covers the previously described authorities and permit concepts, the encapsulation of private data structures, the protection of object references, supervised communication protocols and special security classes (such as copyright, access control). [GeneralMagic 1996] provides a detailed description of the functionalities.

- **System safety and security**. The system security module controls the access of Telescript objects to system resources. Although agents and places have, for example, general access to the local file system (using the Telescript Engine and the storage API), this access can be greatly limited. For example, files can be protected against being copied and can be assigned a copyright. The same control applies for the access to network resources and special system routines.

- **Network security**. A distributed system such as Telescript requires concepts for the network security. The previously described region model that performs a security validation on entering a region represents such a concept. Furthermore, Telescript provides the capability to provide secure transmission channels between regions. Depending on the requirements, a secure channel can have different forms. Telescript permits the use of encryption algorithms such as RSA or DES (see Section 4.5).

Despite the far-reaching concepts Telescript provides for the development of mobile agent systems, it has not yet met with resounding success. This is principally the result of the proprietary development environment and language that are not freely available, and so have significant disadvantages compared with other concepts, such as Java. In particular, the development of heterogeneous applications that are not restricted to a single platform is currently difficult to realize with Telescript. However, these are the particular demands made on an expandable agent language. Consequently, the further development of Telescript could bring changes here.

5.2.4 Tcl/Tk, Safe-Tcl, Agent-Tcl

Tcl (Tool Command Language) a freely available script language that originally came from the UNIX world has met with ever increasing interest since its development in 1987. Not only are there now Tcl implementations for a number of non-UNIX platforms (DOS, Windows 95/NT, OS/2, MacOS), but there are also extensions for special application areas (Agent-Tcl, Tacoma, TKQML).

Tcl consists of a script language and an interpreter. The aim of the development was to produce an interpreter that can be integrated into existing applications with the minimum of effort and so extend these with a Tcl component. The script language permits the development of complex scripts that combine existing application components and their subsequent execution. The principle is the same as for classical UNIX shells, such as the C, Korn or Bourne shell. However, the existence of the interpreter increases the functionality of Tcl in comparison with other shell script languages. The inclusion of a Tcl interpreter in an application makes it possible to structure the application in a set of primitive operations that are combined with a script [SUN 1997d]. Tcl itself is used in this context for the configuration and modification of the individual components.

The Tcl function library has a public interface that hides the Tcl kernel functions. Together with functions to access operating system routines, this library represents a virtual machine within which Tcl programs are executed. New functions (also known as primitives) written in traditional programming languages, such as C/C++ or Java, can be added without difficulty to the Tcl function library. The function itself, for example, is written in C++ and supplied as a new Tcl command. Thus, the functionality of Tcl can be extended without difficulty and the portability of the application increased. A Tcl script adds the existing Tcl primitives to an application. As with all classical script languages, an external program can be started and calls to defined Tcl primitives can be made within a script.

The free availability of Tcl and the consequent large number of developers means that there are now many application-specific extensions to Tcl (in the form of Tcl primitives). Tk (Toolkit), a toolbox for the development of graphical user interfaces is the most widely used extension. Tk provides a set of Tcl primitives that can be used to create and manipulate all important graphical elements of a user interface.

From the viewpoint of agent-oriented systems, Tcl offers a number of advantages [Gray 1995]: It is easy to learn (Tcl uses a language that is similar to C); it is freely available for a wide range of platforms; it is an interpreted language; it can be embedded in existing applications; and it can be freely extended with application-specific functions. However, there are also a number of disadvantages: Tcl is not object-oriented; as with most interpreted languages, it is relatively slow; there is no comprehensive security model; and no support is provided for the migration of agents. Safe-Tcl and Agent Tcl described in the following section attempt to reduce these disadvantages by increasing the functionality of Tcl.

As with the previously described Java and Telescript languages, Safe-Tcl also provides the capability to execute Tcl programs of unknown origin within a pre-defined space and to restrict the activity of a Tcl program to this space. This is achieved through the use of several Tcl interpreters [SUN 1997c]. A so-called master interpreter executes the central application. If the start of an unknown or non-trustworthy Tcl script is required within this application, a new interpreter, called the slave interpreter, is started for this purpose. The slave interpreter possesses only a limited set of instructions. For example, instructions to access the local file system can be removed from the slave interpreter instruction set. The master interpreter determines which instructions the slave interpreter can perform. This decision depends primarily on the origin of the Tcl script to be executed within the slave interpreter. The master interpreter can always make use of the complete instruction set.

The second important concept in Safe-Tcl is the principle of safe calls. If a slave interpreter wishes to access resources that lie outside its access area, it can achieve this with safe calls. The master interpreter provides and monitors such function calls. For example, a master interpreter could provide its slave interpreter with a safe function call to write files in a specific directory. The master interpreter continually monitors the execution of a safe function call performed by the slave interpreter.

Agent Tcl represents a concept that can be used for the development of mobile agents in Tcl. The Tcl extension developed at Dartmouth College pursues several objectives [Gray et al. 1996]:

- The development of a Tcl primitive that permits agents with a single command to migrate from one computer to another (similar to the *Go* command from Telescript).

- The provision of effective security mechanisms for the operation of an agent system.

- Tcl primitives for the transparent communication between agents.

- The creation of a simple script language as central agent language.

Figure 5.2/7 shows the basic architecture of Agent Tcl (which consists of four layers). The lowest layer provides interfaces for all supplied communications protocols. The second layer forms the actual Server Engine that must be installed on every associated computer system. The Server Engine performs the central tasks provided by the management of mobile agents and generally corresponds to the base software described in Section 4.2.2. It receives incoming agents, sends agents to other servers, permits the communication between agents, maintains a log of the agents active on the server at any one time, and protects the agents from system failures by writing them to persistent storage. The interpreters of the supported programming languages form the third layer. Every language has its own interpreter, which in turn consists of four components: a security module; a status mod-

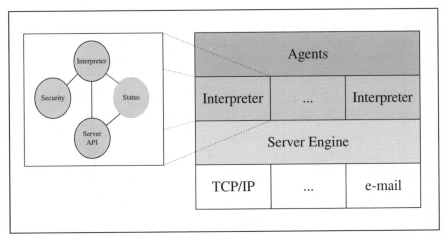

Figure 5.2/7: Architecture of Agent Tcl [Gray 1995]

ule, which maintains the status of an agent and which it recreates after a migration; a server API that is used for the complete interaction with the server during a migration or communication of the agent; and the actual language-specific interpreter. The agents themselves form the highest layer of the Agent Tcl architecture. All services not provided by the Server Engine must be realized within the agents themselves. These include cooperation and negotiation strategies, goal determination, planning and scheduling.

Figure 5.2/8 shows the operation of the first alpha release of Agent Tcl that is currently available.

The Architecture consists of two components: the agent and the server. An agent consists of an extended Tcl interpreter that executes the Tcl agent [Gray 1997a]. As shown in the figure, the interpreter is implemented in three layers: a modified Tcl kernel, which contains primitives for the acquisition and reconstruction of the internal status of a Tcl script as extension to the original Tcl functionality; a number of Tcl extensions, which, in particular, contain the implementation of the *Jump* migration primitive; and the actual agent script.

The server running on every associated computer system forms the second architectonic component. This consists of two fixed modules (Socket Watcher and Agent Tables) and the processes of the active agent on a server. The Socket Watcher monitors a specific TCP/IP port for arriving agents and messages. It also has the task of monitoring the adherence of the security regulations within the

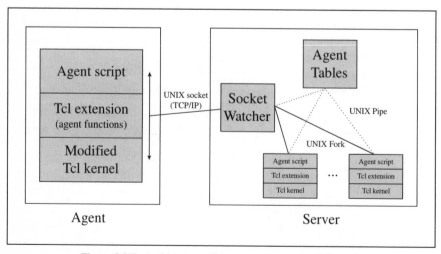

Figure 5.2/8: Architecture of the alpha release [Gray 1997a]

server. When an agent arrives at the server, the Socket Watcher uses the UNIX Fork command to execute a new process. The Socket Watcher forwards incoming messages for buffering in the Agent Table. In addition to storing messages, the Agent Table has the primary task of maintaining a list of the active agents on the server. If messages arrive for a specific agent, these remain buffered in the Agent Table until the agent is ready to receive them. A UNIX pipe is used for the communication. Extensions of the current alpha release are planned for the near future. These extensions are principally concerned with the support of various languages and communications protocols, an improvement in the security concept, the data protection, and the implementation of an event model [Gray 1997b].

Agent Tcl has been tested at Dartmouth College in a number of concrete applications with regard to its suitability for use in practice. For example, a Watcher Agent has been realized that monitors a predefined quantity of remote resources and uses e-mail to inform its user of any changes [Gray 1995]. Various information agents that have been developed in a second scenario search for technical documents, medical data and three-dimensional drawings for mechanical components. The documents are distributed over several computers of a network, which the mobile Tcl agents visit and investigate for information. The agents transport the information items back to their original computers where the data is further processed.

5.3 Component-Based Software Development

The development, the management and the extension of distributed client/server applications represent a very complex task. The subcomponents of a distributed system are generally used in heterogeneous network structures and within different system platforms and operating systems. However, a component should not be developed new for every platform, but rather a high reusability achieved through the creation of standardized interfaces. The aim of component-based software development and standards is to provide mechanisms that permit the interaction of independent, distributed objects in accordance with a number of generally valid rules. Only then is it possible to achieve the desired reusability, the distributed solution of problems, the creation of general service modules, and platform and language independence.

Objects in a component-based system are capable of communicating and cooperating with each other over network and platform boundaries without needing to make allowance for implementation-specific details. The programming language used for the development of an object also should not constitute any hindrance here. For example, component-based standards permit an object developed in Pascal that is executed on a Microsoft Windows platform to communicate with a C++ object on a UNIX workstation or a COBOL object on a mainframe computer. The critical fact is that an object should not need to know where the required contact partner is located within the network or how this was implemented. Instead, the complete communication takes place using a generally-defined interface that is used by all associated objects, independent of their implementation and system platform.

Such a bundling of software into cooperating individual objects or components provides a number of advantages [Nwana/Azarmi 1997]:

- Applications can be developed through the combination of existing components. If a specific functionality is already available as a component, this does not need to be developed a second time, but can be integrated in the application. In the optimum case, a complete application can be designed merely by combining existing objects.

- The components are portable. This means that they can be used on various system platforms. For example, an object developed under MS Windows can run under UNIX or OS/2 without major modifications.

- If a standard for the communication between components is available, objects from various manufacturers can cooperate in heterogeneous system environments. Such a distributed application is characterized by a high degree of interoperability. A client makes a request to a remote server component without having to have knowledge of the basic mechanisms used for the communication.

- Existing systems can be extended with new components by extending them with a standardized interface. Thus, investments in existing applications are largely retained.

The Common Object Request Broker Architecture (CORBA) created by the Object Management Group (OMG) represents one of the two most important standards for component-based software development currently available. The Distributed Common Object Model (DCOM) from Microsoft forms the other concept. For reasons of the wide availability and the advanced concepts, the representation of component-based architectures in the following section uses the CORBA model and the general Object Management Architecture that builds on it. Particular emphasis is placed on the effects of CORBA on the development of agent-based systems.

The OMG is a grouping of currently more than 700 companies and organizations that has the aim to maximize the portability, reusability and interoperability of software, to provide a reference architecture and to offer a discussion forum for the advancement of object-oriented technologies [OMG 1997a]. Thus, the CORBA reference model resulting from the OMG work was conceived from the beginning as an industrial standard, whose future importance, because of the involvement of almost all well-known software companies, can be assumed to be high.

Figure 5.3/1 shows the general architecture of a CORBA-based system. The Object Request Broker (ORB) forms the central module. ORBs provide the basic functions for the communication of the objects within a CORBA system. These include the encapsulation of the objects from implementation-specific details (operating system, programming language, network) and the provision of basic services, such as the determination of other objects or the routing of the messages.

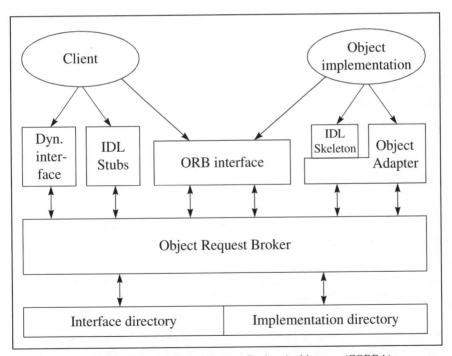

Figure 5.3/1: Common Object Request Broker Architecture (CORBA)

CORBA 2.0 permits for the first time the interaction of ORBs from different manufacturers. Since its availability, many suppliers have developed ORBs for a wide-range of platforms. For example, the Object Broker from Digital is currently available for 20 different platforms, such as Windows 3/95/NT, MacOs, AIX, MVS, OS/2, OS/400, Digital Unix, Open VMS and HP-UX [Montgomery 1997]. With the development of Java ORBs, on which almost all manufacturers are working, and the integration of an ORB in a WWW browser, as is the case for Netscape's latest browser generation, every Internet user has the potential to become part of a CORBA system. The interoperability of CORBA applications is thus already very common and represents one the strengths of the standard.

The Interface Definition Language (IDL) forms the second central module of a CORBA system. The IDL permits every object to make its services externally visible and available as a standardized interface. An IDL is no programming language in the usual sense, but describes the interfaces between distributed components [OMG 1997b]. In a CORBA system, the objects developed in various programming languages and executed on different operating systems have standardized, IDL-based interfaces and thus are capable of invoking methods of other objects independent of the implementation-specific differences. The IDL developed by OMG is a declarative language that is independent of the programming language. The IDL language mappings ensure that objects can be developed in the appropriate programming language and that the communication with other objects can take place in a natural form for the development language [OMG 1997a]. The ORB is given the task here to generate the program code in the appropriate target language from the IDL interface description. For example, if an IDL-to-Java language mapping exists, objects developed in Java can provide external interfaces in a standardized form without having to abandon the features of the Java language. The appropriate Java ORB makes the complete CORBA system available to the interfaces of the Java objects.

If a client application wishes to use the services of a remote object within a CORBA system, this is done in the following manner: the client formulates a request message that contains a reference to the required server object and a specific action that the server object is to perform. The request message is produced when the client calls the routines of the object's IDL stub or dynamically creates the request (see Figure 5.3/1). Irrespective of the chosen variant, the remote server object represents itself to the client as a standardized interface, which is independent of where the object is located in the network and of the development language. The IDL stub or the dynamic interface forwards the request to the ORB. The ORB has the task to localize the site of the actual implementation of the server object and to forward the request there, and then inform the server object appropriately. The ORB passes the control to the server object on completion. When the ORB has processed the request, it returns the results to the invoking client. The control is simultaneously returned to the client.

CORBA is part of a comprehensive architecture, the Object Management Architecture (OMA) (see Figure 5.3/2). As part of the OMA, the services of a system are positioned around the central ORB. Using the analogy of a computer's system bus, the term software bus is often used in this context. In particular, the provided systems are general system services (Object Services and Common Facilities) to provide specific interfaces for a specific application area (domain interfaces) or for an individual application (application interfaces).

The four service categories have the following tasks:

- **Object Services**. The Object Services, also known as CORBAservices, provide general services that are typically required by all CORBA-based applications. These include services such as naming, events, life cycle, persistent objects,

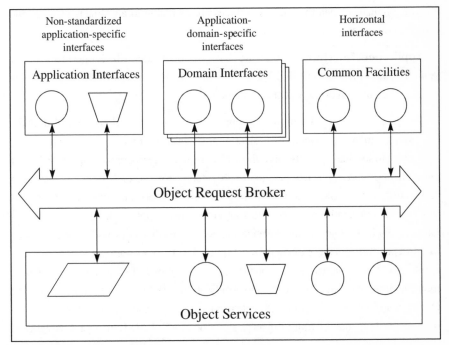

Figure 5.3/2: Object Management Architecture (OMA) reference model [OMG 1997a]

transactions, concurrency control, relationships, externalization, licensing, query, properties, security, time, collections and trader [OMG 1997a]. CORBAservices contain, in particular, services for object management, instance management, and system security. For example, the Security service provides functions for the identification and authentication of objects, for access control, for auditing and for the management of security-relevant information. The Licensing service permits the control of a developer's intellectual property. If, for example, an object is made available within a CORBA system, the Licensing services can be used to define and manage its usage time, group-dependent access rights or access costs.

- **Common Facilities**. The Common Facilities, CORBAfacilities, provide horizontal services that are required by most application categories. General e-mail or printer services are typical examples of CORBAfacilities. Specifically, the CORBAfacilities are the definition of a set of IDL interfaces that an object must provide in order that it can provide or use a specific service.

- **Domain Interfaces**. The Domain Interfaces are application domain-specific services. Domain Interfaces can be specified as a predefined set of IDL interfaces for application areas such as telecommunications, electronic trading, transport, finances or health. These interfaces are available to all objects of an application domain.

- **Application Interfaces**. These are the previously described interfaces of an individual object of a CORBA system. Thus, the Application Interfaces are neither standardized nor application-independent.

The so-called Object Frameworks represent a further central concept of the Object Management Architecture. Object Frameworks consist of a number of cooperating individual objects and thus represent comprehensive, more powerful components, whose services are of direct interest for the end users of a specific application or technology domain [OMG 1997a]. The objects contained in an Object Framework can be grouped into four categories: Application Objects, Domain Objects, Facility Objects, and Service Objects. The objects provide various interfaces depending on the category (see Figure 5.3/3). Application Objects, for example, possess an interface that consists of combinations of Object Services, Common Facilities, Domain Interfaces and Application Interfaces. In contrast, a Service Object interface provides only Object Services. A specific Object Framework always consists of one or more objects or one or more of the four object categories.

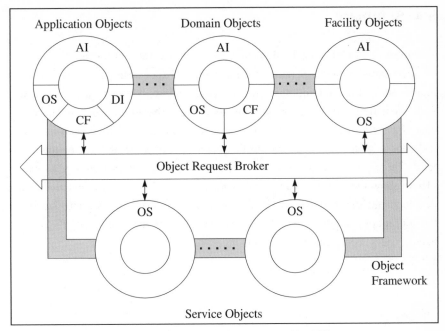

Figure 5.3/3: Object Frameworks [OMG 1997a]

For example, an Object Framework can contain three application objects, four domain objects, one facility object and five service objects.

Because CORBA/OMA is a general standard for the development of distributed client/server applications, the importance of the architecture for agent-oriented system is correspondingly high. The increasing availability of CORBA results in an increased focus on decentralized system structures. These in turn form the basis of all multi-agent systems. Consequently, CORBA is capable of providing direct support and promotion of the development of agent-oriented architectures. It does this through the provision of distributed communications and cooperation mechanisms, but also the development of a specific agent interface (such as the Domain Interface of the OMA) is conceivable. Such a central interface should provide central services and functions required to build distributed agent systems, and so significantly reduce the development effort. The use of CORBA and an IDL also expedites the urgently required standardization process for agent systems. The ADEPT demonstrator from British Telecom represents an example of a currently existing CORBA-based agent interface [Nwana/Azarmi 1997].

5.4 Summary

A number of special considerations must be taken into account for the development of agent-based systems. Traditional methods and tools cannot be used without modification. Both for the analysis and design phase, but also during the actual implementation, the central demands made on agent-based systems have been discussed and illustrated using two existing models of agent-oriented analysis. Many different languages are available for the practical realization of agent-oriented systems. Three selected examples, Java, Telescript and Tcl, have been used as examples to show the major demands and characteristics of the agent-oriented software development; the practical considerations were also analyzed. An introduction in the concept of component-based software development and its effect on the form of agent systems completed this chapter.

Part II: Applications

The second part of the book discusses selected application areas for intelligent software agents. Examples of application areas described in this section are *information retrieval and filtering, entertainment,* and *electronic commerce.* The application areas can be assigned to the three agent categories information agents, cooperation agents and transaction agents and also in the classification matrix for agent systems. Specific applications and research projects, such as *Firefly* or *Kasbah,* are used to describe the form and operation of intelligent agents. Both the concepts of the individual application areas and the base architectures are handled.

6 Application Areas for Intelligent Software Agents[1]

6.1 Introduction

This chapter focuses on the description of selected examples. The representation of selected application areas of intelligent agents shown here deliberately does not follow the viewpoint of a computer scientist or developer of intelligent agents. In contrast to Part I, this chapter aims to use illustrative examples to provide interested readers with an introduction to the complex area of intelligent agents and so permit them to recognize the future potentials of this technology.

The explanations of the individual application areas include an introduction to the area and a listing of current applications to provide a market overview. The description of individual examples, the representation of general concepts and the general architecture follow these sections.

Concepts in this connection are understood to be the representation of the important details and basics of an application area. In particular, they refer to the operation and the functionality of the applications. These concepts have an abstraction level, which through similarities and recurring characteristics, has been represented within the existing examples. If these criteria cannot be found or confirmed for all examples within an application area, they have not been included in the description of general concepts but added to the description of the specific example. The appropriate comment is made at the start of each application area.

The representation of the specific architecture includes the description of the main software components, although no claim is made for completeness. Similar to the representation of general concepts, the similarities and characteristics that fol-

---

[1] This chapter was written by Claudia Schubert and Walter Brenner based on Thorsten Fritsch´s thesis *The Classification of Intelligent Agents Using Application Examples.*

low the description of the architecture are found in most examples of an application area and so represent a certain generality. We omit the description of a general architecture and refer to specific examples that can provide definite details of an architecture. We provide the reader with an appropriate comment at the start of every section.

The model of the classification matrix for intelligent agents (see Figure 6.1/1) produced in Chapter 3 (see Section 3.3) and the grouping into the information agent, communications agent and transaction agent categories serve as basis for the description of the individual application areas.

Every individual application area is shown within the classification matrix, both with the current development state and with the future development objective. This should simplify the reader's task of assigning the application area to the basic properties of *mobility, number of agents* and *degree of intelligence*.

The criterion for the assignment of the application areas into one of the three categories of information agent, communications agent and transaction agent is based on their central task. Previously in Chapter 3 (see Section 3.1) we indicated that the characteristics of all three agent systems are present in an application area. However, their main usage determines the assignment into one of the three catego-

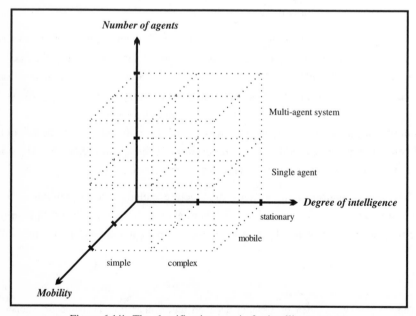

Figure 6.1/1: The classification matrix for intelligent agents

ries. Figure 6.1/2 shows the individual application areas and their assignment to the three categories.

The primary task of an information agent is to support its user in the search for information and in to provide information. It is important here that the individual information items are found reliably and that they are evaluated and filtered in accordance with the user's personal interests. The *information retrieval and filtering* application area supports the user in his search for information in the Internet. The *NewsWatcher* application area combines agents whose aim is the provision of relevant information through the definition of a personal user profile. The agents of the *advising and focusing* application area realize their support for the search for information by observing the user while he works in the WWW. This monitoring is the prerequisite for the presentation of comments and suggestions for the effective and efficient information retrieval in WWW. The *traffic* application area is concerned with supporting the agents in the provision of intelligent services within the travel and transport planning. Such services include the retrieval of information on flight and train connections, and local public transport. The support or acceptance of travel bookings of the user by agents is a further development that places this application area in the transport agent category. Because this area is currently at an early state of development, a special description is omitted.

Specific Task	Application Area
Information agent	• Information retrieval and filtering
	• NewsWatcher
	• Advising and focusing
	• Traffic
Cooperation agent	• Entertainment
	• Groupware
	• Network management/telecommunication
Transaction agent	• Electronic commerce
	• Manufacturing
	• Management of business processes

Figure 6.1/2: The grouping of the individual application areas with regard to their central task

The cooperation agents concentrate on the solution of complex problem situations in which the agents cooperate with other users. The *entertainment* application area uses this cooperation to build an interest profile with which the user can discover new recreational activities or further his knowledge in the fields of interest. The entertainment value of these applications is assigned a high importance. The *groupware* application area is part of the operational and administrative area, and serves to support and provide a number of routine activities that arise within a work group or department. The high communications requirement needed to perform these tasks forces the agents to cooperate with each other. The *network management/telecommunication* focuses on the personal support by agents of the user for the management of tasks within a network. In particular, the support concentrates on the cooperation of the individual agents of the network users. Because there are few information sources for this topic, no additional description is provided.

The transaction agents concentrate on the monitoring and the execution of transactions. The transactions include not only the financial processing of a purchase but also the processing or monitoring of production processes and other business-oriented process actions. The *electronic commerce* application area includes agents that support the user while buying or selling products and services. The *manufacturing* application area focuses on the support by agents in PPS systems. This area concentrates on the realization of multi-agent systems for the planning, control and coordination of flexible and distributed manufacturing processes. This application area is concerned only with the support of production processes. The *management of business processes* application area is concerned with the support by agents in the development of business processes. Both applications are realized that concentrate on the negotiation between the individual agents of the associated business processes and also applications that use a special business process as basis for the agent support. The application area is not part of the description.

Other application areas also exist for intelligent agents. An example is the application area for the military and space industry, in which intelligent agents are widely used, such as for aircraft control. The continuing development of intelligent agents will lead to new application areas, such as in the banking industry and in the financial services sector.

6.2 Information Retrieval and Filtering

6.2.1 Introduction

Applications in the area of information retrieval and filtering support the user during the detailed search for information in the WWW. The rapid increase in the available information requires effective tools for navigation in the various search trees of the WWW to support the user in the specific information retrieval. The navigators, the search catalogs, and the search engines represent such tools. Navigators represent the simplest form of tools that permit a search for information. Examples are the current browsers. Search catalogs include many topic areas in which information is available to the user. Yahoo (www.yahoo.com or www.yahoo.de) is an example of a search catalog. The topic areas are created and managed manually. Search engines in their current form are agent-based software programs that automatically search through the WWW for new information. AltaVista (www.altavista.com) and MetaCrawler (www. metacrawler.com) are two examples of such search engines. These search engines are described in the following sections. Figure 6.2/1 shows the assignment of this application area in the classification matrix (see Section 3.3).

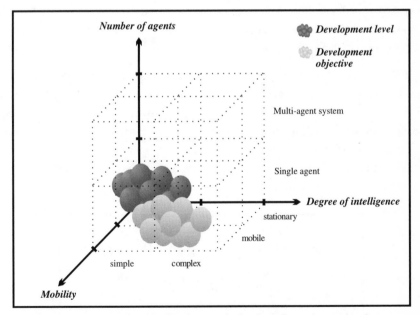

Figure 6.2/1: The classification matrix for the information retrieval
and filtering application area

In accordance with the current stage of development, the agents of this application area operate stationary with limited intelligence. A possible development direction of these agents is in the form of intelligent mobile agents.

The agent-based search engines can be grouped into four different levels corresponding to their stage of development (see Figure 6.2/2).

The simple search engines represent a low level of search tools in the WWW that are realized using the technology of the intelligent agents. Their central characteristic is the storing of all found information in a database, which can be central or distributed. AltaVista (www.altavista.com) or Lycos (www.lycos.com) are representatives of simple search engines. The cycle of the updating of the associated databases for simple search engines forms the major disadvantage of this development level. The continually changing and increasing information offerings result in WWW documents with the same addresses but having different content. The specific search for information cannot be handled reliably and provides the user with insufficiently current documents. Consequently, experienced WWW users normally make use of several simple search engines to increase the reliability and accuracy in the search for information. Pseudo meta search engines can be used to support this technique. Their principle is to provide the user with a collection of known search engines that serve as starting point in the individual search for information. The user is provided with information only from the stored data for the selected search engine. CUSI (Configurable Unified Search Engine) (www.nexor.co.uk/public/ cusi/) is an example of this form.

The meta search engines provide an automation of the simultaneous query to several simple search engines. Meta search engines query automatically several simple search engines in a parallel process. They provide the user with the results of the associated search query in a compressed and improved form compared with the simple search engine. Because the meta search engines do not use their own database to store the information, they access and process the stored data of the

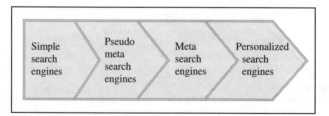

Figure 6.2/2: The development levels of search engines

simple search engines. Representatives are SavvySearch (guaraldi.cs.colostate. edu: 2000/form) and MetaCrawler (www.metacrawler.com). A possible development direction of the meta search engines is based on the concept of the personalization of the result sets. Experience shows that the search for information covers the special areas of interest of the user, with the result that the contents of the result sets exhibit certain similarity. This permits the creation of a personalized data base that can be used to provide specific information. A further development of the Meta-Crawler at the University of Washington, Seattle, USA [Selberg/Etzioni 1995] is a prototype of this evolution stage.

The descriptions of the application area are restricted to the representation of the simple search engines and the meta search engines. A differentiation between simple and extended search queries is assumed. Simple search queries normally permit the search for a term without the definition of additional search criteria. An example for a simple search query is the search for the term Internet. Here no restriction is made regarding the specific areas of interest within the Internet nor the contents. The user receives a result set that contains all documents having this search term. Additional search criteria that permit a restriction to the search term are part of an extended search query and normally use logical operations and an exact string. Logical operations exist between the various words of the search expression. The specific forms are AND, OR and NOT. They permit the specification of a search query. AND permits the search for documents that contain all words of the search query, whereas OR presents only those documents that contain at least one of the specified words. NOT supplies only those documents that do not contain the word of the search term excluded by NOT. The identification of the search term as an exact string permits an exact search. Only those documents are presented that contain exactly the specified word form. Every search engine has different forms and limitations for simple and extended search query, as noted in the individual examples.

6.2.2 Simple Search Engines

6.2.2.1 Market Overview

Figure 6.2/3 lists a selection of the current simple search engines with name and WWW address.

This description concentrates on the simple search engines WebCrawler and HotBot. WebCrawler represents the first agent-based search engine in the WWW

Simple Search Engines	WWW Address
AltaVista	www.altavista.com
WebCrawler	www.webcrawler.com
Excite	www.excite.com
HotBot	www.hotbot.com
InfoSeek	www.infoseek.com
OpenText	www.opentext.com
Lycos	www.lycos.com

Figure 6.2/3: Selection of the current simple search engines

and thus is a classic example for the simple search engines, whereas HotBot represents one of the most advanced search engines currently available. Both search engines are demonstrated using the search expression **TU Bergakademie Freiberg**. The aim of the search query is to retrieve the homepage of the TU Bergakademie Freiberg.

6.2.2.2 WebCrawler

The WebCrawler was created as research project at the University of Washington, Seattle, USA, and has been available since April 1994 as free, simple search engine. WebCrawler was sold to America Online in 1995. Since the end of 1996 the search engine belongs to Excite Inc., which itself offers a simple search engine with the name Excite (www.excite.com).

The WebCrawler homepage is divided into two main areas (see Figure 6.2/4). The first central area contains all functions that permit the user to perform a detailed search. The second area permits the user both the simple and clear navigation within the WebCrawler and also the use of the services of the Excite search engine that he can use together with those of the WebCrawler. Five buttons are used for the navigation within the WebCrawler: *Search*, *Guide*, *Services*, *Fun* and *Help*; the selected button is indicated by an arrow.

The WebCrawler has a single search mode that can be used for both simple and extended search queries. Simple search queries permit the processing of the search term without using the exact string of the individual words. The extended search query can restrict or extend the result set through the use of a detailed specification

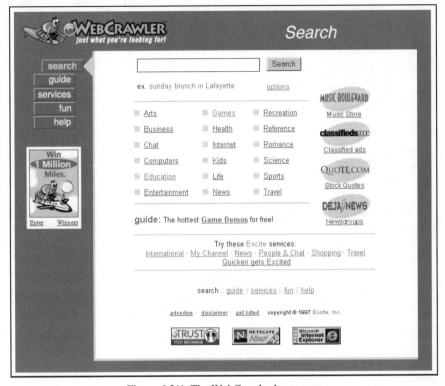

Figure 6.2/4: The WebCrawler homepage

of the search expression. WebCrawler offers with the *Help* button the user notes for the specification. The user also has the capability to search for information on explicit topics in the specified categories.

The *Options* reference located directly below the text field permits the user to individually specify the representation of the result set (see Figure 6.2/5). *Titles or Summaries* are used to specify the presentation of the found documents; *Number of Results per Page* specifies the number of found documents per page. *More*, the third field, selects the display form for the navigation within the result set. Browser support for cookies, which permits defined preferences to be stored locally, is a prerequisite for the specification of these options. Cookies are program components in which information on the current WWW page is stored. The browser informs the user if it does not support the use of cookies.

The following section uses the previously specified search term "TU Berga-kademie Freiberg"to explain the WebCrawler by demonstrating the simple and the

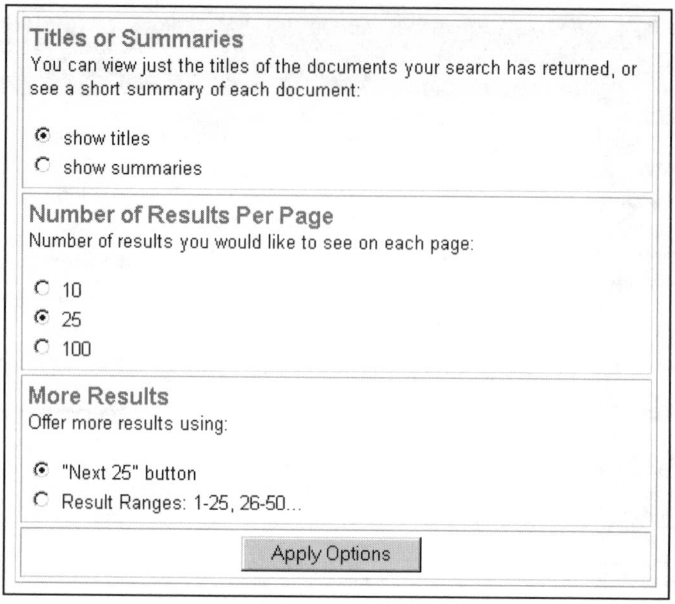

Titles or Summaries
You can view just the titles of the documents your search has returned, or see a short summary of each document:

    ⊙ show titles
    ◯ show summaries

Number of Results Per Page
Number of results you would like to see on each page:

    ◯ 10
    ⊙ 25
    ◯ 100

More Results
Offer more results using:

    ⊙ "Next 25" button
    ◯ Result Ranges: 1-25, 26-50...

[Apply Options]

Figure 6.2/5: The setting of the preferences

extended search query. Because of its extending character, a search for categories is omitted.

- **Simple search query**. The specified words of the query in this alternative are searched without taking account of the sequence. The WebCrawler automatically searches for documents that contain all or just single words of the search term. This simple search query has the form **TU Bergakademie Freiberg** (see Figure 6.2/6).

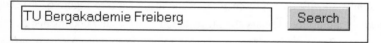

Figure 6.2/6: Text field of the simple search query

This search query produced a result set of 8,142 hits (see Figure 6.2/7). These hits are sorted in the relevance value order that WebCrawler specifies for every document. The relevance values symbolize the degree of matching between the search query and the found documents. They show the probability as percentage for the matching of the found documents with the search query.

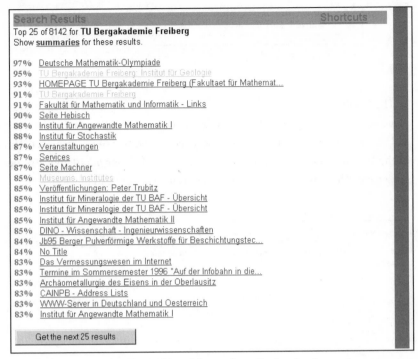

Figure 6.2/7: The first 25 hits of the result set for the simple search query

WebCrawler determines these relevance values by assigning a higher relevance for those documents that contain all words of the user's search term. Such documents have a higher position than those documents that do not contain all words of the search query. The number of documents that have just a link to the homepage of the university is determined during the evaluation of the determined results. The document with the highest relevance represents one of the continuation pages of the **TU Bergakademie Freiberg** homepage. The actual homepage (www.tu-freiberg.de) with 91% is at the fourth position.

The extended search uses additional search criteria to limit the size of the result set for the simple search query and so achieve a higher relevance for this search query.

- **Extended search query**. The search terms in the extended search query can be combined with the AND, OR and NOT logical operators. Furthermore, quotation marks can be used to specify that the search term represents the exact string. This example uses an AND combination of the terms "**TU Bergakademie Freiberg**" and "**Deutschland**" and the quotation marks for the definition of the exact term sequence (see Figure 6.2/8).

"TU Bergakademie Freiberg" AND "Deuts   Search

Figure 6.2/8: Text field of the extended search query

The result set consists of seven hits, which again are sorted into relevance value order (see Figure 6.2/9). The restriction of the search term as exact string and the specification of the country greatly reduce the size of the result set. Three of the seven documents contain only links to the **TU Bergakademie Freiberg** homepage. The homepage of the university is not contained in this result set.

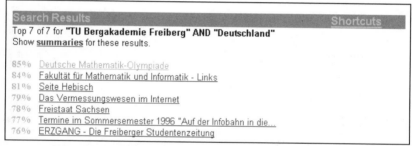

Figure 6.2/9: The result set of the extended search query

6.2.2.3 HotBot

HotBot was developed as part of a research project of the Computer Science Division of the University of California Berkeley, USA. Since 1996, Inktomi Corp. and the Wired magazine have provided HotBot as free commercial search engine. The HotBot data base consists of more than 50 million WWW documents and more than 4 million Usenet articles [HotBot 1997].

The HotBot homepage is divided into three central areas (see Figure 6.2/10). In addition to the text fields for the search query, the upper central part contains an advertising window and three links to the pages of Bigyellow (www.bigyellow.com), which is a special search service for e-mails, people and telephone numbers. The second central area shows as buttons the individual categories to determine the additional search criteria. There are also special buttons required for the navigation and the additional services of the HotBot search engine. The lower area contains certain links to WWW pages of the WiredSource content provider (www.wired-source.com) of Hotwired Inc. and also the two links to the supported browsers.

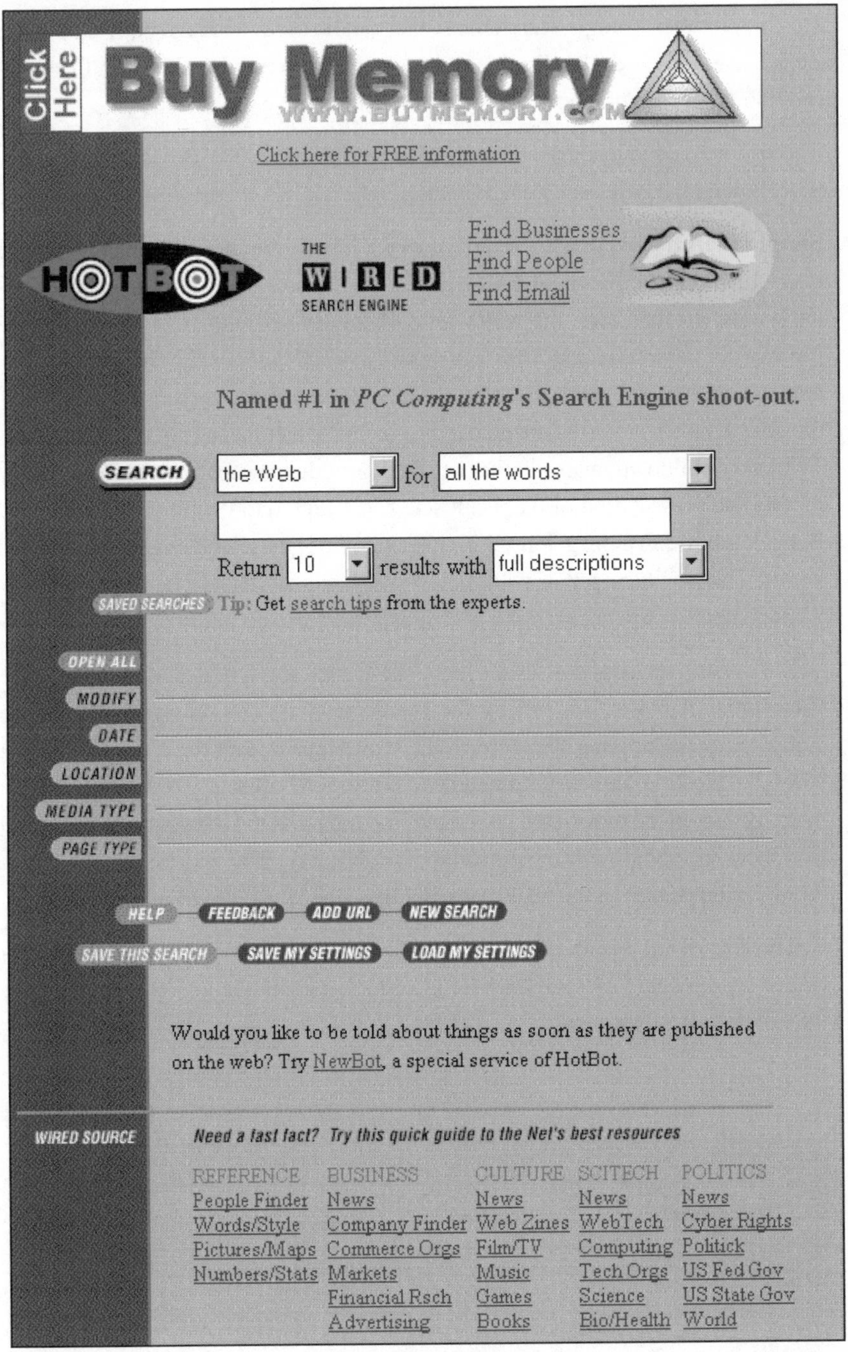

Figure 6.2/10: HotBot homepage

HotBot provides a single search mode that can be used to realize both simple and extended search queries. HotBot mainly uses pulldown menus, shown in the upper area of the homepage, to define the two search alternatives.

The following section uses the specified search term 'TU Bergakademie Freiberg' to explain the two search alternatives.

- **Simple search query**. This search query can use the specified words for the query both with and without taking consideration of the sequence of the individual words. Furthermore, the AND and OR logical operators can be used in the form of the alternatives *all the words* and *any of the words*. The definition is made in a pulldown menu that also permits the search for persons or WWW addresses. Another pulldown menu can be used to select the required search space. Two other pulldown menus in the text field provide the capability to individually modify the presentation of the result set. The search query with the wording **TU Bergakademie Freiberg** is used in this example. The search engine uses all the words. The results, together with their WWW address, should be displayed with 25 documents per page. Figure 6.2/11 illustrates these definitions.

This result set contains 1,469 hits. These hits are sorted into the relevance value order that was defined by the search engine. The relevance values are computed by comparing the word in the search query with the frequency of the words in the title and in the document. The more often a word in the search query occurs in the associated document, the higher is the relevance of the found document weighted with regard to the search query. The address we seek is at the seventh position in the result set with the value 99 % (see Figure 6.2/12).

The size of the result set for the simple search query is restricted in the extended search query by searching for information about the university relating to the economics department.

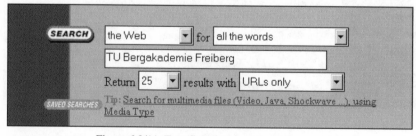

Figure 6.2/11: Text field for simple search query

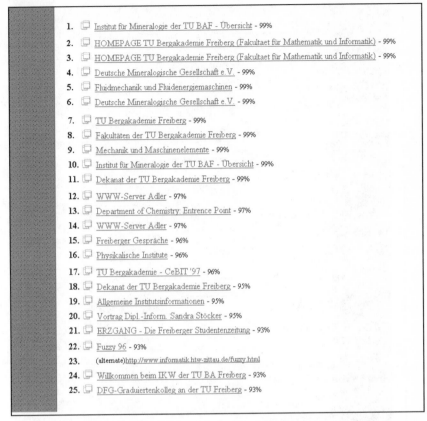

1. Institut für Mineralogie der TU BAF - Übersicht - 99%
2. HOMEPAGE TU Bergakademie Freiberg (Fakultaet für Mathematik und Informatik) - 99%
3. HOMEPAGE TU Bergakademie Freiberg (Fakultaet für Mathematik und Informatik) - 99%
4. Deutsche Mineralogische Gesellschaft e.V. - 99%
5. Fluidmechanik und Fluidenergiemaschinen - 99%
6. Deutsche Mineralogische Gesellschaft e.V. - 99%
7. TU Bergakademie Freiberg - 99%
8. Fakultäten der TU Bergakademie Freiberg - 99%
9. Mechanik und Maschinenelemente - 99%
10. Institut für Mineralogie der TU BAF - Übersicht - 99%
11. Dekanat der TU Bergakademie Freiberg - 99%
12. WWW-Server Adler - 97%
13. Department of Chemistry: Entrence Point - 97%
14. WWW-Server Adler - 97%
15. Freiberger Gespräche - 96%
16. Physikalische Institute - 96%
17. TU Bergakademie - CeBIT '97 - 96%
18. Dekanat der TU Bergakademie Freiberg - 95%
19. Allgemeine Institutsinformationen - 95%
20. Vortrag Dipl.-Inform. Sandra Stöcker - 95%
21. ERZGANG - Die Freiberger Studentenzeitung - 93%
22. Fuzzy 96 - 93%
23. (alternate)http://www.informatik.htw-zittau.de/fuzzy.html
24. Willkommen beim IKW der TU BA Freiberg - 93%
25. DFG-Graduiertenkolleg an der TU Freiberg - 93%

Figure 6.2/12: The first 25 hits of the result set for the simple search query

- **Extended search query**. The HotBot search engine offers the user five different categories for the specification of his search query. The input of the search term in the text fields of the simple search query is the prerequisite for this extended specification. The first category, *Modify*, permits the modification of the search query by adding limiting terms to the original search term. The user can specify in the two pulldown menus how these terms are to be used by the search engine. The *Date* category can restrict the search to within a specified time interval, whereas the *Location* category permits the specification of the search space to geographic places or domains, such as *.de* for Germany. The user can specify with the *Media Type* category that the search is to be restricted to the file types that can contain the sought document. The final category, *Page Type*, specifies a selection of the search query using the page type of the sought document (see Figure 6.2/13).

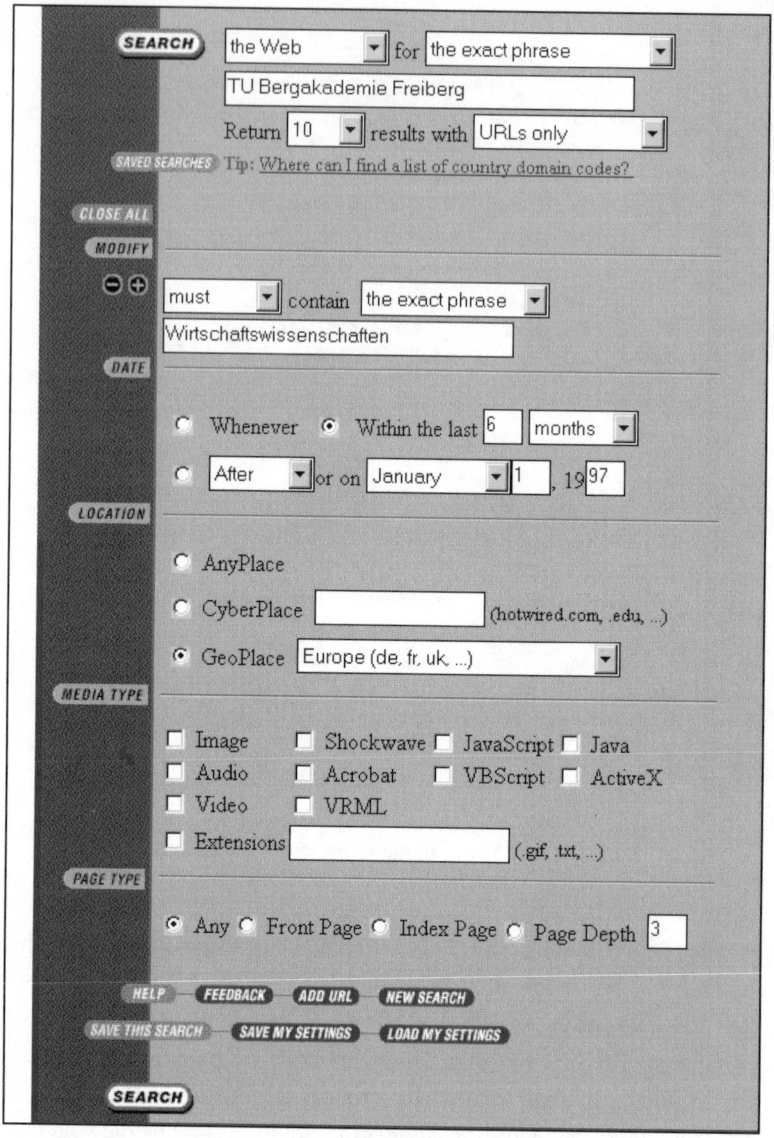

Figure 6.2/13: Text fields of the extended search query

In this example, the **TU Bergakademie Freiberg** search query is selected as exact string and is restricted by the following categories: the sought documents must contain references to the **Economics** department, must not be older as **six months** and must originate from **Deutschland**. The data type and the page type have no significance.

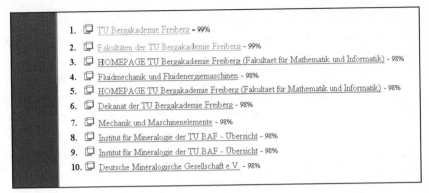

1. 🖥 <u>TU Bergakademie Freiberg</u> - 99%
2. 🖥 <u>Fakultäten der TU Bergakademie Freiberg</u> - 99%
3. 🖥 <u>HOMEPAGE TU Bergakademie Freiberg (Fakultaet für Mathematik und Informatik)</u> - 98%
4. 🖥 <u>Fluidmechanik und Fluidenergiemaschinen</u> - 98%
5. 🖥 <u>HOMEPAGE TU Bergakademie Freiberg (Fakultaet für Mathematik und Informatik)</u> - 98%
6. 🖥 <u>Dekanat der TU Bergakademie Freiberg</u> - 98%
7. 🖥 <u>Mechanik und Maschinenelemente</u> - 98%
8. 🖥 <u>Institut für Mineralogie der TU BAF - Übersicht</u> - 98%
9. 🖥 <u>Institut für Mineralogie der TU BAF - Übersicht</u> - 98%
10. 🖥 <u>Deutsche Mineralogische Gesellschaft e.V.</u> - 98%

Figure 6.2/14: The first 10 hits of the result set of the extended search query

The result set contains 663 hits that are sorted in relevance value sequence. Figure 6.2/14 shows the first ten references. The reference to the University's homepage appears as the first entry with the same reference value as for the simple search query. The document with references to the individual departments follows as the second entry with a relevance value of 99%. This document was at eighth place in the simple search query. This specification of the search query, in addition to the large reduction in the size of the search set, changed the order of the presented individual results to favor the sought document.

6.2.2.4 Concepts

The operation of simple search engines is based on three main concepts. Although these concepts exist in most of the current agent-based simple search engines, they exhibit large similarity to the concept of the simple search engine WebCrawler [Koster 1995, Pinkerton 1997].

- **Input of information**. Simple search engines require many information items to build their database. They use an original list of all known WWW documents that have a large number of links to unknown documents. This permits the search engine to track the contained links. This tracking of previously referenced documents is an important characteristic of agent-based search engines and is called recursive tracking. In addition, WWW addresses can be entered manually in most of the current search engines. The "What's New" section of many WWW documents and the mailing list archives form other sources for the input of information.

The Robot Exclusion standard provides another possibility to acquire specific WWW documents. This standard permits the developers of WWW documents to create a table of contents over the complete documents of a server or individual documents [Koster 1994]. The use of this standard follows two aims. Firstly, marked WWW documents can be excluded from the acquisition by the search engines. Secondly, the search engines are provided with a qualitative selection of information. The search engine is informed while visiting the associated WWW documents as to which text sections are suitable for a subsequent indexing because of their content relevance.

One of the aims of the acquisition of information is to obtain as large a number of unknown WWW documents as possible. This step forms the basis for the selection of the documents for possible indexing and storing in the database.

- **Indexing of information and storing in the database**. Indexing of WWW documents means the syntactical analysis of selected documents and their preparation for storage in the database. The aim of the indexing is to make the contents available and to permit the specific location of the WWW documents. The syntactical analysis serves to include the contents of the documents and is handled differently by the search engines. All simple search engines determine the main contents. Some search engines, such as Lycos (www.lycos.com) form a compressed, content summary of the document, whereas others use the complete content (full text) for syntactical analysis. WebCrawler and Hotbot are examples of such search engines. All search engines then check the contents for so-called stop-words and perform the selection. Stop-words have limited connection to the actual content of the document. They are excluded from the indexing and so must be analyzed. Stop-words can be words such as 'and' and 'the'. Every search engine uses different criteria to determine stop-words. Knowledge of the type of stop-words can be of major importance for the user of search engines, because the incorrect use in the search query can severely limit the relevance quality.

The created index is stored in the database of the search engine and forms the prerequisite that the indexed documents can be found. The indexed contents of the documents, the WWW addresses and the previously mentioned lists of known WWW documents are normally stored in separate databases.

- **Retrieval of information for the user-specific defined search queries and ranking**. The retrieval of documents is the primary aim of the agent-based search engines. The comparison of documents and contents of the search query is used to determine those WWW documents that may be appropriate. They are represented using their relevance value. The determination of relevance values should represent the accuracy and completeness of the found documents. The process to determine the relevance values is designated as ranking. The general aim of all ranking methods is to achieve a very high reliability for the agreement of search query and result set. All retrieved documents are checked with the search query and the relevance values determined. The result set represents a sorting of the WWW documents for reference values. Some search engines represent these values as percentages, as shown in the two examples. Other search engines use the mathematical system of the natural numbers to represent a weighting in the result set.

The type of the definition of the search query can affect the result set in the previous examples. The size and the selection of the documents to be retrieved largely depend on the definition of the search query.

6.2.2.5 Architecture

The architecture of the simple search engines consists of four main components as shown in Figure 6.2/15. These components have a strong relationship to the architecture of the simple search engine WebCrawler [Pinkerton 1997, WebCrawler 1997]. The knowledge gained from the analysis of the publications makes it possible to use the components on the other current simple search engines.

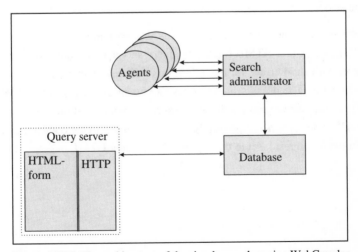

Figure 6.2/15: The architecture of the simple search engine WebCrawler

- **Search administrator**. The two main tasks of the search administrator are the initiation and control of the information acquisition, and the indexing. The individual steps required for the indexing of documents have already been described in the conceptional area. The search administrator is responsible for the syntactical analysis and also for the storage and administration in the database. Exact instructions supplied to the agents initiate the information retrieval. The relevance values are determined for all found documents, which are then forwarded to the query server, which then converts the retrieved addresses into an HTML list.

- **Agents**. The primary task of the agents is the retrieval of indexed documents. Because this task represents the main objective of search engines, this component has a central importance. The individual search engines, such as WebCrawler, use several agents in separate, parallel processes to reduce the duration of the retrieval of documents. The operate exclusively on behalf of the decision maker, the search administrator. The agents navigate independently with an exactly specified objective in the WWW to retrieve the required documents. They communicate with the search administrator only for the task assignment and to present the results.

- **Database**. The database is responsible for the permanent storage of the index. In addition to the full-text index, as built by the majority of search engines, the WWW addresses and the references to the not yet indexed documents are stored in the database. The search administrator uses them as starting point for the expansion of the data base. The database can be located either on a server or on different servers.

- **Query server**. The query server consists of two major software components, HTTP protocol and HTML form. The query server is responsible for providing the user with an interface for the definition of his search query and to present the found results. The user's search queries can be specified with the HTML form. The two described examples illustrate specific layout capabilities of such forms. The HTTP protocol is required to forward the queries to the database and to represent the found result set to the user in a subsequent HTML page.

6.2.3 Meta Search Engines

6.2.3.1 Market Overview

Figure 6.2/16 lists a selection of the current meta search engines with name and WWW address.

Meta Search Engines	WWW Address
MetaCrawler	www.metacrawler.com
MetaGer	meta.rrzn.uni-hannover.de
SavvySearch	guaraldi.cs.colostate.edu:2000/form

Figure 6.2/16: A selection of current meta search engines

This description concentrates on the MetaCrawler and MetaGer search engines. MetaCrawler represents one of the first available meta search engines, whereas MetaGer serves primarily the German-language countries. Both search engines are demonstrated using the **TU Bergakademie Freiberg** search term. The aim of the search query is to retrieve the university's homepage.

6.2.3.2 MetaCrawler

The MetaCrawler was developed at the University of Washington, Seattle, USA. It is freely available to every user of the Internet since 1995. MetaCrawler has been offered by go2Net Inc. (www.go2net.com), a content provider, since the end of 1995. The MetaCrawler serves the user with parallel queries of the simple search engines AltaVista, Excite, InfoSeek, Lycos, WebCrawler and the Yahoo search catalog. There were 150,000 queries per day to the MetaCrawler in 1996 [Selberg/ Etzioni 1997].

The MetaCrawler homepage is divided into two main areas (see Figure 6.2/17). The central area contains all functions that the user requires for a detailed search. The second, and left area, provides the go2Net services, which are also available using the buttons in the homepage heading. Four possible functions offered under the *go2search services* keyword for help and information are shown in the lower area on the left side.

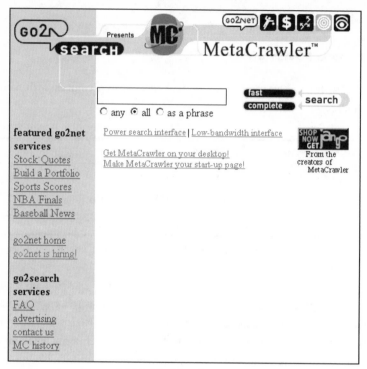

Figure 6.2/17: The MetaCrawler homepage

The MetaCrawler uses a special search mode for the simple and the extended query. The simple search query is realized using the *standard search interface*. It is standardized by the MetaCrawler and has a search duration of 30 seconds and a maximum result delivery per query of ten documents per search engine.

The extended search query permits an extension or restriction to the search duration. The *Power bandwidth interface* below the text field is used to change into this mode. The *Low-bandwidth interface* mode permits a reduction of the bandwidth, because the contained references of go2Net in the user interface are contained in neither the query nor the result set. Because the size of the result set is not affected, this mode is not demonstrated.

The following section uses the previously defined search term "TU Bergakademie Freiberg" to demonstrate both the simple and extended search query.

- **Simple search query**. The *as a phrase* button determines whether the sequences of the individual words of the specified words in this query are to be used. The *any* and *all* buttons permit the use of the OR and AND logical operators. The

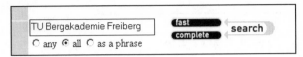

Figure 6.2/18: Text field for the simple search query

fast button reduces the predefined standard search of 30 seconds and ten results per search engine. The query with the **TU Bergakademie Freiberg** wording in this example defines that all words are to be used in the query. Figure 6.2/18 shows this definition.

The result set (see Figure 6.2/19) of this query contains 37 hits. These hits are sorted into the relevance value order determined by the MetaCrawler. It assigns a new value in the range 0 to 1000 to the relevance values for the simple search engines. If the same individual documents occur more than once in the result sets, the relevance values are corrected with the number of duplicates and assigned to the document.

The sought WWW address with a relevance value of 1000 is at the first position and was supplied by the AltaVista simple search engine and the Yahoo search catalog.

The *Power search mode* is described in the extended search query.

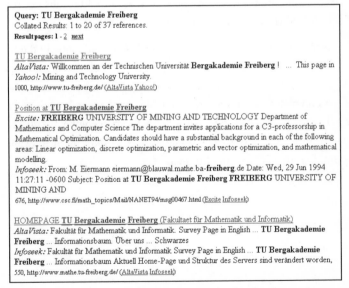

Figure 6.2/19: The first hits of the result set for the simple search query

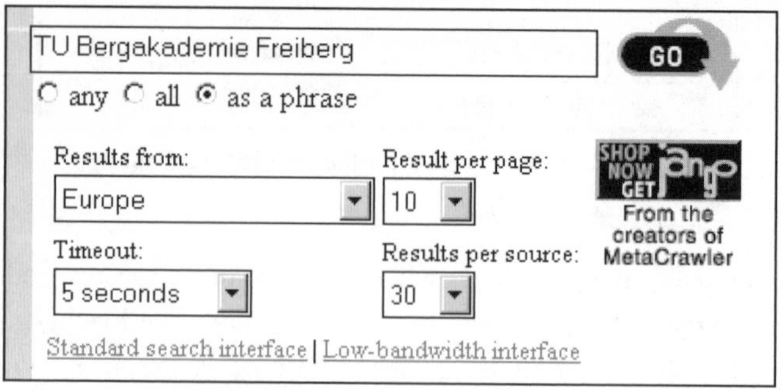

Figure 6.2/20: Text fields of the extended search query

- **Extended search query**. This alternative permits changes to be made to both the search duration and also to the maximum possible number of individual results per search engine. A geographic restriction and a modification to the presentation of the result set are also possible. The shorter the time range selected for the delivery of the documents, the larger is the result set and the less reliable is the agreement of the found documents with the search query. These settings are made using pulldown menus. The selection of the logical operators for the search term and its wording correspond to the definitions of the simple search query. The exact string of the words in the search term and a time limitation of the search duration to five seconds are used for this example. The use of the exact sequence should increase the agreement of WWW documents and the search query. The maximum result set has been increased to 30 results per search engine. Figure 6.2/20 shows these specifications.

The result set contains 87 hits. The sought document, namely the university's homepage, is at third position with 795 points. The relevance with regard to the search query has fallen because of the time restriction, because the MetaCrawler could not completely search all the available simple search engines. In addition to the extension of the maximum result set per search engine, the specification of the search term as exact string has achieved a suitably high relevance for the document. Figure 6.2/21 shows this result set.

```
Query: TU Bergakademie Freiberg
Collated Results: 1 to 10 of 87 references.
Result pages: 1 - 2 - 3 - 4 - 5 - 6 - 7 - 8 - 9  next

HOMEPAGE TU Bergakademie Freiberg (Fakultaet für Mathematik und Informatik)
AltaVista: Fakultät für Mathematik und Informatik. Survey Page in English ... TU Bergakademie
Freiberg ... Informationsbaum. Über uns ... Schwarzes
WebCrawler: Fakultät für Mathematik und Informatik. Veranstaltungen (Vorträge, Workshops,
Tagungen. Services (Bibliotheken, Datenbanken, elektronische Fachinformation. Forschung.
Publikationen. Lehre (Studienordnung, Prüfungsordnung, Vorlesungsverzeichnisse. ). von,
Infoseek: Fakultät für Mathematik und Informatik Survey Page in English ... TU Bergakademie
Freiberg ... Informationsbaum Aktuell Home-Page und Struktur des Servers sind verändert worden,
1000, http://www.mathe.tu-freiberg.de/ (AltaVista WebCrawler Infoseek)

Deutsche Mathematik-Olympiade
WebCrawler: Die DEUTSCHE MATHEMATIK-OLYMPIADE wird unterstützt aus Mitteln des
SÄCHSISCHEN STAATSMINISTERIUMS FÜR KULTUS. Schirmherren der Olympiade sind der
BÜRGERMEISTER DER STADT FREIBERG und der REKTOR DER TU BERGAKADEMIE
FREIBERG. Die TU Bergakademie Freiberg ist
Lycos: TU BERGAKADEMIE FREIBERG Fakultät für Mathematik und Informatik Deutsche
Mathematik-Olympiade 1...
Infoseek: 1995 vom 7. bis 10. Mai 1995 in Freiberg Informationen zum Programm Preisträger der
DeMO 1995 (Presseinformation vom 10. Mai 1995) Die DEUTSCHE
MATHEMATIK-OLYMPIADE (DeMO) ist der H
979, http://www.mathe.tu-freiberg.de/AMM1/demoinfo/demoinfo.html (WebCrawler Lycos Infoseek)

TU Bergakademie Freiberg
AltaVista: Willkommen an der Technischen Universität Bergakademie Freiberg !  ... This page in
WebCrawler: No summary available. http://www.tu-freiberg.de/ 91%  Fakultät für Mathematik und
Informatik - Links Hier findet man eine Auswahl von weltweiten Angeboten zu den jeweiligen
WWW-Servern, geordnet nach den Gruppen: Verlage; Buchhandlungen; Zeitschriften, Magazine;
Zeitungen; Weiteres zum Buch. Kostenlose Direktbuchungen mit Sofortbestätigung, zur Zeit 15.000
Lycos: Herzlich Willkommen bei uns, der Technischen Universität Bergakademie Freiberg Wir möchten
Sie ...
795, http://www.tu-freiberg.de/ (AltaVista WebCrawler Lycos)
```

Figure 6.2/21: The first three hits of the result set for the extended search query

6.2.3.3 MetaGer

The meta search engine MetaGer was developed at the regional computer center of the Hanover University, Germany, and, through use of German simple search engines, primarily serves the German-language user of the Internet. Figure 6.2/22 shows the simple search engines used for the search operation listed in the lower area of the homepage.

The MetaGer homepage is divided into two main areas (see Figure 6.2/22). The central upper area contains all functions that permit the user to define his search query. The MetaGer uses a common search mode for the simple and extended search queries. A time and quality specification is possible for the extended search query. The simple search engines used for the search operation are listed in the lower area of the homepage. Although MetaGer in the default setting has activated all specified search engines for the query, the range of possible search engines can be restricted manually.

The following section uses the specified search term "TU Bergakademie Freiberg" to demonstrate the MetaGer search by making use of both search alternatives.

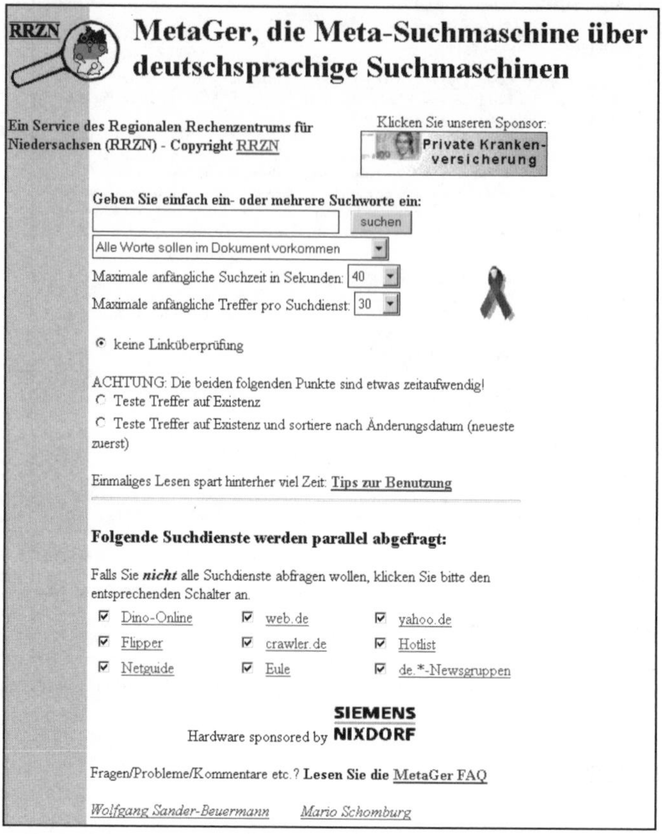

Figure 6.2/22: The MetaGer homepage

- **Simple search query**. In this search query, the search can use the specified
  words of the search query both with and without consideration being made of the
  sequence of the individual words. Furthermore, the words of the search query
  can be combined using AND and OR. These are specified in a pulldown menu.
  The predefined standard search takes 40 seconds and permits 30 results per
  search engine. The search is aborted if this time is exceeded during the search.
  The search query with the wording **TU Bergakademie Freiberg** defined for this
  example uses all words of the search query. Figure 6.2/23 shows this definition.
  The default settings for the time range and result set are not changed.

  The result set contains 78 hits. The references to the found documents are
  specified without relevance values, because MetaGer does not make any judgment of the documents with regard to the search query. The individual docu-

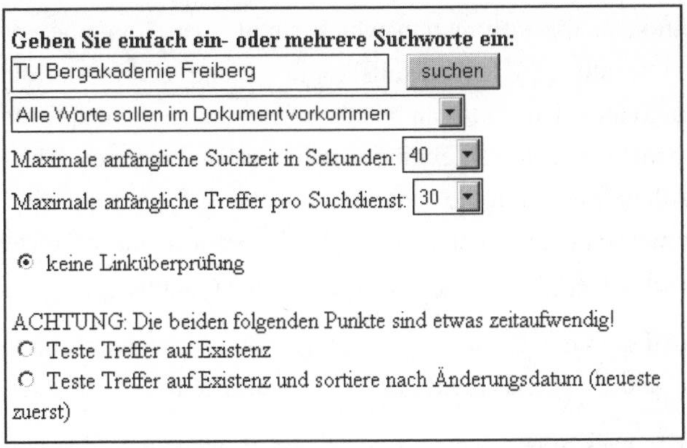

Geben Sie einfach ein- oder mehrere Suchworte ein:

| TU Bergakademie Freiberg | | suchen |

| Alle Worte sollen im Dokument vorkommen | ▼ |

Maximale anfängliche Suchzeit in Sekunden: 40 ▼

Maximale anfängliche Treffer pro Suchdienst: 30 ▼

⦿ keine Linküberprüfung

ACHTUNG: Die beiden folgenden Punkte sind etwas zeitaufwendig!
○ Teste Treffer auf Existenz
○ Teste Treffer auf Existenz und sortiere nach Änderungsdatum (neueste zuerst)

Figure 6.2/23: Text fields for the simple search query

55) **TU Bergakademie Freiberg**

http://www.tu-freiberg.de/
    ○ *(Yahoo.de)*

Figure 6.2/24: The importance of the sought document in the result set
of the simple search engine

Search service	Hits (total)	including duplicats	including equival.	Hits (effective)	Existence tested	Time out during test	untested	not present
Crawler.de	6	0	0	6	0	0	6	0
Eule	10	0	1	9	0	0	10	0
Fireball	10	0	0	10	0	0	10	0
Netguide	30	0	0	30	0	0	30	0
Yahoo.de	22	11	0	11	0	0	11	0
Total result	78	12	1	65	0	0	66	0

Figure 6.2/25: Result set in tabular form for the simple search query

ments are shown with an increasing numbering. The sought document is at position 55, as shown in Figure 6.2/24. If relevance values are contained in the result set, these represent the specified relevance of the quoted simple search engine.

This search engine also provides a static analysis of the result set, as shown in Figure 6.2/25.

In addition to the information which simple search engines have produced how many results and hits, details of the found *Dubletten* (duplicates) and *äquivalente* (equivalent) hits can be taken from this table. Duplicates in this case are documents that a search engine supplies more than once. They are listed as count and then ignored in the subsequent analysis. Equivalent hits contain identical documents on different servers. These produce the corrected number of documents in the *effektive Treffer* (effective hits) column.

An extended search query uses the specification of search criteria to improve the quality of the search set with regard to the relevance of the search query.

- **Extended search query**. The extended search query provides the capability of influencing the result set by changing the time range for the search and the maximum number of possible results per search engine. Two pulldown menus are used for the selection. Furthermore, the search engine can check the existence of the found results. Figure 6.2/26 shows these options in the form of buttons. The search term **TU Bergakademie Freiberg** is defined as exact string and the maximum search time limited to 20 seconds for this search request. The results should also be checked for their existence, which means those WWW documents that no longer exist will be eliminated from the result set.

The extended search query produces a result set of 55 hits. The checking for duplicates, equivalent hits and existence reduces the result set to 53 hits. The sought document is presented at position 17 (see Figure 6.2/27).

Figure 6.2/28 shows this result set in tabular form. The *Existenz getestet* (existence tested) column contains a series of numbers. These specify how many of the maximum found documents have been tested from the *Treffer gesamt* (total hits) column. The *Timeout beim Test* (time-out during test) column contains the number of documents for which the time range was exceeded during the check.

Geben Sie einfach ein- oder mehrere Suchworte ein:

| TU Bergakademie Freiberg | suchen |

| Worte als String in Titel oder Kurzbeschreibung ▼ |

Maximale anfängliche Suchzeit in Sekunden: | 20 ▼ |

Maximale anfängliche Treffer pro Suchdienst: | 30 ▼ |

○ keine Linküberprüfung

ACHTUNG: Die beiden folgenden Punkte sind etwas zeitaufwendig!
○ Teste Treffer auf Existenz
⊙ Teste Treffer auf Existenz und sortiere nach Änderungsdatum (neueste zuerst)

Figure 6.2/26: Text fields for the extended search query

17) **TU Bergakademie Freiberg**

http://www.BA-Freiberg.de/
  ○ *(Eule)* Willkommen an der Technischen Universitaet Bergakademie Freiberg ! ... This page in
    English ... Français Die aelteste Bergakademie der Welt hat sich zu einer modernen technischen Univer
    Status: Existiert (Last Modified: Thu Mar 13 08:51:05 1997)
http://www.tu-freiberg.de/
  ○ *(Yahoo.de)*
    Status: Existiert (Last Modified: Thu Mar 13 08:51:05 1997)

Figure 6.2/27: The status of the sought document in the result set
of the extended search query

Search service	**Hits** **(total)**	including duplicats	including equival.	**Hits** **(effective)**	**Existence** tested	Time out during test	untested	not present
Crawler.de	8	0	0	8	8	0	0	0
Eule	6	0	1	5	6	0	0	0
Fireball	4	0	0	4	4	0	0	0
HarvestUniHannover	2	0	0	2	0	0	2	0
Netguide	25	0	0	25	22	1	0	2
Yahoo.de	1	0	0	1	1	0	0	0
web.de	9	0	0	9	8	1	0	0
Total result	55	1	1	53	48	2	2	2

Figure 6.2/28: Result set in tabular form of the extended search query

6.2.3.4 Concepts

The operation of the meta search engines is based on two main concepts. The representation of the details and fundamentals of the meta search engines are largely based on the conception of the MetaCrawler [Selberg/Etzioni 1995, 1997].

- **Adaptation of the smoothed search query to the interfaces of the simple search engine**. The aim of the meta search engines is to supply high quality results through the parallel query of the databases of simple search engines. The meta search engines must have an algorithm that adapts the standardized query to the predefined query criteria of the simple search engines. A syntactical analysis forms the central component of this algorithm. A syntactical analysis investigates the structure of the search term by determining the position of the individual words of the search query to each other. The prerequisite for the effective processing of this analysis is the knowledge of the individual search criteria of the simple search engines. This permits the parsed search term to be adapted to the criteria and the capabilities of each simple search engine. If a simple search engine cannot satisfy a criterion, the meta search engine must convert the defined search query into the allowed specifications. This, however, means a reduction of the quality of the expected result set.

  A short example is used to explain this analysis methodology. The meta search engine MetaCrawler uses the database of the WebCrawler amongst other things. If a search query to be processed as exact string is given to the WebCrawler, the user specifies this in a text field. WebCrawler can realize this definition only through the use of quotation marks. To permit the term to be found in the WebCrawler database with a high relevance, the MetaCrawler must adapt the query to the restrictions of the WebCrawler before it starts the search.

- **Analysis, evaluation and presentation of the aggregated result set**. Meta search engines receive a large quantity of different information items from the simple search engines. It is possible that the information of the individual search engines overlap to some degree. Result sets that contain copies of identical documents then eventuate. Consequently, the meta search engines must further analyze and evaluate the supplied individual results. The aim of this task is to check the individual results with regard to their relevance to the placed query and the recognition and elimination of duplicates.

  The first concept of meta search engines stated that the search queries must be adapted to the restrictions of the simple search engines. This requires that the received individual results are subjected to a relevance check. The originally defined search query is used as criterion for the check. Those documents far outside the required search space resulting from the modified search query are rejected and no longer appear in the aggregated result set. Simultaneously, the documents with relevance value are evaluated, provided the meta search engine supports such an evaluation.

The analysis for the recognition of the duplicates and their evaluation is performed using a content-related investigation of the received documents. The WWW addresses of the documents to be compared are first checked. This is done by comparing the wording and path details. The complete contents of the selected documents are checked in a second step. If these analysis steps are positive, the meta search engine can, with a high probability, recognize and eliminate the duplicates. Some simple search engines, such as Lycos, do not index the complete content of the documents, and so no unique validation of duplicates can be made for the documents of such search engines. Consequently, the result sets of meta search engines often contain duplicate hits.

The selected documents are presented to the user in a standardized form after these processing steps.

6.2.3.5 Architecture

The architecture of the meta search engines consists principally of the four components shown in Figure 6.2/29. Although this architecture applies for most of the current meta search engines, its main components are largely based on the architecture of the MetaCrawler [Selberg/Etzioni 1997].

- **Search administrator**. The two main tasks of the search administrator cover the analysis and evaluation of the individual results. It is responsible for the recognition and elimination of the duplicates. It also passes the modified search query to the simple search engines and the aggregated result set to the query interface.

- **Modular platform**. The central function of this platform is the grouping of the selected simple search engines. The tasks required to perform this function are concerned with checking the capability of the modified search query being performed by the simple search engine and also in passing the document references to the agents of the meta search engine. The platform also supplies status information, such as the throughput times of the individual search engines, to the

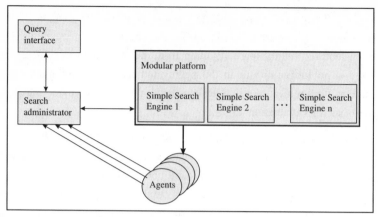

Figure 6.2/29: Architecture of the meta search engines

search administrator. The modular form ensures that it can be extended with additional simple search engines.

- **Agents**. The primary task of the agents is the retrieval of the referenced documents. The agents perform this work in parallel and separate processes. The agents process the specified references of the modular platform and navigate independently with an exactly specified objective in the WWW to retrieve the required documents. These documents are passed to the search administrator.

- **Query interface**. The query interface is responsible for the definition of the search query and for the presentation of the aggregated result set. It also performs the adaptation of the smoothed search query to the specification of the individual search engines.

6.3 NewsWatcher

6.3.1 Introduction

The aim of the user area of the NewsWatcher is the specific grouping and automatic updating of user-specific messages and information items in the Internet. The definition of a personal user profile provides the user with the capability to be individually supplied with the latest news and information. Figure 6.3/1 shows the assignment of this application area in the classification matrix (see Section 3.3). In accordance with the current development level, the agents operate stationary with

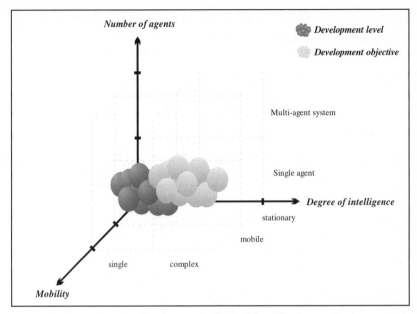

Figure 6.3/1: The classification matrix for the NewsWatcher application area

limited intelligence. A possible development direction of these agents is in the form of mobile agents with high intelligence.

Pull technologies designate the applications for which the information retrieval takes place using a number of individual, separate information providers or content providers. The user himself pulls the information from the net and has only a limited influence on the quantity and content of the information. This type of information retrieval is currently performed by most users of the WWW, such as in the form of search engines. Push technologies have reversed the process of the information retrieval; here a single provider specifically supplies (pushes) the user with user-specific tailored information. The push technologies have already being described in Section 4.7, so that only a reference is made here to this section (see Section 4.7.2). The most important characteristic of this technology is the time-related separation of the processing of the information retrieval and the viewing of this information. The push technologies are part of these discussions. NewsWatcher combines the personalization of the news with the characteristics of the push technologies. The specific applications can concentrate their operation on one of the two technologies. PointCast Network (www.pointcast.com) or Backweb (www. backweb.com) have their strength in the personalization of news, information and other services, whereas Marimba (www.marimba.com) or the Microsoft Internet

Explorer 4.0 (www.microsoft.com/ie/ie40/) concentrate on the push technologies. This division is not further discussed in the following sections.

6.3.2 Market Overview

Figure 6.3/2 lists a selection of current NewsWatcher applications with name and WWW address.

NewsWatcher	WWW Address
After Dark Online	www.afterdark.com
Backweb	www.backweb.com
Marimba - Castanet Tuner	www.marimba.com
Intermind Communicator	www.intermind.com
PointCast Network	www.pointcast.com
FreeLoader	www.freeloader.com
Netscape Netcaster	www.netscape.com
Microsoft Internet Explorer 4.0	www.microsoft.com/ie/ie40/

Figure 6.3/2: Selection of current NewsWatcher applications

The following section describes the two applications PointCast Network and FreeLoader. PointCast Network is the first application in this application area. It is currently one of the leading applications in wide use. FreeLoader belongs to the first developments that can supply off-line information through the use of agent-based technologies.

6.3.3 PointCast Network

The PointCast company was founded in 1992 in California, USA. PointCast provides a free Internet news service for the detailed and automatic distribution of news and information of mainly American character. The definition of a personal user profile permits the required information for the user to be filtered from the total quantity of provided news items and information. Information providers such as CNN, The New York Times and the Wired magazine are contracted to PointCast in Version 1.1.

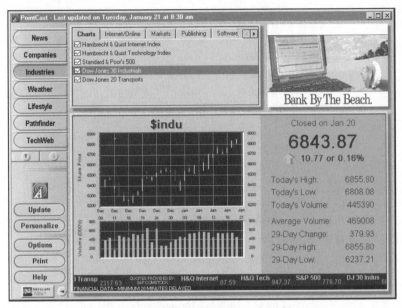

Figure 6.3/3: The PointCast user interface

The central screen that is visible in every PointCast Network application (see Figure 6.3/3) presents itself with three windows (the register, the display and the advertising window), and a menubar in the form of a channel bar and toolbar. This user interface can be used to view the user-specific messages and information and also set the user profile. This page organizes the incoming information into channels and presents them to the user.

The user can select the individual channels with the channel bar in the left upper area of the user interface. Figure 6.3/4 shows the two representation variants of this channel bar.

All information provided by the PointCast Network is organized by topic into channels. The following six basic channels are currently available: news, companies, industries, weather, pathfinder and TechWeb. In addition, other services such as The Boston Globe, CNN, The LA Times, Internet or The New York Times can be selected. The number of standard available channel is growing continually. The groups defined within most channels also contain individual digital publications.

The register window in the upper left area (see Figure 6.3/3) permits the selection of a group within the selected channel. The individual publications of a group appear as list of headings under the group title. After a publication is selected from

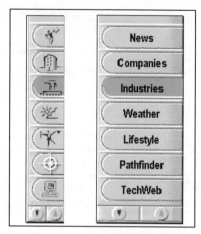

Figure 6.3/4: The two variants of the PointCast channel bar

the list, it appears in the display window that occupies the largest area of the user interface. This window is used to display the contents of the publication. The advertising window is located in the upper right area (see Figure 6.3/3). Various companies and service organizations present themselves in this window. The user can select an advertising area to jump directly to the linked WWW pages.

Some channels are supported by tickers for the presentation of news and information. For example, the sport channel or stock market news are shown using their own ticker.

A toolbar is used to select the channels tailored to the information requirements with their news. Figure 6.3/5 shows the two layout forms of the toolbar.

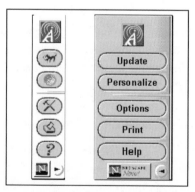

Figure 6.3/5: The two variants of the PointCast toolbar

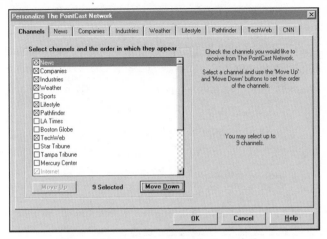

Figure 6.3/6: The *Personalize* button window

The toolbar contains functions to update the user-specific information, to define preferences for printing, for the organization of the user interface and for help. The *Update* button permits the activation of the transmission of the latest news and information to the user. The user receives information on the current status of the transmission. Figure 6.3/6 shows the window for the definition of the areas of interest. This window contains all available channels as register. Various groups can be selected within a channel, each of which is built from a maximum of ten groups, which themselves can contain up to 25 articles. The definitions can be changed at any time.

The *Option* button of the toolbar can be used to define the operation of the user interface and also make the settings for updating the news and information (see Figure 6.3/7).

In particular, this user interface contains the registers to control the screen-saver, for the update mechanism, for the definition of the connection to the Internet, for the definition of proxies for access to the WWW within a firewall, and for the possibilities for the registration of the user.

The settings for the use of a screen-saver are made in the *SmartScreen* register. PointCast also provides a screen-saver in addition to the interface for the detailed representation of the news and information (see Figure 6.3/8). This screen-saver presents the latest news and information during the work breaks of the local computer. A mouse click on the animation area activates the central user interface and so provides access to more detailed information.

Figure 6.3/7: The *Option* button window

Figure 6.3/8: The PointCast screen-saver

The *Update* register of the *Option* window (see Figure 6.3/7) permits the definition of the mechanism used to update the news. The user can choose between four different forms. If the user selects the alternative for the user-specified definition of the update times, the two small windows below are activated. Both the time and the weekdays for the automatic update must be specified. The other three alternatives that are visible as selectable menu items in the upper area of the *Update* window are assigned by PointCast and cannot be changed.

The *Internet* register of the *Option* window (see Figure 6.3/7) is used to define the connection to the Internet and the e-mail parameters required to establish the connection. The settings for the proxy functions are made in the *Proxies* register. The user sets his personal data, such as age, origin or e-mail address, in the *Registration* register.

The *Print* button of the toolbar (see Figure 6.3/5) permits the user to print his current articles. The *Help* button can invoke an interactive help for working with PointCast. The button above the toolbar is designated as the *Pointcast radio tower icon*. If the button changes its appearance by taking the form of another icon, a new version of PointCast is available and can be activated to update the current version. Clicking on this button automatically loads the latest version, which then replaces the old version. The defined user profile is retained.

6.3.4 FreeLoader

The FreeLoader company was founded in 1995 in California, USA. FreeLoader was taken over in mid-1996 by Individual Inc., a company that provides customer-specific services in the news area. As with PointCast, FreeLoader automatically provides the user with the latest news and information, partially supported with multimedia contents, relating to his areas of interest. The most important difference between the two applications is that FreeLoader supplies only the contents of the WWW pages of the previously defined providers, whereas PointCast also uses sources that have their own WWW address that is not present in the Internet.

FreeLoader uses either the Netscape Navigator or Microsoft Internet Explorer browser to display the required information. The use of a browser provides the graphical capabilities of the selected browser in addition to the central user interface of FreeLoader. Figure 6.3/9 shows this user interface with the Netscape Navigator.

The FreeLoader user interface is divided into three central areas. The left part of the user interface contains the channel bar. The user can select those user-specific channels whose contents are to be presented in the central display window. The currently available basic channels include, among others, art and style, music, science and health, computers, politics, marketplace, and travel.

As with PointCast, specific information providers (such as US Today, Hotwired, Sportsline, MSNBC or ZDNet) support these channels. The individual information offerings are limited to American and English language speakers. The central display window shows the articles of the selected channel as short summaries as a list

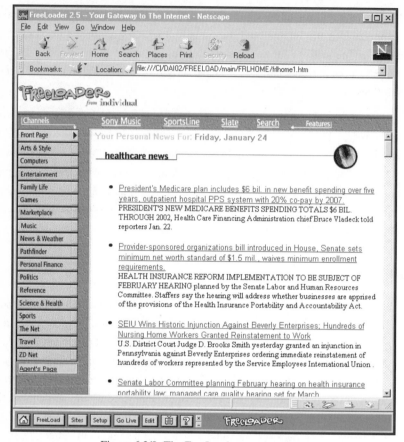

Figure 6.3/9: The FreeLoader user interface

and provides references to switch to the detailed contents of the articles. The use of the *back* and *forward* buttons from the associated browser improves the navigation within the individual articles.

The upper area of the user interface of FreeLoader (see Figure 6.3/9) contains a bar that provides the user with the selected channel, the predefined information sources for the application, a search facility and *Features* as an information aid for the application. The lower area of the user interface contains a toolbar that can be used to select the individual channels and to make the settings for the automatic updating.

The *Home* button of this toolbar returns the user to the front page (see Figure 6.3/9). The *FreeLoad* button can be used to include current WWW pages in addi-

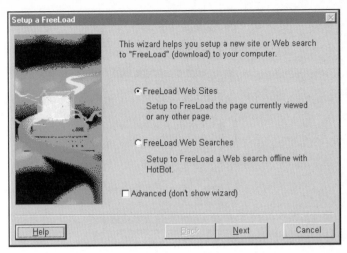

Figure 6.3/10: The *FreeLoad* button assistant

tion to those automatically updated by the FreeLoader. The aim of this option is to provide the user with a continuously extendible range of information sources. Although this acquisition can be made using an assistant (wizard) or manually by the user, this form of acquisition should be reserved for the advanced user. Figure 6.3/10 shows the support provided by an assistant in the acquisition of current WWW pages.

Registers must be used to make these definitions if an assistant is not used. Figure 6.3/11 shows this window. The *Add Site* register makes the assignment to the

Figure 6.3/11: The manual input of new WWW pages

Figure 6.3/12: The *Sites* button dialog window

channel and the automatic acquisition of the current WWW page with title and WWW address. The user determines the frequency of updating and the search depth. The user can enter a search option in the *Add Search* register. The register corresponds to the second alternative with the use of the assistant. The storage requirements and duration of the updating are defined in the *Limits* register. The *Info* register contains a number of status information items pertaining to Free-Loader.

The *Sites* button of the FreeLoader toolbar (see Figure 6.3/9) activates a dialog window that lists the current channels, the contained WWW pages and the current status (see Figure 6.3/12). The user can make changes in this additional window to the input WWW pages, the current status and the assignment to the individual channels.

The user makes settings for the configuration of the application with the *Setup* button (see Figure 6.3/9). These definitions can also be made by selecting an assistant or with manual settings in the form of registers (see Figure 6.3/13).

The *Settings* register specifies the browser used, the maximum available disk storage capacity on the local computer and the time limit for the update operation. The register contains information on the loading of the available resources and the time required until now.

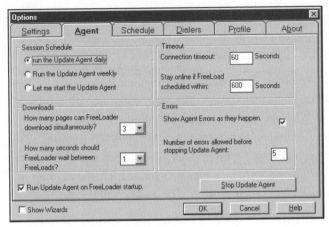

Figure 6.3/13: The *Setup* button dialog window

The *Agent* register specifies the operation of the agents. This includes the error handling, and the number of pages to be loaded concurrently. The *Schedule* register creates the update times of the agent. The settings permit an hourly, daily, weekly or monthly entry. The *Dialers* register notes the type of the connection to the Internet. The *Profile* register stores individual user data, such as name, age, salary and origin, whereas the *System* register contains all system settings, such as processor identification, main memory, and connection type, that are required for the use of the application. The *About* register shows the version number and contact addresses.

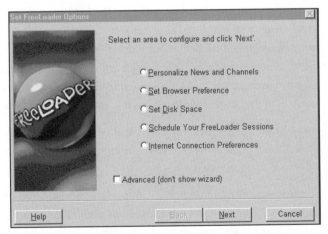

Figure 6.3/14: The *Setup* button assistant

If the assistant is used, this navigates the user through the individual areas and successively prompts for the individual parameters. Figure 6.3/14 shows the assistant.

The *Go Live* button of the toolbar (see Figure 6.3/9) returns the user for WWW pages similar to the entered page. The application uses the term similar pages to refer to WWW pages that, for example, have been implemented in various languages. The *Edit* button in the toolbar (see Figure 6.3/9) performs all the entries for a WWW page registered by FreeLoader. The corresponding dialog window of the *FreeLoad* button opens after the button is pressed. The button with the TV icon in the toolbar activates the screen-saver. The button with the question mark icon activates a help tool for working with this application.

6.3.5 Concepts

The NewsWatcher operation is based on two main concepts. These are strongly related to the operation of the PointCast application. Most of the current applications in this area are characterized by having a similar operation, which can be seen by the addressing of news and information as channels.

- **Personalization of the news channels**. The continually increasing availability of online information was a factor in the rapid development of the NewsWatcher application area. The central task of the applications is to filter those items of personal interest to the information seeker from the mass of news items and information available. The definition of the personal interests for each individual user is the prerequisite for the realization of these applications. The two examples have already shown that predefined channels exist for the better grouping of the individual interest areas from which the user can select specific topics. These predefined channels are supplied by the provider of the news and information. Every provider uses different information. The available channels are adapted to the individual information requirements by personalizing the individual topic areas. This produces a subset of the news and information that is tailored to the user.

  The personalization of the news channels that is realized using the automatic information matching is the most important prerequisite for the user-specific distribution of news and information.

- **Automatic information matching**. The automatic information matching guarantees a continuous availability of the latest news and information. The prerequisites are the specification of the updating parameters, such as time and type of the connection, and a platform that provides the latest news and information. The user can determine the time and period for updating the news and information through the specification of the updating parameters. This is similar to choosing a daily or weekly magazine. The process of transmission of these news and information items takes place without any direct user action. The specification of the updating parameters has been shown in the two examples.

6.3.6 Architecture

The architecture of the applications in the NewsWatcher area is based on the client-server principle (see Section 4.1.3). This principle is the basis of most of the current applications. In particular, the architecture consists of the following components (shown in Figure 6.3/15).

- **Channel viewer**. The channel viewer is responsible for organizing the incoming news and information items into channels, and then presenting these data. The channel viewer has the capability of organizing the news and information items so that they are presented in a clear and standardized form. The information must be adapted to the application-specific user interface. To permit the work of the channel viewer, every application uses a conventional or self-developed browser to provide the user access to the Internet.

- **User agent**. The user agent is responsible for initiating the transmission of the latest news and information items. The unambiguous definition of the required parameters, such as time or duration of the transmission, is the prerequisite for performing this task. The user agent requires these specifications to initiate the transmission of the current news and information by the server. The user agent operates independently without further instructions from the user.

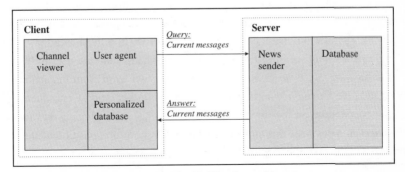

Figure 6.3/15: The NetWatcher architecture

- **Personalized database**. The personalized database is responsible for storing locally the personalized news and information supplied from the server so that the channel viewer can access this information at any time. It receives the latest news and information tailored for the user. An update replaces the previous news and information with the incoming items. The required storage space on the user's local hard disk can be individually adapted and is normally based on the system-specific requirements of the associated client's computer system.

- **News sender**. The news sender is responsible for processing the update queries of the various user agents and of ensuring the transmission of the required news and information. The user agent informs the news sender of the type of the required news and information at the start of update phase. It can then select suitable news and information from the server's database and send these items to the client's personalized database.

- **Database**. The database contains all news and information of the provider that are made available for the application as information source. The specific news providers have been mentioned in the two examples. These databases can be considered to be catalogs that are built as hierarchical topic directories. They represent the maximum number of channels available for the user. The reader is requested to consult the discussions in Section 4.6 concerning the administration of meta data (see Section 4.6.2.1).

6.4 Advising and Focusing

6.4.1 Introduction

The two previous application areas, information retrieval and filtering and NewsWatcher, show that the user can use both search engines and push technologies for the specific provision of required information. In a third area that follows the goal of searching for information, personal assistants help the user in his work with the browser. By observing the user, the assistants learn from his actions (advising) and give him advice and information for his further work. Consequently, the user can concentrate on the important work (focusing). The advising and focusing application area provides this support. Figure 6.4/1 shows the position of the application area in the classification matrix (see Section 3.3).

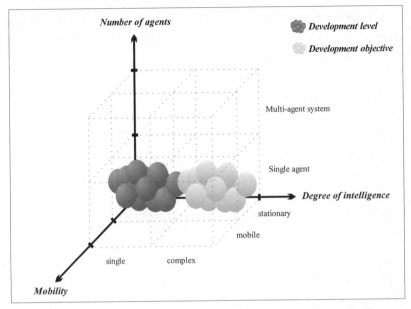

Figure 6.4/1: The classification matrix for the advising and focusing application area

In accordance with the current level of development, the agents operate stationary with a limited degree of intelligence. An increase in the intelligence is a demand for the future development of agents in this application area.

Applications in the advising and focusing area permit the acceptance and evaluation of the information search. They combine these tasks with the automation of time-consuming activities of the user while working with the browser. They can also create a personalized user profile adapted to the information needs of the user. The majority of the tasks in this application area assigned to agents demand a high degree of intelligence from them, which makes itself particularly apparent in a high capability of learning. Learning capability in this context means that the agents monitor and imitate the user's behavior, and they can adapt their own behavior using the communication capability with the user. The agents can be trained by the user with examples and can also communicate with other agents [Maes 1994a]. The potential of the current developments is mainly concerned with the area of monitoring and the independent reasoning resulting from the behavior of the user, and also the communication with the user.

The theoretical basis of the Letizia application is available to describe the concepts for the representation of the operation of the architecture for the applications in the advising and focusing area. Consequently, the description of the Letizia prototype is extended with the representation of the basis concepts. No statements are made regarding the architecture.

6.4.2 Market Overview

Figure 6.4/2 lists with name and WWW address a selection of current applications in the area of advising and focusing.

The description in the following section concentrates on the Web Browser Intelligence and Letizia applications. Whereas the Web Browser Intelligence displays some of the mentioned development potentials, Letizia is a research project still in progress.

Advising and Focusing	WWW Address
Web Browser Intelligence	www.networking.ibm.com/wbi/wbisoft.htm
Letizia	lieber.www.media.mit.edu/people/lieberary/
	Letizia/Letizia.mov
Basar	GMD research project
Webdoggie	rg.media.mit.edu:80/projects

Figure 6.4/2: A selection of current applications of advising and focusing

6.4.3 IBM Web Browser Intelligence

The Web Browser Intelligence was developed within the research division of IBM Corporation and is freely available. The Web Browser Intelligence is a personal assistant that helps the user in his work with the browser. The Web Browser Intelligence's help support supplies the user with the visited, changed or forgotten WWW pages [Gilbert 1997].

Once the installation is complete, the toolbar of the Web Browser Intelligence appears for every subsequent use of the selected browser (see Figure 6.4/3).

Figure 6.4/3: The Web Browser Intelligence toolbar

The *History* button provides the user with a list of the previously visited WWW pages (see Figure 6.4/4). The individual WWW pages are sorted according to access frequency and access speed. The access frequency results from the number of visits per page and is assigned automatically by the Web Browser Intelligence. The more often a page is visited, the higher this page is positioned in the ranking list of the Web Browser Intelligence. The access speed is the time period between activating the connection to the server that contains the selected page and the successful completion of the transmission. The *Score* column shows this sorted with numbers in the range 0 to 100; these numbers are assigned to the associated references.

The Web Browser Intelligence has the capability to search for contents in the previously visited WWW pages. Either the text field in the upper area of the user interface or the pulldown menu at the side can be used for this purpose. The *All*, *Title* or *URL* criteria can be specified for the search term in the menu.

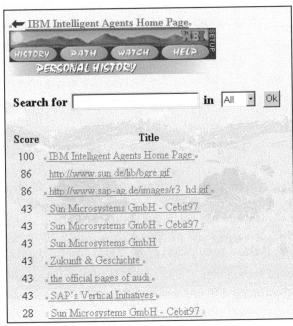

Figure 6.4/4: The *History* button user interface

Figure 6.4/5: The *Path* button user interface

The Web Browser Intelligence uses a color marking (*web traffic lights*) to emphasize the classification of the pages with regard to access. The user manually activates this marking. The Web Browser Intelligence checks the speed of the transmission of the WWW pages and flags for the user the access speeds per page with the color green, yellow or red. WWW pages marked green or yellow have a high or medium access speed, respectively. No access was possible for the WWW pages marked red.

The *Path* button in the toolbar displays a user interface with which the user can trace all previously used links back to the original pages. This permits him to reconstruct the path from the start of his information search through to the current WWW page. Figure 6.4/5 shows the user interface of the *Path* button. The user is in the 'trends online' WWW page when he invokes this button. He reached this page by making the links *Kurzmeldungen*, *TV Projekte*, and finally *Querschnitt*.

The *Watch* button can be used to select various WWW pages to be monitored by the Web Browser Intelligence (see Figure 6.4/6). The Web Browser Intelligence checks frequently used WWW pages for changes and informs the user accordingly. Furthermore, it is possible to view the pages already selected for monitoring and to exclude from monitoring those pages no longer favored. The text field in the middle of the user interface can be used to enter new WWW pages. The current WWW page is automatically entered into this text field when the user interface is called. The personalization of WWW addresses and their contents is similar to that of the NewsWatcher (see Section 6.3). The *Yes* or *No* button is used to make the decision for the future monitoring. The user can specify in the lower part of the user interface any previously selected pages that are to be excluded from future monitoring.

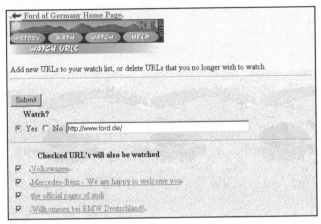

Figure 6.4/6: The *Watch* button user interface

If the Web Browser Intelligence has registered a change to a WWW page, it informs the user with the *Look Here!* marking above the *Watch* button (see Figure 6.4/7).

The Web Browser Intelligence in this example informs the user that two of the above selected WWW pages have been changed. It automatically checks the links contained in the changed pages to make an assignment for the access speed. The *Look Here!* button disappears from the toolbar once the user has viewed the changed addresses.

The *Help* button provides the user with a general or context-sensitive help. The former is used to describe the individual functions of the application, whereas the context-sensitive help provides explanations for the user interfaces developed by the Web Browser Intelligence, such as *Path* or *Watch*.

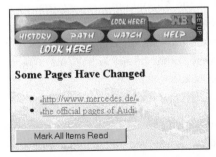

Figure 6.4/7: The *Look Here!* button user interface

WBI Setup

To set up WBI, fill in and then submit this form.

Make these changes? [Yes]
WBI Listens on Port 8088

Socks Server		Port	1080
Proxy Server	www2.mms-dresden.telekom.de	Port	80
No Proxy For			
Cache Size	50	Files	
Show WBI Toolbar in	no frame		

WBI Module Setup

On	Module Name	Module Description
✔	Personal History	Allows querying of personal web history, watches pages for changes, adds shortcut links
✔	Web Traffic Lights	adds colored dots around links indicating network speed to server

Figure 6.4/8: The *Setup* user interface

All important parameters are set by the user in the *Setup* user interface. Figure 6.4/8 shows the *Setup* user interface.

Both the prerequisite technical and system specific details required for the network the selection of the Module Personal History and Web Traffic Lights are specified in this user interface.

6.4.4 Letizia

Letizia was developed at the Media Lab of the Massachusetts Institute of Technology in Cambridge, USA as prototype for the automation of the user's work with the Netscape Navigator and Mosaic browsers. Letizia, by permanently observing the user's actions and their imitation, can provide suggestions and information for the future work with the browser. Letizia also permits the automatic search for information. The relevance of the results with regard to the required user's search is based on the results of the observations.

In addition to the browser's original window, Letizia opens two other windows that the application requires to perform its work. Figure 6.4/9 shows these three windows. The left window is reserved for the user's work.

The ability to learn and autonomy are two of the most important characteristics of intelligent agents (see Section 3.2). Applied to this application, Letizia can be considered to be an autonomous interface agent [Lieberman 1997]. Autonomous interface agents permit both the realization of the principle of the indirect manipulation and also the delegation of user tasks.

In direct manipulation, the user himself must perform all steps required to achieve his objective. The browser is the graphical interface that permits the processing of the specified actions. The user must check the results of the processing before he can decide on the initiation of some further action. The interface agents permit the change to the indirect manipulation. They can influence the execution of actions and also check their results without requiring the explicit intervention of the user. Because the interface agent can intervene independently, it influences the user's processing sequence. The autonomy of the interface agents provides the user with the advantage of delegating a number of tasks to the agents. The agent is independent, continuously active and not dependent on instructions from its user.

The left area of the user interface (see Figure 6.4/9) corresponds to the functionality of a traditional browser user interface and is exclusively reserved for the

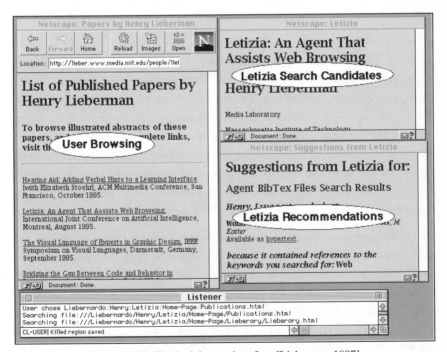

Figure 6.4/9: The Letizia user interface [Lieberman 1997]

user. He can either enter known WWW pages or analyze a number of unknown WWW pages. Letizia observes this behavior. This forms the basis for the future presentation of recommendations for the consideration of unknown WWW pages. These recommendations are displayed for the user in the lower right part of the user interface (see Figure 6.4/9).

To enable Letizia to make reliable decisions, Letizia must have access to a knowledge base that permits conclusions to be made from this behavior. The simulation of the browsing process of the user and the assignment of its associated handling form the basis.

The principle of the browsing process lies in the user following the links of a page that has already met his interests. He normally follows the individual links back to the original page and adds the new interesting links to his bookmark list. Letizia simulates these steps by checking the individual links in a significantly shorter time period than the user, while the user checks the contents for a possible relevance. In particular, those links can be determined that do not have any content and which the user has reported as being 'dead-ends'. Letizia can use this independent checking of all links to determine which of the links could be relevant for the user's further work. The upper right area of the user interface shows the links that Letizia is currently searching, the so-called search candidates (see Figure 6.4/9).

Letizia analyses the user's individual actions as the second basis for a reliable reasoning. The evaluation is based on a priority assignment with the aim of being able to make decisions on the relevance of the individual WWW pages. Letizia's action with the highest priority with regard to the user's interest is the storage of a WWW page in the bookmark list. Letizia also assigns a high priority to the tracing of a link and the time range for the visit to this page; in particular, the frequency and the time duration are the necessary criteria for determining how interesting this page is for the user. The number of the traced links per page provides a certain degree of importance. The higher the number of links traced per pages, the more interesting these pages can be assumed to be for the user.

Letizia stores all checked links in its knowledge base. This contains specific keywords that are used to decide whether a document is of interest to the user. Letizia does not use percentage values to specify the exact relevance for the importance for the user, but lets the user decide by offering him all recommendations for evaluation. To increase the acceptance of the recommendation, Letizia presents the user with an additional overview that contains documents with similar content. Letizia also autonomously checks the permanence of interest by using the time since the last visit as criterion for the assignment to the current area of interest. To check the individual links, the relevance for the current document is first defined before the individual links are tested.

6.5 Entertainment

6.5.1 Introduction

Applications in the area of entertainment aim to support the user in the selection of recreational activities that match his interest profile. In particular, help should be provided in the areas of online shopping, and movies, music and television. All these recreational areas are characterized by an almost unlimited amount of information being available in the Internet and demand a time-consuming search for information from the user. Entertainment applications attempt to relieve the user of this information search by building a personal user profile. The applications have the task of presenting the personalized information. Figure 6.5/1 shows the assignment of the application area in the classification matrix (see Section 3.3).

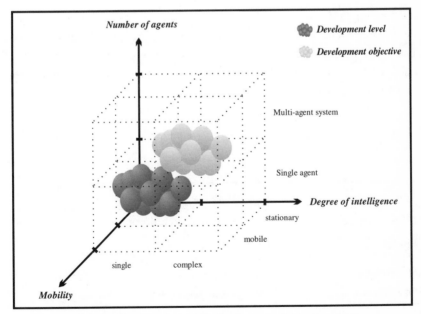

Figure 6.5/1: The classification matrix for the entertainment application area

In accordance with the current stage of development, the agents operate stationary with a limited degree of intelligence. The reason for the assignment of the current applications at this development level lies primarily in their limited capability to cooperate. This capability means that several agents can work together to meet their individual tasks and so permit the solution of complex problem situations. To obtain comprehensive knowledge on the user's areas of interest and preferences, the agents must be able to compare individual user profiles with each other in addition to communicating with the user. Firefly is the only current application that has this capability.

The theoretical basis of Firefly is available to describe the concepts to represent the operation and architecture of the entertainment area. Consequently, the description of the Firefly application is extended with the representation of the basic concepts. No generalizations can be made on the architecture. Other previously described concepts relate to the clustering analysis (see Section 4.6.2.4) and matching (see Section 4.6.2.5).

6.5.2 Market Overview

Figure 6.5/2 lists a selection of current applications in the area of entertainment with name and WWW address.

The description in the following section concentrates on the LifestyleFinder and Firefly applications. LifestyleFinder is an agent-based application from Andersen Consulting and provides the user with an interest-related selection of available online shopping alternatives. Firefly is one of the leading applications in the area of agent-based entertainment in the movie and music areas, and shows the potential for future developments.

Entertainment	WWW Address
LifestyleFinder	lifestyle.cstar.ac.com/lifestyle/
Firefly	www.firefly.com
Netradio	www.netradio.net
OpenSesame	www.opensesame.com

Figure 6.5/2: A selection of current entertainment applications

6.5.3 LifestyleFinder

LifestyleFinder was developed by the research institute for intelligent agents at Andersen Consulting in cooperation with Claritas, Inc. Claritas provides the demographic data required for this application. The aim of LifestyleFinder is to determine the life style pattern and so provide recommendations for the visits to various online providers.

The creation of the personal profile by LifestyleFinder begins for the user with the answering of several questions. These questions are related to the areas of cars, home, travel, recreation, television, newspapers, beverages and music and are shown as diagrams that express the content of the associated question. Within these categories, the user is provided with six different ways to answer the question according to his area of interest. Figure 6.5/3 shows one of these eight categories.

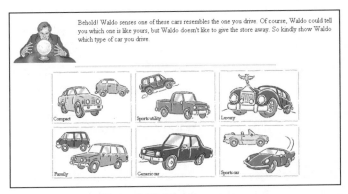

Figure 6.5/3: The cars category

The personal profile that results from the answer given to the individual categories is shown in an overview (see Figure 6.5/4).

Figure 6.5/4: The user profile

Waldo's description of you may be crazy, but Waldo's crystal ball still shows you enjoying the following Web pages. The point
of the LifestyleFinder research project isn't to write fortune cookies but rather to suggest URL's, so Waldo would appreciate
knowing whether you like the following. Just select the Y or N next to each link you check out. Then press the **tell me more**
button at the bottom to hear how LifestyleFinder has the power to change the Web as you know it.

Things you can buy
   ⊙ Y ⊙ N The Golf Circuit - everything you want to know about golf. Information about the British Open, the Michelob
Championship and more!
   ⊙ Y ⊙ N Hops Internationale - an imported beer lover's club. Outstanding feature: the weekly newsletter.
   ⊙ Y ⊙ N Honda/Acura Integra Performance - find out more about the Acura Integra.
   ⊙ Y ⊙ N Fidelity Investments: Online Investor Center - a good one-stop information source on personal finance. Features:
Retirement Calculator and Commission Calculator.
   ⊙ Y ⊙ N Homelite Chainsaws - detailed information about Homelite chainsaws, with pricing info.

Places you can go
   ⊙ Y ⊙ N Sara's City Workout: give the Internet a workout - find out about the latest aerobics seminars and conventions
from Sara.
   ⊙ Y ⊙ N Preview Vacations: about Puerto Rico - browse through this page for Puerto Rico attractions, travel tips and
more!
   ⊙ Y ⊙ N Travel Org: welcome to France - your trip begins here! Here's everything about travel in France.
   ⊙ Y ⊙ N Virtually San Francisco - this virtually entertaining, sightseeable, hospitable Web site invites you to visit the world's
second most visited city.
   ⊙ Y ⊙ N Hokeo Hawaii: Welcome to the Islands - where you can enter to win your own customized Hawaii Vacation!
Learn more about the islands, or find out about accomodations.

Stores you can shop at
   ⊙ Y ⊙ N Internet Shopping Network - good one-stop shopping for computer hardware and software - visit this site and
get hot deals.
   ⊙ Y ⊙ N Virtual Vineyards - excellent online store for rare wines and gourmet food. Also featuring the Sizzlin' Summer
Sampler!
   ⊙ Y ⊙ N Wal-Mart Stores--store information, corporate information, SAM'S Club information, community involvement
and so forth.
   ⊙ Y ⊙ N Time Warner's DreamShop - an online collection of well-known catalogs. You can shop by store or by category
with "Personal Shopper."
   ⊙ Y ⊙ N Fashion.Net - a global meeting point for the world of fashion; you'll find links to fashion magazines, online
shopping as well as links to other fashion and beauty sites.

Figure 6.5/5: The list of recommendations

LifestyleFinder also presents an overview with those online providers that it considers can best satisfy the user's interest areas and preferences (see Figure 6.5/5).

Recommendations for specific products and selected online businesses, and for
the general WWW pages are provided. The user can use a link to visit each of these
recommendations.

The user can increase the usefulness of his profile by using the *Yes* and *No* buttons of the recommendation list to rate the individual providers. The user can also
supply additional details concerning his person, such as age. This additional information then can be sent to the LifestyleFinder to be used to improve the user profile.

6.5.4 Firefly

The Firefly application is a product of Firefly Network Inc., Cambridge, Massachusetts, USA and is available for every user after they have registered. The aim of

Firefly is to provide the user with a guided navigation to information and products. The creation of a personal profile enables the user to receive personalized information and to communicate with other users of the application having similar interests. The registration of every member or user permits the creation of a virtual community as prerequisite for an interactive communication between the members.

The definition of the user-specific interests in the areas of movies and music forms the basis for the creation of a personal profile. These two areas also form the starting point for the communication with other members.

The user's personal directory, shown in Figure 6.5/6, is activated once the user has been registered. This directory serves the user during his navigation within the application and remains active as its own window for the period of participation by the user.

This directory contains two central registers, *Personal* and *Directory*. The upper area contains the name of the user, in this case the test-agent pseudonym. The lower area of this directory contains four buttons, *talk*, *help*, *messages* and *exit*.

The *Personal* register contains five selection fields, *profile*, *notifications*, *message screening*, *member page* and *privacy policy*. They are used for the administration of the user's operation with Firefly.

 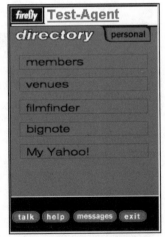

Figure 6.5/6: The user's personal directory

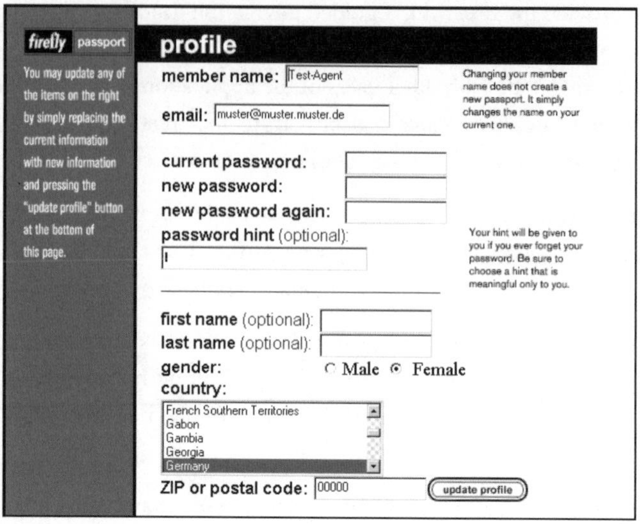

Figure 6.5/7: The *profile* user interface

The user can enter and change his personal data in the first selection field, *profile*. Figure 6.5/7 shows this user interface.

The second selection field, *notifications*, permits the user to define a list within the areas of movie, artist, member and interest/hobby to which the user wishes to obtain new information, changes or opinions of other users for these topics (see Figure 6.5/8). He can also specify his special interests in these areas. The Firefly

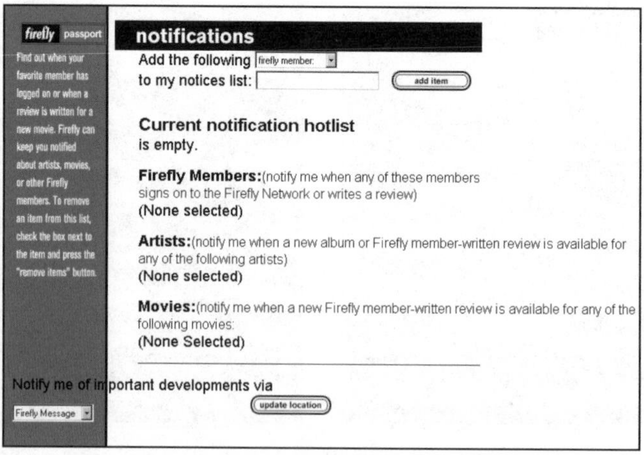

Figure 6.5/8: The *notifications* user interface

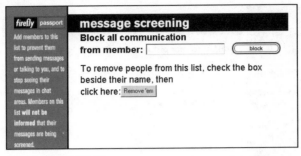

Figure 6.5/9: The *message screening* user interface

then supplies the user with every new information item or change that affects these specified forms.

The user can use the *message screening* selection field to stop other members from communicating with him (see Figure 6.5/9). The entry of the selected member then inhibits this member from sending messages to the user.

The *member page* selection field permits the user to create his own homepage and to include his previous homepage with a link. The particular aim of this selection field is to make his personal interest areas available to the other users and so achieve a preselection for a possible exchange of ideas with users having similar interests. Figure 6.5/10 shows the *member page* user interface.

The operator of the application uses *private policy*, the last selection field of the *Personal* register, to inform the user of the data protection for his personal data.

The second register, *Directory*, contains the five selection fields *members, venues, filmfinder, bignote* and *My Yahoo!* (see Figure 6.5/6). The user can use this register to search for other members and to define his interests in the movie and music areas and to make an evaluation within these two areas. A platform is also available for the users to communicate over various topics.

The user can use the first selection window, *members*, to search for other members with whom he would like to contact. The user is provided with several areas within which he can search for other users. The members are selected with the user's personal profile. Figure 6.5/11 shows this user interface. The user is presented with a list of possible participants if the search is successful.

The second selection field, *venues*, permits the user to exchange information with other participants in the forums of various interest areas. This user interface is comparable with the discussion lists in the Internet. The user can register or deregis-

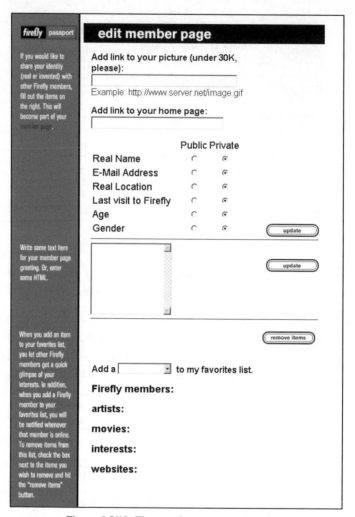

Figure 6.5/10: The *member page* user interface

ter himself from the many available forums or also open new forums. The user is provided with six channels to simplify his navigation. The majority of the users maintain their discussions in these channels. Figure 6.5/12 shows these channels.

The search function in the lower area of the user interface can be used to determine the other possible forums. The *venues chat* function permits discussion of special topics with users who are online at the time of the visit. The user can also join existing group discussions or open new discussions. The user can restrict the number of participants by defining the new discussion as being a *private room*.

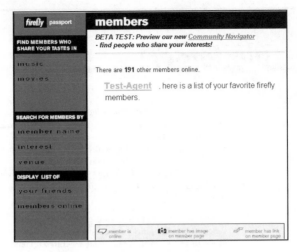

Figure 6.5/11: The *members* user interface

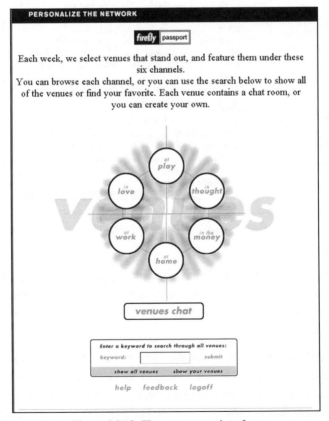

Figure 6.5/12: The *venues* user interface

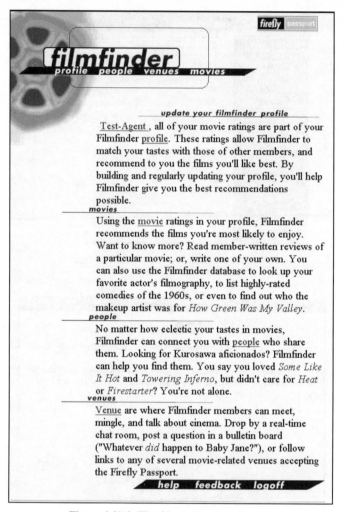

Figure 6.5/13: The *filmfinder* user interface

The *filmfinder* selection field forms a central area within Firefly. The rating, checking and recommendation of movies that are the major functions of this user interface are used to define a personal profile. Figure 6.5/13 shows the *filmfinder* user interface.

The *profile* button is used to rate the movies. This button presents a new user interface, in which the user can rate a range of movies and also suggest other movies for a future rating. The larger the number of movies rated, the more reliable are Firefly's recommendations for new movies. The user obtains these movies with the *movies* button. They are based on the individual ratings that have been made previously. Firefly provides the user with a list of suggestions that match the specified interest profile for movies. He can rate these suggestions and so improve his personal profile. A range of supplementary information is available for every movie, such as information on the actors, directors or producers. In addition to rating movies, the user can also write his own opinion on the movies he has rated, which is then available to every other Firefly user.

The *people* button can place the user in contact with other members that have similar movie interests. This user interface corresponds to the operation of the *member* selection field of the *Directory* register. The *venues* button provides the previously described *venues* user interface and their features.

The *bignote* selection field of the *Directory* register provides the user in the music area with the similar functions as for the *filmfinder* selection field. In addition to these functions, Bignote supports the user in ordering the selected music. The user can also listen to selected titles and so simplify the rating. The only difference between the two selection fields is the layout of the individual user interfaces. Figure 6.5/14 shows the *bignote* user interface.

The *My Yahoo!* user interface that Firefly provides in the last selection field of the *Directory* register permits the user to perform a general search for information.

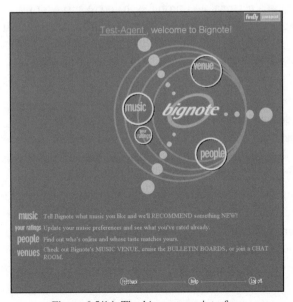

Figure 6.5/14: The *bignote* user interface

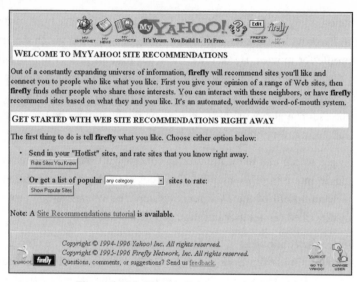

Figure 6.5/15: The *My Yahoo!* user interface

The search results of the Yahoo search catalog can be adapted to the personal profile formed by the evaluation within the movie and music areas. Thus, they promise improved success for the relevance of the search query and results. Figure 6.5/15 shows the *My Yahoo!* user interface.

The building of a personal user profile is the prerequisite for the specific support during the personalized search for information and its selection within the user's interest areas. Firefly uses two concepts to achieve this objective: High Performance Profile Management Architecture and Advanced Collaborative Filtering [Firefly 1997a]. The High Performance Profile Management Architecture concept provides the basis to build a useful user profile. This user profile contains both demographic data and details of the user's personal preferences. The user can enter his personal data and preferences in the *profile* and *member page* user interfaces in the *Personal* register, and in the Filmfinder *profile* and the Bignote *music* user interfaces within the *Directory* register. The comprehensive and detailed user details concerning his interests and preferences normally permit a reliable and trustworthy construction of the user profile. The existing user profiles are used to present personal information. Consequently, the user can move within the relevant information and in the corresponding participation circles. The *venues* user interface is used for the communication between the members, whereas the Filmfinder *movies* and the Bignote *your ratings* user interfaces provide the personalized information in the form of recommendation lists. The reliability of these recommendations determines the degree of usefulness to the user.

The Advanced Collaborative Filtering concept is used in those areas in which the user's decisions for a specific interest are highly dependent on a subjective assessment. This is often the case in the movie and music areas. The concept is based on the theory that the preferences and interests of the members of a community can be used to predict other preferences or interest areas of an individual user [Firefly 1997b]. The comparison of the specific user profile with the other profiles of the Firefly users permits the user to be provided with detailed predications and recommendations regarding his main interests. The application also has comprehensive data files containing information on the movie and music areas. These data are also used as basis for the above mentioned comparison. These data are not formed from the contents of the individual user profiles but contain the information from which the user can define his areas of interest. The Filmfinder *profile* and the Bignote *music* user interfaces provide these functions. The resulting user profile is then compared with the other user profiles of Firefly users to produce recommendations for the user. In addition, the user's communication with other participants having similar interests ensures that the user can receive additional information and recommendations within his areas of interest. The members' personal experiences and interests permit them to learn from each other [Firefly 1997b].

The Advanced Collaborative Filtering concept that resulted from the development of this application and its objectives permits the user to be presented with highly useful personalized information. This information can in the future use other areas that have a high subjective rating. The High Performance Profile Management Architecture permits a simple increase in the number of users without losing the application capability [Firefly 1997a].

6.6 Groupware

6.6.1 Introduction

Groupware applications or workgroup computing systems provide support for teams and work groups during the processing of a common, relatively unstructured task [Mertens et al. 1995]. From the economic viewpoint, groupware systems create contents and information that are grouped and analyzed, and distributed within the workgroup [Hansen 1996]. The specific forms of the groupware applications in-

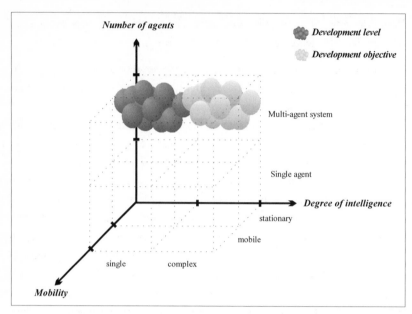

Figure 6.6/1: The classification matrix for the groupware application area

clude computer conference systems, such as e-mail, decision-support systems and appointment scheduling programs [Mertens et al. 1995].

Agent-based applications, in particular, provide support in this area for the information retrieval and decision making within the problem solution process. They permit the supply and administration of important information and content for all members of the group and the acceptance of routine work within this group [Maes 1994a]. Figure 6.6/1 shows the position of this application area in the classification matrix (see Section 3.3). The applications in the groupware area are currently characterized by a limited intelligence and normally consist of several cooperating agents. Future applications will be particularly characterized by a higher intelligence.

The handling and processing of the electronic mail within a workgroup form an ideal operational area for agents. Their use permits the handling of a large part of the routine work, such as reading, deletion, printing or forwarding of e-mails. In the area of scheduling, they can usefully support the process of scheduling work assignment, conferences and meetings. They help the individual workers in the solution of problems and in the decision-making process.

Groupware	WWW Address
MAXIMS	lcs.www.media.mit.edu/groups/agents/research.html
Lotus Notes Mail	www.lotus.com
PLEIADES	www.cs.cmu.edu/softagents/pleiades/
Calendar Agent	lcs.www.media.mit.edu/groups/agents/research.html

Figure 6.6/2: A selection of current groupware applications

Although the following examples are not based on a potential use within the groupware applications, they well illustrate the possible application areas. Because most of the current applications are only prototypes, no separate description is provided for the concept and architecture; these are, where appropriate, described in the individual examples.

6.6.2 Market Overview

Figure 6.6/2 lists a selection of current groupware applications with name and WWW address.

The description in the following section concentrates on the Lotus Notes Mail, MAXIMS and PLEIADES applications. Whereas Lotus Notes Mail represents a commercial application that uses the agent-oriented technologies, MAXIMS is a research project that illustrates the basic concepts. In the area of agent-based scheduling, the description is limited to the PLEIADES research project that has been designed as a distributed agent system. Because the Calendar Agent project is based on the same concepts as the MAXIMS application, no separate description is provided here.

6.6.3 Lotus Notes Mail

Lotus Notes Mail is the agent-based component for the management and processing of e-mails within the Lotus Notes 4.5 groupware application. Lotus Notes is produced by the Lotus Development Corporation.

The aim of Lotus Notes Mail is the automatic processing of e-mails by allowing the agents to communicate and cooperate with the user. The agents receive predefined task assignments from the user and attempt to support the user during the

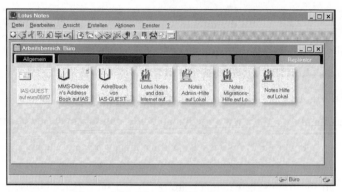

Figure 6.6/3: The Lotus Notes work-area

daily work with his e-mails by independently performing this work. The work-area
provides the Lotus Notes user interface (see Figure 6.6/3).

The user invokes the *Agent* menu item from the *Create* menubar. This menu item
permits the user to define the agent. The following section uses the creation of an
agent to demonstrate the operation of the Lotus Notes Mail component. The agent's
task is to answer incoming e-mails and then send a copy to him and other users.

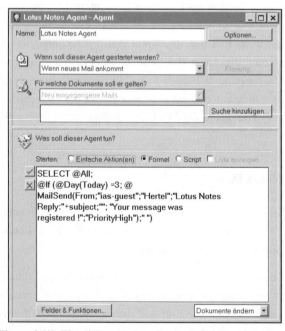

Figure 6.6/4: The dialog window for the definition of the agent

Figure 6.6/5: Dialog window for the initialization of the agent

A dialog window for the definition of the agent opens after activating the *Agent* menu item (see Figure 6.6/4). This dialog window is used to define the name of the agent, and the time and option for the activation of the agent. The *Formel* button can be used to specify the exact operating instructions for the agent. These instructions contain details for the specific time for the agent's activity, March in this case. It is also specified that a brief reply is supplied for all arriving e-mails and that a copy is sent to the users. This brief reply exists in the e-mail body from the *Your message was registered!* wording and the header in addition to the original text from the *Lotus Notes Reply*.

The definitions of the agent are stored in the database that is visible in the *General* register of the user's work-area (see Figure 6.6/3). This database is also used for the simultaneous initialization of the defined agent. Figure 6.6/5 shows the initialization of the agent.

The agent and user communicate using the protocol user interface. All the agent's processing steps are maintained in this user interface, where they are also documented for the user. Figure 6.6/6 shows the agent's protocol.

The user must define a single agent to provide support for each task. Such tasks can be the generation of e-mails at a fixed time, the answering of the e-mails, or the forwarding to particular application users. The *Agent Manager* is responsible for the coordination of the individual agents (see Figure 6.6/7).

This Agent Manager is located on the application's server system. It is possible to define the persons who can activate the individual agents, the maximum execution duration, the possible execution period, the number of currently operating agents and the maximum resource load. Figure 6.6/7 shows the Agent Manager.

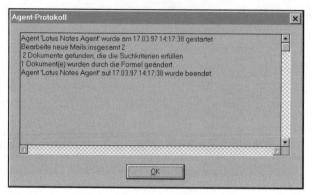

Figure 6.6/6: The agent protocol

Agent-Manager			
Agent-Einschränkungen	**Wer kann -**	**Parameter**	
Persönliche Agents starten:		Agent-Cache aktualisieren:	00:00
Eingeschränkte LotusScript Agents starten:			
Nicht-eingeschränkte LotusScript Agents starten:			
Tagesparameter		**Nachtzeit Parameter**	
Startzeit:	08:00	Startzeit:	20:00
Endzeit:	20:00	Endzeit:	08:00
Agents gleichzeitig max.:	1	Agents gleichzeitig max.:	2
Max. Laufzeit LotusScript:	10 Minuten	Max. Laufzeit LotusScript:	15 Minuten
Max % belegt vor Verzögerung:	50	Max % belegt vor Verzögerung:	70

Figure 6.6/7: The Agent Manager

6.6.4 MAXIMS

MAXIMS is a research project of the Media Lab at the Massachusetts Institute of Technology. This application is freely available and requires the local installation on an Apple Macintosh with the Eudora 1.3 e-mail software. This software is extended with the agent component and is available in the Eudora 1.3ag version [Metral 1997].

The aim of MAXIMS is to support the user in the management of his e-mails. In particular, the acceptance of several routine work, such as the deletion and forwarding of messages, and the sorting and archiving of the user's individual e-mails [Maes 1994a]. MAXIMS's capability to learn (see Section 4.4), made possible by

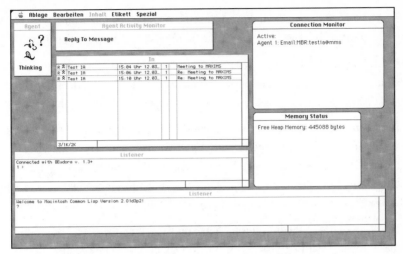

Figure 6.6/8: The individual work windows of the application

the existence of a memory, is the prerequisite for this support. The basic concept is designated the Memory Based Reasoning and is based on an algorithm used to register all situations and actions of the user, which are then stored as situation/action pairs in the memory [Lashkari et al. 1994]. In addition to the storage of the specific examples with the situation/action pair, the resulting knowledge base permits the creation of a user-specific behavior pattern. This can be the basis for future situations to be analyzed by agents and the appropriate actions suggested to the user.

Figure 6.6/8 shows the individual windows that are required for the operation of the agent. MAXIMS consists of three software components, the MAXIMS agent, the Central Knowledge Base (CentralKB), and the Agent Bulletin Board (AgentBB).

The MAXIMS software component is the heart of the application and permits the configuration of the agent and the construction of its knowledge base. The *Agent Activity Monitor* window and the upper of the two *Listener* windows belong to this software component. The current action suggested by the agent is shown in the *Agent Activity Monitor* window, whereas the *Listener* window is used for the communication with the Eudora e-mail program.

The CentralKB permits the storage of the persons who work with the MAXIMS application, together with their names, the position within the workgroup and their e-mail address. This component is normally installed locally on each user's computer. The lower *Listener* window shows the communication with the MAXIMS software component. The user entry is the prerequisite for the agent operation.

Several agents in this application can use the AgentBB to cooperate with each other and thus their users. The central installation of the CentralKB is the prerequisite for this cooperation. No multi-agent environment is provided in this example.

The *Agent* and *In* windows belong to the Eudora e-mail program. The *In* window shows all arriving e-mails, whereas the *Agent* window is used for the visual communication of the agent and user. The associated mimic of the agent symbolizes a specific state of the agent, such as thinking, working, unsure or suggestion. The two right windows are status windows that provide the user with a control function.

The observation of the user during his daily work with the e-mail program forms the basis for the learning process. MAXIMS monitors every situation that occurs and thus the associated user action. Every situation is uniquely described using a specific range of properties. Such properties include the sender, the receiver, and the e-mail subject title. It is also determined whether the message was read, forwarded or answered directly. The Automatic Feature Selection algorithm permits a selection of relevant properties by the agent [Lashkari et al. 1994], because many possible criteria can be used to describe the situation. The fewer the number properties required for the unique description, the faster MAXIMS can react, even though a higher number of properties increases the accuracy of the agent [Metral 1997].

The storage of the situation, and the associated actions, permits the prediction of the agent's future actions. This prediction of future actions is based on a comparison of the new situations with the previously stored situations. This comparison is performed using a weighting of the individual properties of the stored situations with regard to the importance of the associated activities. The assignment of the appropriate actions to the new situation is the basis for the prediction of the specific activities. A further step should replace the prediction by an automatic completion of the activities by the agents.

The reliability of the prediction for the user is of central importance to satisfy this objective. Only when there is an appropriately high level of reliability for the prediction can the user permit the agent to independently perform the tasks. Two limit cases are available to determine the reliability: the do-it and the tell-me area. The agent in the do-it area is permitted to automatically perform the associated action without confirming with the user. It informs the user in a report on the performed action. The agent in the tell-me area suggests an appropriate action to the user for every occurring action. The agent does not independently perform the action. The confidence of the user in the tell-me area is the prerequisite for the independent work of the agent in the do-it area.

Every action in the do-it and tell-me areas is represented by confidence levels within the range 0 to 1. Because the knowledge base does not exist at the start of the learning process, the application provides basic settings that the user can change if necessary. The basic settings for reading a message are 0.1 for the tell-me and 0.6 for the do-it area. This means that the reading of a message is suggested relatively quickly to the user, whereas the agent has a high confidence in the area of the automation. The agent never becomes active for a confidence level below 0.1. Only during the course of the learning process does the agent build its own knowledge, which results from the monitoring of the user and the stored situation/action pair. This knowledge base and the repeated acceptance of a suggested action permit the entry at the associated confidence level in the tell-me area. If the confidence level in the tell-me area corresponds to the confidence level of the do-it area, the agent automatically completes the suggested actions. In general, the confidence level for the automation for an action is higher, the more important and decisive an action is. The confidence value then represents a value near the limit value 1.

To accelerate the learning process, the user can train MAXIMS by evaluating hypothetical situations. The user monitors the agent's operation. Another possibility is that the agents communicate with each other, because they are connected with each other using the AgentBB and CentralBB. The agents of the user with a high degree of experience send descriptions of the individual situations to the new agent and so give it the possibility to learn. Maes describes this multi-agent communication as being an effective method for the knowledge transfer within a workgroup [Maes 1994a].

6.6.5 PLEIADES

PLEIADES has been produced as part of the RETSINA (Reusable Task Structure-based Intelligent Network Architecture) of the Carnegie Mellon University (CMU), Pittsburg, PA. The aim of the research project was to develop a distributed, reusable system architectur of intelligent agents in which the agents cooperate to perform their individual tasks. The cooperation of the associated agents applies to the specific supply of information and its integration as prerequisite for the solution of a number of decision tasks [Sycara et al. 1996].

PLEIADES represents a specific application example of the RETSINA project and was designed as the Visitor Hosting System for the planning of visits within the CMU research institutes. PLEIADES consists of several agents that possess a precisely defined task area and cooperate to fulfill this. In particular, that of the Visitor Host Agent, the Personnel Finder Agent, the Interest Agent and the Visitor Scheduling Agent. The research facilities of the CMU are partially represented by Calendar Agents.

The Visitor Hosting Agent is the link between the university and the visitor. It accepts the visitor's request, coordinates the process of the information retrieval and scheduling, and provides the visitor with a detailed schedule. It requires the Interest Agent and the Personnel Finder Agent to provide it with more detailed information on the individual research facilities and on the personal data of the employees and visitors. To collect the required information, the Interest Agent and the Personnel Finder Agent contact the Internet and various university databases that contain data on the research areas and the individual employees. The Internet is searched for more detailed information about the employees, the exact title of the visitor, his position within his organization and his e-mail address. The retrieved information is passed to the Visitor Host Agent. This turns to the individual Calendar Agents that accept the suggested appointment dates from the Visitor Host Agent. The Calendar Agents match the suggested dates with possible appointments of the employees, and return the resulting suggestions. The determination of the suggestions depends largely on the position of the visitor within his organization. This permits the assessment of the potential interest of the visitor with regard to the requested meeting. A Visitor Scheduling Agent is available to avoid conflicts arising during the final scheduling of the meeting. It matches any possible employee appointments with the appointment suggestions of the visitor. The Visitor Scheduling Agent can independently make contact with the agents of the research institute to clear any remaining differences. Its work results in a detailed schedule that is transferred to the visitor.

The developers of RETSINA have formed three groups of agents to permit the unique classification of the individual agents and for the task assignment: the Interface Agents, the Task Agents, and the Information Agents. The Interface Agents communicate with the user, they receive his request and provide the required response. The Task Agents are responsible for fulfilling the task that the query sent to the system. They require the Information Agents for the reliable solution; the Information Agents supply the information required for this task from a number of available databases. The individual agents cooperate both within their group and with each other. The group of Task Agents mainly operates together to integrate the retrieved information in the process to solve the task. The Information Agents cooperate to compare and evaluate the individual information items. Modeled on the PLEIADES, the Visitor Agent belongs to the Interface Agents, the Personnel Finder Agent, the Visitor's Scheduling Agent and the individual Calendar Agents belong to the Task Agents, whereas the Interest Agent can be considered to be an Information Agent [Sycara et al. 1996].

6.7 Electronic Commerce

6.7.1 Introduction

The description of the agent-based applications in the area of electronic commerce is restricted to the subarea concerned with the buying and selling of products and services in the Internet. Agents support the buying and selling of products and services in the Internet for their users [Chavez/Maes 1996]. The use of agents in this area can act as a catalyst for their further development. Figure 6.7/1 shows the position of this application area in the classification matrix (see Section 3.3). In

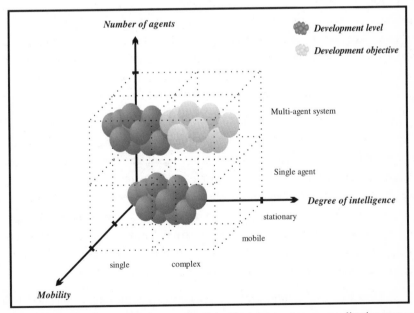

Figure 6.7/1: The classification matrix of the electronic commerce application area

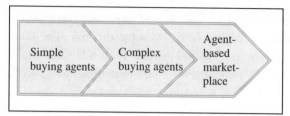

Figure 6.7/2: The development levels of the agent-based electronic commerce

accordance with the current stage of development, the agents work partially mobile with a limited degree of intelligence. An increase in the intelligence level and the form as mobile multi-agent systems are demands on the future development.

The initial aim at the start of the development of agent-based applications for the electronic commerce was to support the user in the specific search for products and services in the Internet (see Figure 6.7/2). The simple buying agents access the product files of the supplier and use this information to provide the user with the requested product information. The result of this search is a product overview that permits a comparison with the prices of offered products provided by the selected suppliers. The range of available virtual suppliers is normally fixed and relates to the previously specified product group.

The support of the purchasing action is not the highest priority for this development stage. The user must himself locate the appropriate supplier for the product he wishes to buy. Representatives of this area include the BargainFinder (bf.star.ac. com/bf/) and the BargainBot (www.ece.curtin.edu.au/~saounb/bargain/bot). This concept is comparable with the previously discussed price agencies. On request, the employees of a price agency determine the market prices of the product required by the customer and supply him with a price comparison.

The complex buying agents go one step further by providing support for the purchase in addition to the search and the price comparison. The support for the purchase in the current forms is performed using the local storage of the user's personal data; these data contain details of the purchasing preferences and for the financial processing of the transaction. If requested by the user, the complex buying agents can buy the selected product. This they do by independently and autonomously making contact with the appropriate supplier and then processing the transaction. Jango (www.jango.com) is a representative of this development level.

The agent-based marketplaces are an extended concept for the support of the user in the buying or selling of products and services in the Internet. Electronic marketplaces as preliminary stage for agent-based marketplaces are characterized by the representation of the supplier, manufacturer, requester and service provider as part of a common platform [Brenner/Zarnekow 1997]. The Internet represents this platform in the current developments. These market users in agent-based marketplaces are represented by their individual agents that perform tasks on behalf of their user. A number of different agents exist, such as buying agents and selling agents, as well as payment agents or advertising agents. The principal difference between the simple and complex buying agent is that agents represent the demand and the supplying party. Whereas the buying agents at the two lower development levels use the static information of the individual product files of the supplier to fulfill their tasks for the user, the user's agents communicate with the supplier's agents. The negotiating capability of the individual agents of the market user has priority here. Kasbah (kasbah.media.mit.edu/), the Personal Electronic Trader as research project of the Multimedia Software GmbH, Dresden, Germany and the DAI lab of the Technical University of Berlin, Germany are representatives of this development level.

6.7.2 Simple Buying Agents

6.7.2.1 Market Overview

Figure 6.7/3 lists a selection of the current simple buying agents with name and WWW address.

Simple Buying Agents	WWW Address
BargainFinder	bf.cstar.ac.com/bf
BargainBot	www.ece.curtin.edu.au/~saounb/bargainbot/
Fido	www.shopfido.com/
AdHound	www.adone.com/

Figure 6.7/3: A selection of the current simple buying agents

The description in the following section concentrates on the BargainFinder and the BargainBot simple buying agents. They are the best known representatives of this evolution level. These two agents are used to show the potential of intelligent applications for the area of the electronic commerce during the search for suppliers and the information retrieval. Both applications apply to a specific product group.

6.7.2.2 BargainFinder

The BargainFinder was created as part of "Smart Store Virtual" study by Andersen Consulting. The objective of this application was the price comparison of music CDs for various virtual suppliers.

CDnow, Tower Records and CD Universe belong to the ten suppliers selected by BargainFinder. After making a search through the information files of these suppliers, BargainFinder provides the user with the capability to select the cheapest CD. The purchase is made directly with the selected virtual supplier.

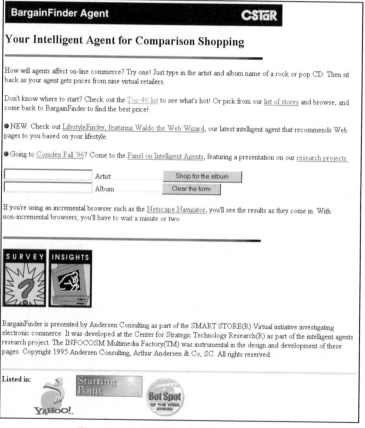

Figure 6.7/4: The BargainFinder homepage

Figure 6.7/4 shows the BargainFinder homepage. The user can find on this page information about the application and also additional offerings, such as a list of the Top 40 music CDs or the available online suppliers. The user can select three further links recommended by BargainFinder in the lower part of the homepage. The central area of the homepage contains two text fields that are reserved for the definition of the search query using Artist and Album.

The following section demonstrates the operation of the application based on the search for the Music Box album sung by Mariah Carey.

The singer Mariah Carey is entered in the upper text field *Artist* and the title of the music CD, Music Box, entered in the second text field *Album*. Figure 6.7/5 shows the input of the search query. The *Clear the form* button permits editing of the input; the *Shop for the album* button starts the BargainFinder search.

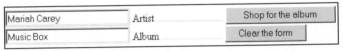

Figure 6.7/5: The text fields for the input of the search query

In addition to this specification, the user can also search for the required artists within the Top 40 list. The link is located in the upper part of the homepage (see Figure 6.7/4). This can be used to significantly shorten to the search time, provided that the required music CD is located within this repertoire.

The BargainFinder searches through the available suppliers for the required music CD and determines the corresponding offerings. The results with price and supplier are presented to the user in a new window (see Figure 6.7/6). Because only

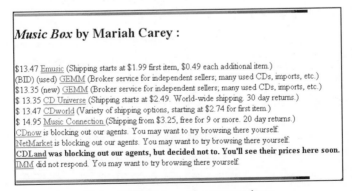

Figure 6.7/6: The search query result set

6.7/7: The WWW page of the selected supplier

some of the price details are shown with the various conditions of payment for the individual suppliers, an offer that appears reasonable at first glance may differ significantly from the net price shown when the payment conditions and shipping costs are taken into consideration (especially for European users). For this reason, the user should check the individual conditions of the supplier before finally choosing the product.

Some of the selected suppliers for this search query have blocked the application from accessing their data files. This is made apparent with the expression "*is blocking out our agent*". The "*did not respond*" message is returned to the user if the BargainFinder exceeds the time duration for individual suppliers during the search query.

The user can change directly to the associated supplier using links. Figure 6.7/7 shows the WWW page of a supplier.

This step completes the work of BargainFinder. The supplier now accompanies the user from the confirmation of the selection through to the shipping of the order.

6.7.2.3 BargainBot

BargainBot was created as research project of the IMAGE Technology Research Group of Curtin University of Technology, Australia. The application was developed with the aim of the simultaneous price comparison for selected online book-

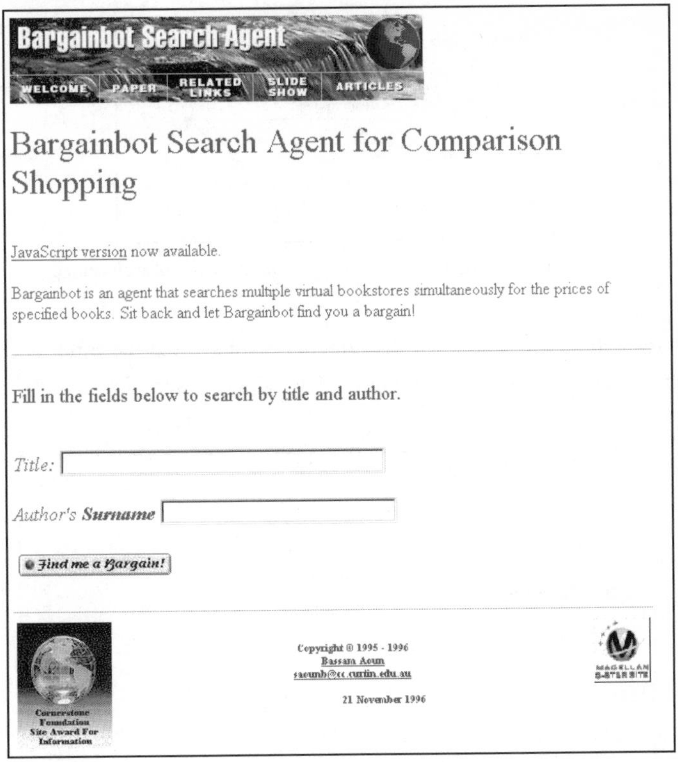

Figure 6.7/8: The BargainBot homepage

stores. The current totals of twelve virtual suppliers of books include the market leader, Amazon.com, Book Stacks Unlimited and Bookserve.

Figure 6.7/8 shows the BargainBot homepage. This page contains both general information on BargainBot and also development-relevant notes. The central area of the homepage contains two text fields for the input of the search query for book title and author.

The following section demonstrates the operation using the search for the book The Importance of Being Earnest by Oscar Wilde.

The input of the title and the book author are specified as the criteria used to search for the required book (see Figure 6.7/9). The Importance of Being Earnest is entered in the upper text field *Title* and Wilde is entered in the lower text field *Author's Surname*. The *Find me a Bargain!* button starts the search.

Fill in the fields below to search by title and author.

Title: The Importance of Being Earnest

Author's **Surname** Wilde

● *Find me a Bargain!*

Figure 6.7/9: The text fields for the input of the search query

BargainBot starts the search for the relevant results when the input is confirmed. The determined result set is presented in a new window (see Figure 6.7/10).

CompuBooks Bookstores

Sorry no books were found.

Staceys Bookstores

Sorry no books were found.

WordsWorth Bookstores

3 books found:

IMPORTANCE OF BEING EARNEST , WILDE,O , Price: 0.91

IMPORTANCE OF BEING EARNEST , WILDE,O , Price: 3.60

IMPORTANCE OF BEING EARNEST & OTHER , WILDE,O , Price: 6.26

Figure 6.7/10: Extract from the result set for the search query

The individual results are sorted according to bookstore and contain the price, and normally the publisher and the book form. Because the various payment conditions of each supplier are not specified for the price details, an offer that appears reasonable at first glance may differ significantly from the net price shown when the payment conditions and shipping costs are taken into consideration (especially for European users). For this reason, the user should check the individual conditions of the supplier before finally deciding the product. Some suppliers provide a direct link to the required book.

The user can change directly to the corresponding supplier using the link. Figure 6.7/11 shows the WWW page of a supplier.

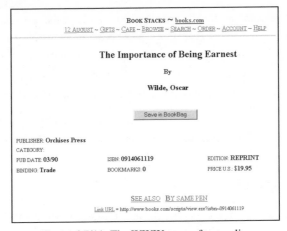

Figure 6.7/11: The WWW page of a supplier

This step completes the work of BargainBot. The supplier now accompanies the user from the confirmation of the selection through to the shipping of the order.

6.7.2.4 Concepts

The operation of the simple buying agents is based on two concepts. The representation of the content and basis of the simple buying agents are heavily oriented on the BargainBot concept [Aoun 1996].

- **Support of the search**. The aim of the simple buying agents is to support the user in the specific search for a required product. The prerequisite for achieving this support is the use of the data or product files of the selected server. Once the user has defined his search query, the simple buying agents access the data files of the individual suppliers, gather the required product information items and pass these to the user in a standard form of representation. The current application examples in the area of the simple buying agents can search for product information only within a specified group of suppliers. The user has the capability of asking the buying agents to search for information in this product group. The product groups are music CDs for BargainFinder and books for BargainBot.

- **Price comparison**. The found results for the sought product of the user are presented as a priced representation of the supplier. Short product descriptions are sometimes added. The two examples discuss the form to each product presentation. The aim of this presentation is the price comparison of the required product between the various suppliers. Consequently, the user can achieve significant time savings. However, this type of price comparison is incomplete, because the simple buying agents are not capable of specifying the shipping costs that are added to the product price. The result of this incorrect price representation is a change to the net price and an incorrect product selection by the user.

The user can order his selected product with the direct links to the individual online suppliers. The simple buying agents do not support the actual purchase.

6.7.2.5 Architecture

The architecture of the simple buying agents consists essentially of the three components shown in Figure 6.7/12. Although this architecture applies for the two described applications of simple buying agents, its principal components are based on the architecture of BargainBot [Aoun 1996].

- **Query interface**. The query interface permits the definition of the required product and the presentation of the result set. The specified search queries are forwarded, and the determined result set is presented to the user.

- **Subagents**. The subagents are responsible for performing the search query and transferring the result to the administrator. The subagents have the task to mak-

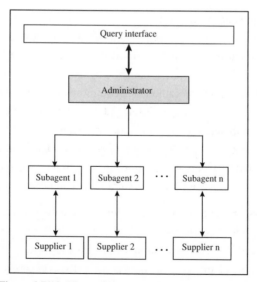

Figure 6.7/12: The architecture of simple buying agents

ing contact with the appropriate online suppliers and searching their databases for the required product. They forward the received results to the administrator. The process of information gathering by the subagents is performed in parallel. This means that every subagent tests only a single online supplier, which significantly reduces the search time.

- **Administrator**. The administrator is responsible for the coordination of the subagents and also for the organization of the search query and result set. It possesses the knowledge on all registered online suppliers and all available subagents. In accordance with the user's specified product request, it forwards this query to all subagents. The administrator combines these results by sorting them according to price. This result is transferred to the query interface, which presents the result to the user.

- **Supplier**. The online suppliers reached by the buying agents provide their data and product files. This permits the subagents to search for the relevant information. Each supplier handles the ordering and payment. The simple buying agents do not have any effect here.

6.7.3 Complex Buying Agents

6.7.3.1 Market Overview

Complex buying agents are characterized by the support for the complete purchase. Only the client-based Jango application is described in this category. Because of the few available references, the concepts and the architecture are not described here.

6.7.3.2 Jango

Jango was produced as part of the Intelligent Assistant Technology research division of Netbot Inc., Seattle, USA, a company founded in 1996. Jango is currently freely available.

The aim of this application is to provide the user with a simple, powerful and fast access to a number of online suppliers using a standardized user interface. Virtual traders and manufacturers, content providers, and selected search engines belong to the selected suppliers. The user can currently select from ten product groups. Depending on the selection of the product group that contains the user's product, the application selects the supplier to be used to determine the product.

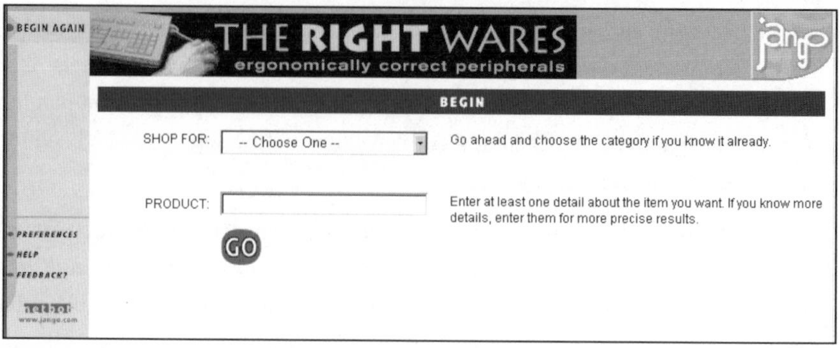

Figure 6.7/13: The Jango start user interface

The Jango start interface is divided into the two central areas shown in Figure 6.7/13.

The central area of the start user interface presents the user with two text fields for the specification of his search query. The meaning of the text fields is shown in a short text next to them. The user in the upper text field *Shop for* can select a pull-down menu for his required product group. Jango offers a number of product groups, such as books, computer hardware, computer software, wine, movies or jewelry. Some of these product groups are not currently available. The form of the *Product* text field changes in accordance with the selected product group. This field is one-dimensional in the initial situation and is normally extended with up to three text fields for the specific product description.

The *Begin Again* button in the left part of the user interface is used to represent the previously described central area of the start user interface. This button permits the user to directly change to any window of this application and so redefine his search query.

The *Preferences* button is used to enter the registration parameters (see Figure 6.7/14).

The user can specify details about himself or payment conditions in the individual registers. Although the user is prompted for these details after the installation of the software, he can leave these open and enter them later in this user interface.

The *Help* button uses the contents of the homepage www.jango.com to provide the user with notes on the operation of Jango. The user can also use the button to obtain information on the application and its design. The *Feedback* button also uses

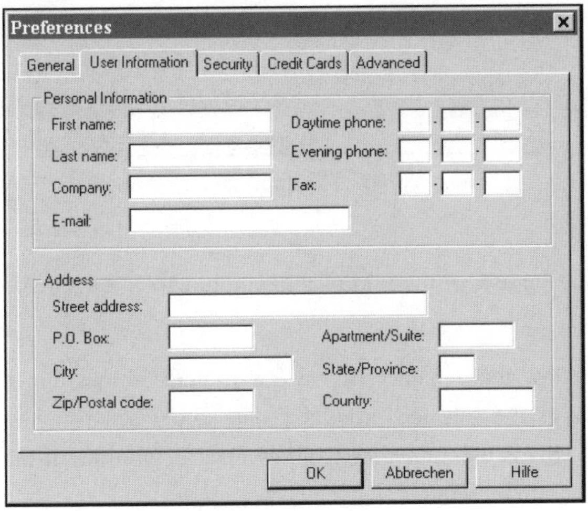

Figure 6.7/14: The registration window

this link to the homepage to provide the user with the capability to send his comments or notes as e-mail to the developers.

The following section uses the Books product group and the Being Digital book by Nicholas Negroponte to demonstrate the operation of Jango.

Figure 6.7/15 shows the specific definition of the search query. Once the *Books* product group has been selected, the original text field of the product is extended with three product description characteristics: *Title*, *Author* and *Subject*. Because the exact designation of the book and the author are known, there is no need to enter a keyword in the *Subject* text field. The *Go* button starts the search query.

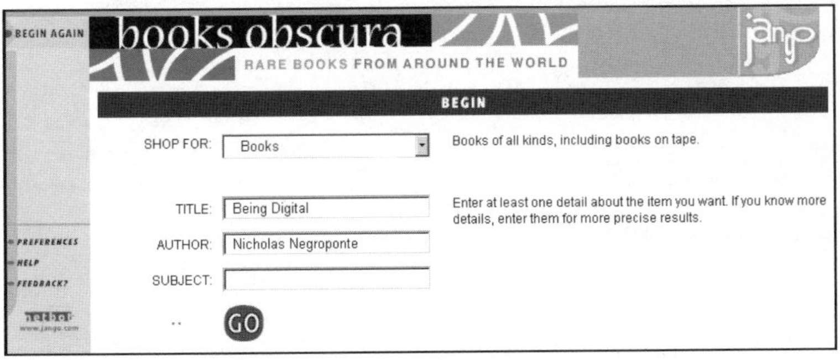

Figure 6.7/15: Text fields of the specific search query

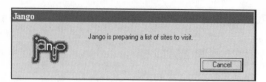

Figure 6.7/16: The information window

Jango informs the user of the start of the search with an information window (see Figure 6.7/16).

The new window that appears after a few minutes shows the currently visited online suppliers of the selected product group sorted according to category (see Figure 6.7/17). This is the *Summary* window and, as with the displayed categories (*Products/Prices, Makers/Seller, Reviews, Miscellaneous Hits*), shown as button in the lower area of the window. The user can use these links to change to the various display windows of the result set. The four category windows contain detailed information about the selected product.

The *Summary* window contains the time remaining for the search and also the sought product with the specified product description characteristics and the product group. The application also provides an advertising spot (in an advertising window) appropriate for the selected product group.

The total number of suppliers is shown in the summary heading. A differentiation of these suppliers is also made. A characteristic relates to the number of suppliers to which a contact (*Contacting* column) exists, although no result is sup-

Figure 6.7/17: The *Summary* window

plied. *Answered* relates to the supplier who has already successfully answered, whereas *No answer* specifies the number of suppliers for which the product was sought without success. These three differentiation criteria are also shown in different colors.

The other lines contain the four previously mentioned categories to differentiate the suppliers.

The *Products/Prices* category contains all online suppliers of the selected product group (see Figure 6.7/18).

The upper area of this window contains the number of the found results for the sought product. The first column of the overview lists the designation of the author as maintained by the individual suppliers and the corresponding book title. *Format*, the second column, specifies the format of the book, provided this information is available from the supplier. *Store*, the third column, contains the specific supplier

PRODUCTS / PRICES			
SHOPPING FOR: "Being Digital Nicholas Negroponte" (Books)			
FOUND: 38 ITEMS			
PAGES: 1			
NEGROPONTE,N	FORMAT	STORE	PRICE BUY
BEING DIGITAL		The Booksmith	12.00 ⊘
Negroponte, Nicholas	FORMAT	STORE	PRICE BUY
Being Digital	Paperback	Powell's Books	7.95 ⊘
Being Digital	Paperback	Powell's Books	8.00 ⊘
Being Digital	Hardback	Powell's Books	9.00 ⊘
Being Digital	Paperback	Books Now	10.80 ⊘
Being Digital	Paperback	Books Now	10.80 ⊘
Being Digital	Hardback	Powell's Books	10.95 ⊘
Being Digital	Audio Cassette	Books Now	12.60 ⊘
Nicholas Negroponte	FORMAT	STORE	PRICE BUY
Being Digital	Paperback	BarnesandNoble.com	9.60 ⊘
Being Digital	Audio Cassette	BarnesandNoble.com	15.00 ⊘
Being Digital	Hardback	Amazon.com	17.50 ⊘
Being Digital	Hardback	BarnesandNoble.com	17.50 ⊘
Being Digital (Cd)	Hardback	Amazon.com	15.00 ⊘
Being Digital O M	Paperback	BarnesandNoble.com	7.00 ⊘
Nicholas Negroponte, Marty Asher (Editor)	FORMAT	STORE	PRICE BUY
Being Digital	Paperback	Amazon.com	9.60 ⊘
Nicholas Negroponte, Penn Jillette	FORMAT	STORE	PRICE BUY
Being Digital	Audio	Amazon.com	9.80 ⊘

Figure 6.7/18: The *Products/Prices* window

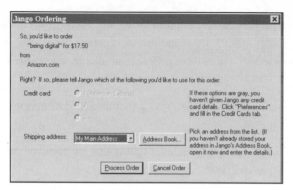

Figure 6.7/19: The order window

as link. The user reaches the supplier's homepage if he activates this link. A link to
the direct ordering page of the supplier is not possible and also not desired by
Jango. The price of every found product is specified in the fourth column *Price*.
The user can click on the arrow to directly order the most favorable variant in the
last column, *Buy*. A new window appears in which the options required for the
order can be entered. Figure 6.7/19 shows this order window.

Both the credit card to be used for the purchase and the delivery address must be
entered in this window. If these parameters have not yet been specified, they can be
specified with the *Preferences* button in the left area of every window.

The *Makers/Sellers* category shows those suppliers that can provide further descriptions and more detailed information (see Figure 6.7/20). Because not every
supplier has this capability, not all suppliers specified in the *Products/Sellers* cate-

Figure 6.7/20: The *Makers/Sellers* window

Figure 6.7/21: The *Reviews* window

gory are contained in the category. The user can use the links to change to the corresponding supplier where he can obtain detailed information about the product.

The *Reviews* category contains those magazines and periodicals that can provide information on the sought product in the form of reviews. The user can also change directly to this supplier using the link.

The last category, *Miscellaneous Hits*, lists some of the current search engines that supply the user with a number of results for the sought product. These categories complete the information range that Jango provides the user within the selected product group. Figure 6.7/22 shows a section of this window.

Jango is a client-based application of a complex buying agent and permits both the specific supply of the product information and the support of the purchase. The delivery process for the required information is performed simultaneously and must

Figure 6.7/22: The *Miscellaneous Hits* window

be coordinated. The coordination covers the grouping of the various information sources to permit the supply of all the necessary information for the required product.

The determined and grouped results are analyzed before they are present to be user. The checking and analyzing of the gathered information should ensure that identical information is recognized and eliminated. The results are then sorted and evaluated with regard to their relevance to the user's search query.

The found results for the sought product are presented as the supplier's price information. It is also possible to display the found number of products according to other criteria.

Because Jango's support of the purchase means that it adopts the role of an intermediary, the user does not need to make direct contact with the final supplier. Jango combines the supplier's trading advantages with the benefits of an intermediary. The user is supported during the transaction handling and does not need to concern himself with the conditions of each individual supplier.

6.7.4 Agent-Based Marketplace

6.7.4.1 Market Overview

Figure 6.7/23 lists a selection of the current agent-based marketplaces with name and WWW address.

Agent-based Marketplace	WWW Address
Kasbah	kasbah.media.mit.edu
Personal Electronic Trader (PET)	research project
Bazaar	guttman.www.media.mit.edu/people/ guttman/reseach/bazaar/bazaar.html

Figure 6.7/23: A selection of the current agent-based marketplaces

The description in the following section concentrates on the agent-based marketplaces Kasbah and Personal Electronic Trader (PET). They represent very effectivly the potentials of agent-based marketplaces.

6.7.4.2 *Kasbah*

Kasbah was developed at the Media Lab of the Massachusetts Institute of Technology as prototype for an agent-based marketplace with name and WWW address and is available without charge as experimental marketplace. The aim of this development was to simulate a virtual marketplace through the use of autonomously operating buying agents and selling agents. The negotiating capability of the individual agents forms the central module of the operation of this marketplace. Kasbah currently offers trading in nine products, such as CDs and cameras.

The user's participation on Kasbah starts with his membership. Figure 6.7/24 shows the entry page of the virtual marketplace with these options. A prerequisite for the communication within the marketplace is the knowledge of the user's e-mail address. The user enters the marketplace by activating the *click here!* button.

Figure 6.7/24: The Kasbah entry page

Once connection has been established, the user is first provided with his personal start page (see Figure 6.7/25). The central functions of this page are represented as buttons in the upper area. They are primarily used to navigate within the marketplace. The *home* button takes the user to this start page. The user is already at his homepage in this case. The *messages* button permits the user to view the e-mails of his individual agents. This particular start page shows a message directly after this toolbar indicating that the user has not received any messages. The *kasbah* button provides the user with notes, information and help functions. The *agents* button has central importance for the user; he creates new agents with this function. The *logout* button removes the user from the marketplace. The lower part provides the user with additional information on working with Kasbah and also the capability to use links to access functions that are shown with their own buttons.

The following section uses two agents that negotiate with each other to demonstrate the operation of Kasbah. Beethoven's Ninth Symphony as music CD has been chosen as product.

Figure 6.7/25: The user's personal start page

The user first uses the *agents* button to activate a new window that contains five different options to specify the agents. Figure 6.7/26 shows this user interface. The *Create a new selling agent* menu item permits the definition of all important parameters for a selling agent. The *Create a new buying agent* menu item is used to specify the criteria for a new buying agent. The *Create a new finding agent* menu item is used to define an agent who searches the virtual marketplace for products and presents the results to its contracting party.

The *See your currently active agents* menu item provides the user with the capability to check his active agents; he is provided with a status report of the objectives and the degree to which these objectives have been achieved. The last menu item *Browse the marketplace* provides information to the user on the agents active in Kasbah; the user can select the required presentation of the agents.

To define a selling agent, the user activates the *Create a new selling agent* menu item and receives a form in which all parameters can be specified. Figure 6.7/27 shows the upper part of this user interface.

Kasbah Agents Menu

DAI01, please select what you would like to do:

- Create a new selling agent.
Your selling agent will find and negotiate with any interested buying agents in the marketplace. It will try to find the best offer available, and will send you messages asking for approval when it begins negotiation or strikes a deal.

- Create a new buying agent.
Your buying agent will find and negotiate with any interested selling agents in the marketplace. It will try to find the best deal available, and will send you messages asking for approval when it begins negotiation or strikes a deal.

- Create a new finding agent.
Your finding agent will search the marketplace for a good or type of good, and report back to you with the item description, either when it finds something which might be of interest to you, or at certain time intervals, depending on which you prefer. It will continue to send you reports until its termination.

- See *your* currently active agents.
From here you can have a look at all of your agents which are presently active, as well as their descriptions. Besides this, you can also see what they are doing, change their parameters, or terminate them.

- Browse the marketplace.
This feature allows you to check out any agents in the marketplace at present. You can choose to view agents which fit a very specific description only, or you can look through every agent in the marketplace. It all depends on what you want!

Figure 6.7/26: The *Agent* menu user interface

Fill out the form below to create a selling agent that will sell your *music* for you. Please enter all information as accurately as possible, so that your agent will be able to find matches for you more easily. Remember to click the "Create Agent" button at the bottom of the form when you've finished.

Click to clear form: [Clear]

Each agent has its own identity, and so it must have its own unique name. What would you like to name your agent?

[Alpha]

Description of Music to sell:

- I am trying to sell a [CD ▾]
  of the following music genre: [Classical ▾]

(Note: *The Genre you enter does not affect negotiations or matching between buying and selling agents. It is used only to help finding agents who might be browsing for music of a particular genre.*)

- The title of this recording/album is:
[9th Symphony]

- and the Artist is:
[Beethoven]

- The recording is in the following condition: [Used but not damaged ▾]

- Description:
(*Optional: Enter anything which you think might help your agent find matches*)
[ ]

Figure 6.7/27: The upper part of the selling agent form

The user must specify in the first text field of the form a name for the selling agent. The name in the example is Alpha. The product and the music genre then must be defined in the two following text fields. The title or the album and the artist now must be specified before the user defines in a further pulldown menu whether the product is to be new or used, undamaged or damaged. The user can optionally enter further descriptive characteristics in a large text field. The CD Beethoven's Ninth Symphony from the classical genre, used but undamaged has been selected in this example.

In addition to these parameters, the user must also specify the required sales date, the price and the negotiation strategy. Figure 6.7/28 shows the lower part of the form.

The user selects the first pulldown menu to define when the sale is to be made; both the date and the time can be set in this pulldown menu. The user must also specify an ideal price and a lowest possible price as negotiating capability for the agent. The two text fields: *What is your desired price?* and *What is the lowest pos-*

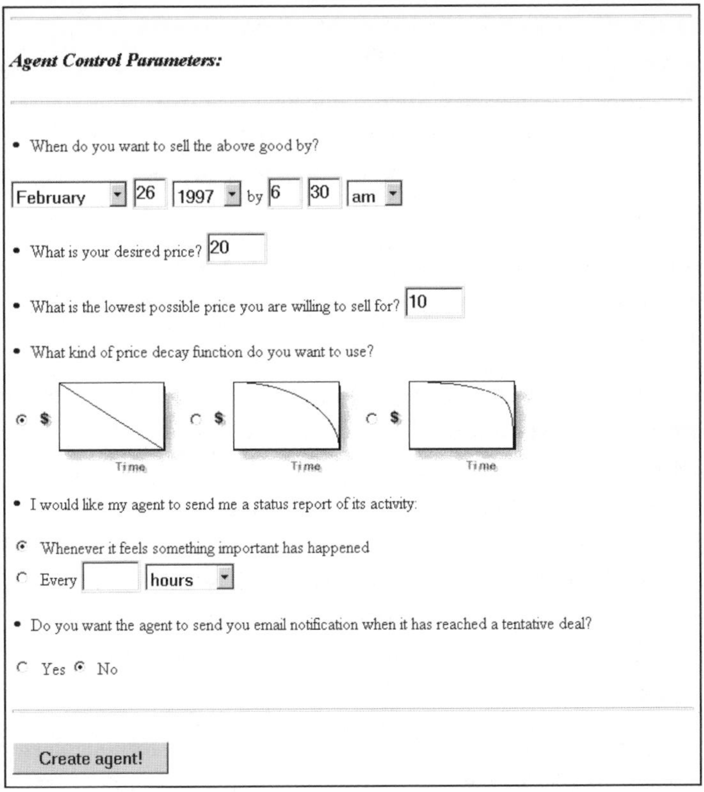

Figure 6.7/28: The lower part of the selling agent form

sible price you are willing to sell for? are used for this purpose. Three price-time curves (one linearly decreasing, one quadratically decreasing, and one cubically decreasing) are available to the user to choose the required negotiating strategy for the selling agent with other buying agents.

The user selects a linearly decreasing characteristic of the price-time curve as strategy in the first graphic. To achieve its objective, the agent will linearly decrease the required price to a minimum possible price over the course of time. It behaves anxiously. The agent tends to behave in a more restrained manner if the cubically decreasing curve is chosen. It is prepared to make larger price concessions to its negotiating partner only towards the end of the selling phase. The user's choice of the quadratically decreasing curve provides its agent with a negotiating strategy that lies between the two extremes [Chavez et al. 1997].

Several criteria for the communication between agent and user are specified as the last parameters. The *Create Agent!* button is used to activate the Alpha selling agent that is to sell Beethoven's Ninth Symphony at a maximum price of 20 US dollars and a minimum possible price of 10 US dollars using a linear selling strategy. The time of sale is specified as 6:30 AM on February 26, 1997. The user is to be informed of all agent actions.

To permit the selling agent to find a trading partner in this example, a buying agent is defined in a second phase. The starting point is the menu user interface of the agents as shown in Figure 6.7/26.

A similar form to that for the selling agent appears when the user selects the *Create a new buying agent* menu item. The differences relate to the price agreements and the specification of the negotiating strategy. Buying agents have the capability to negotiate using the linearly increasing, quadratically increasing or cubically increasing strategies. The buying agent is assigned the name Beta and should buy Beethoven's Ninth Symphony as CD on behalf of the user. Although this CD can be used, it must be undamaged. The desired price is 15 US dollars with 25 US dollars as the maximum possible price. A cubically increasing price-time curve is selected as negotiating strategy.

The *See your currently active agents* menu item of the *agents* button (see Figure 6.7/26) permits the user to check his agents. Figure 6.7/29 shows the status report of the two agents.

The user is informed if either of the agents finds a trading partner. The user can view these messages with the *messages* button. The message contains the request whether the agent should buy or sell. If the user responds positively, the agent completes its negotiations and sends the result as a message to the user. The Alpha selling agent in this example informs the user that it has found a buying agent. Figure 6.7/30 shows the contents of the message.

The owner of the buying agent is identified from the e-mail address (because both the buying agent and the selling agent have a common owner in this example, this address is the e-mail address of the current user of the application). Because the products must be shipped conventionally, the address of the owner is used instead of its buying agent's name; the owner of the selling agent can contact the buying agent if necessary.

Your Agent **Alpha** with ID #32 is trying to sell the good with the following description:

GOOD TYPE: *MUSIC*
music type:*CD*
genre:*Classical*
title:*9th Symphony*
artist:*Beethoven*
condition:*Used but not damaged*
description:

- Deadline to sell by *Wed Feb 26 06:30:00 EST 1997*;
- Trying to sell it for *20* dollars;
- Willing to sell for as low as *10* dollars;
- Will NOT send you email messages.
- Click here to change the agent's control parameters.

- Current asking price is *20* dollars;
- Currently negotiating with *1* agents.

- If you want to "terminate" this agent, click here

Your Agent **Beta** with ID #34 is trying to buy the good with the following description:

GOOD TYPE: *MUSIC*
music type:*CD*
title:*9th Symphony*
artist:*Beethoven*
condition:*Sealed/Mint OR Used but not damaged OR Playable but slightly damaged OR Good to own but not to play*
keywords:

- Deadline to buy by *Wed Feb 26 06:30:00 EST 1997*;
- Trying to buy it for *15* dollars;
- Willing to buy for as high as *25* dollars;
- Will NOT send you email messages.
- Click here to change the agent's control parameters.

- Current asking price is *15* dollars;
- Currently negotiating with *1* agents.

- If you want to "terminate" this agent, click here

Figure 6.7/29: The status report for the two agents

The owner uses the *Acknowledge* button to confirm the agent's work. Because its task is now complete, this action also terminates the agent's existence.

If only e-mail has been defined in the form to determine the parameters for the transmission of the messages (see Figure 6.7/29), the owner of the agents receives the information using an e-mail interface that is external to the application (see Figure 6.7/31).

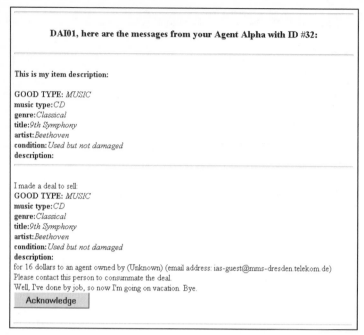

Figure 6.7/30: The result of the negotiation

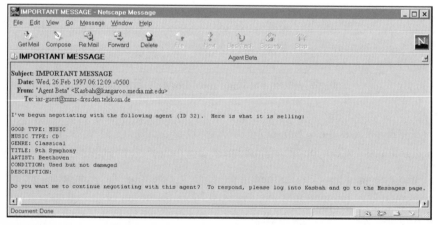

Figure 6.7/31: The transfer of the messages using an external e-mail user interface

6.7.4.3 The Personal Electronic Trader (PET)

The Personal Electronic Trader (PET) was developed as part of a research project of the Multimedia Software GmbH, Dresden, Germany and the DAI lab of the Technical University of Berlin, Germany. The aim of this agent-based marketplace is the provision of personal buying agents to support the purchase of mobile telephone equipment and the selection of a telephone tariff. The definition of the personal buying preferences, such as maximum price and product descriptions, permits the personal buying agents to determine the products that best correspond to the user's buying profile. The marketplace is not freely available as prototype.

Four traders for mobile telephones and one provider of general mobile telephone services for T-Mobil are represented in the marketplace of the current version of PET. Each of the four traders represents one or more mobile telephone providers and offers the associated products. Specifically, traders for the Ericsson, Sony/ Siemens, Motorola and Nokia brands are active in the marketplace. The provider of general mobile telephone services offers the various D1 tariffs.

The current realization of the marketplace requires a local installation of the access software. This software provides the user with four input user interfaces. The details of his special requirements form the prerequisites for the specification of the personal agents that support the user during the selection of the tariff and the mobile telephone.

The two arrows directly below the window used to specify the parameters are available to switch between the four input user interfaces. The *Agenten abschicken* (send agent) button is used to define the personal agent. The user is not required to complete all four input user interfaces. The *Agenten zurückstellen* (reset agent) button discards the details previously made for the user. The three lower buttons permit the user to obtain help for the application, save current agents and load agents for reuse. These functions are available for every input user interface.

Figure 6.7/32 shows the first user interface for the specification of the parameters. This window is used to specify the details of the monthly telephone duration of the tariffs. The monthly telephone duration in this example is 70 hours. The user can also directly select a D1 tariff using the third question. Because there is no possibility to obtain the exact conditions of the specified tariff alternatives, the user must have previous knowledge of these. The user has chosen the ProTel D1 tariff in this example.

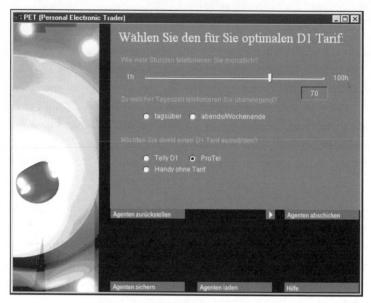

Figure 6.7/32: The first user interface

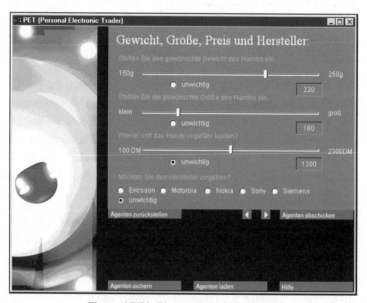

Figure 6.7/33: The second user interface

The second user interface permits the specification of the physical characteristics of the required mobile telephone (see Figure 6.7/33). In this example, a mobile telephone with a weight of 220 g and a size of 160 has been specified as being the optimum unit. Because the price and the manufacturer do not play any role in the search for a suitable mobile telephone, these two selection criteria have been marked as being unimportant. This completes the first part of the definition of the required parameters.

The user can provide details for the required functionality of the mobile telephone in the third input user interface. This affects both the battery loading capacity with regard to telephone duration and stand-by mode, and also the form of the display. An active telephone duration of 150 minutes and receiving capability of 34 hours in stand-by mode have been selected in this example. The detail on the number of lines on the display is considered to be unimportant. The fourth input user interface is provided for other technical criteria for the definition of the required mobile telephone. The user can specify whether his mobile telephone is to be able to transfer data and fax massages. Because the user has selected the ProTel D1 tariff in the first user interface, it is possible to use this service. In addition, the user's future mobile telephone should be capable of sending short text messages that can be entered using the telephone's keypad. The maximum number of telephone numbers that can be stored is not important in this example. The third and fourth input user interfaces are not shown.

Once the individual parameters have been entered and checked by scrolling through the four user interfaces, the user can define the personal agent and send it to perform its task. The agent returns the result of its work to the user as a suggestion for a tariff and a suitable telephone in the form of three result interfaces. As for the input interfaces, the user can navigate with the arrows. Figure 6.3/34 shows the presentation of the tariff as the first result interface. Specifically, this means that the user would pay a connection price of DM 49 and a base price of DM 69. This tariff has a minimum duration of 12 months. The user is also presented with the individual prices for the call charge units (differentiated between the various nets).

The second result interface shows one of the suggested mobile telephones (see Figure 6.7/35). This suggestion applies to a Motorola d460 mobile telephone. Details are provided for both the physical characteristics and the technical functions of this alternative.

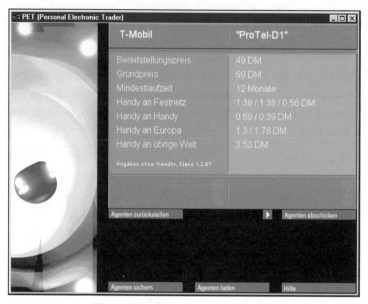

Figure 6.7/34: The first result interface

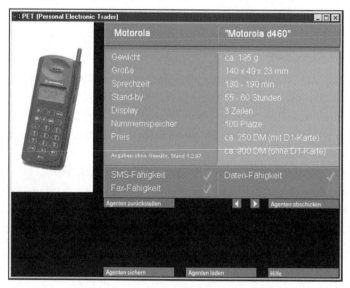

Figure 6.7/35: The second result interface

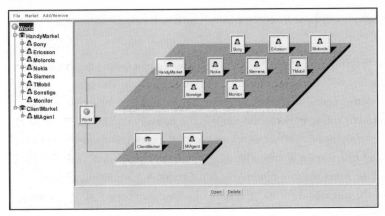

Figure 6.7/36: The marketplace monitor

This scheme applies for the presentation of all product variants. The second product is a mobile telephone of the type Hagenuk Global Handy supplied by Hagenuk. The physical characteristics and the technical functions are specified in the same form as for the first offering.

The user can observe in real-time using a monitor window the activity of his agents on the agent-based marketplace (see Figure 6.7/36). He sees both the existing mobile telephone market with his representatives and also the client side where his personal agent is located. This structure is also shown in a directory level.

6.7.4.4 Concept

The operation of an agent-based marketplace is based on a single important concept: the cooperation between autonomous agents. This concept shows the greatest potential for the future developments in this area. The specific form makes itself apparent in the negotiation capability of the individual agents (see Section 4.3.5). Both the described examples possess this capability.

The central task of an agent-based marketplace covers the capability of negotiation with the individual agents. The agents of an agent-based marketplace have the objective to fulfill the tasks specified by the user. The decisive difference between simple buying agents and an agent-based marketplace lies in the communications capability of the marketplace agents. Simple buying agents can access only the static data and product files. Their actions are limited by this restriction. Both the user and the suppliers are represented by agents in a marketplace. This permits more complex tasks to be accomplished, such as the negotiation over a product or a service.

The specific form of the negotiation phase can in a simple case cover the successive contact with the aim of buying or selling a product. The agents for both parties can initially request and evaluate information, and then negotiate over price in a second step, before they discuss the specific delivery conditions. The use of negotiating strategies is a further development of the communications processes. These strategies provide the agents with a certain degree of freedom that permits them to fulfill their tasks in an optimum manner. Section 4.3.5 contains a detailed description of the individual forms. The individual agents operate autonomously of each other in both forms.

Because both supplier and manufacturer are represented by agents, it is relatively simple for them to access such markets. No changes are required to their data files.

6.7.4.5 Architecture

The architecture of agent-based marketplaces consists of two central components as shown in Figure 6.7/37.

The central components, user and marketplace, are formed from several individual components, the interaction of which determines the central components.

The user side consists of a user interface, the user agents and the base software. The agent-based marketplace consists of the marketplace agents and the base software. To fulfill the tasks, the marketplace agents access the product files of the individual suppliers (who are normally located outside the marketplace).

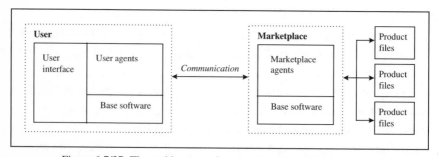

Figure 6.7/37: The architecture of marketplace-based buying agents

- **User interface**. The task of the user interface covers providing the parameters that the user requires to define his agents. This interface also serves as communication between agent and user. The two described examples have shown that this user interface can be used as local software and from a browser.

- **User agent**. The primary task of the user agent is to support the user for the buying or selling of products. The user agents gather information, negotiate with the agents of the marketplace and present the results to the user. The prerequisite for the support is the clear definition of its tasks, which the user passes with the user interface. The user agents contact the marketplace agents using the base software .

- **Base software**. The task of the base software covers both the supply of various basic functions for the complete functionality of the agents that build on this software and also the integration in the complete system (see Section 4.2.2.3). The form of the base software is identical for both parties. The base software also supports the other agents of a marketplace (such as payment agents or advertising agents) in the communication.

- **Marketplace agents**. The primary task of the marketplace agents is to provide support for the associated supplier during the selling of products, services and information. If requested, the marketplace agent supplies the user agent information about the products being offered, negotiates with the user's agents and initiates the delivery of the product by the supplier on successful completion of the purchase. The ability of a marketplace agent to access the data or product files of each supplier is a prerequisite for this support. Normally every supplier in a marketplace is represented by a specific agent.

- **Product files**. The product files contain the required information about every product of the supplier. These files are not normally contained in the marketplace but are stored decentrally. The marketplace agent of the supplier has access to these files.

6.8 Manufacturing

This application area concentrates on providing support for the planning and control of production processes using multi-agent systems. Distributed PPS systems form the basis for this support.

Conventional PPS systems are considered to be computer-supported systems for the planning, control and monitoring of technical processes and whose specific application areas are the manufacturing processes of the production area. Their main aims are the reduction of the throughput times, ensuring that the delivery date is met, maintaining low stock levels, and providing a high and consistent loading of the available capacity [Kurbel 1993]. The data management and the disposition belong to the most import specific tasks [Hestermann/Pöck 1995]. The disposition is divided into a strategic and an operative planning, and covers, in particular, complex activities, such as the capacity requirement calculation. Whereas the strategic planning is long-term, the operative planning contains the short-term and middle-term planning time horizons [Kurbel 1993]. A further development of the conventional PPS systems into distributed PPS systems takes place using electronic control stations, etc. [Hestermann/Pöck 1995]. They permit the transition to distributed production processes in the area of short-term manufacturing control. This also caters for the demand for improved flexibility in the manufacturing area [Kassel 1996]. The central element of distributed PPS systems is the autonomous satisfying of subtasks and the integration to a complete manufacturing process.

Multi-agent systems permit the specific realization of distributed PPS systems using agent support (see Section 4.1.2). The agents of this system consider themselves to be autonomous units that cooperate as subsystems to fulfill the tasks of the complete system [Kassel 1995, Zelewski 1997]. The focus of the task completion of the agents can lie on the disposition (in particular in the operative area) and on the process coordination, as shown by some current research projects [Hestermann et al. 1997, Zelewski 1997]. Figure 6.8/1 shows the positioning of this application area in the classification matrix (see Section 3.3)

The multi-agent system support in the planning, control and coordination in PPS systems has been intensively discussed in German-language literature for some time. Knowledge-based systems and expert systems in the area of manufacturing processes supply the preliminary work for the current research activities. These concepts that originally came from the classical artificial intelligence (see Section 4.1.1) have been further developed through the potential of the distributed artificial

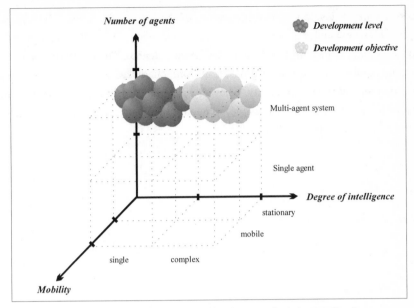

Figure 6.8/1: The classification matrix for the manufacturing application area

intelligence and find their use in many current research efforts. These projects normally relate to distributed PPS systems and flexible manufacturing systems.

[Müller 1993] and [Klauck/Müller 1995] describe a number of research projects. These include the SOPP project (self organizing production processes) of the Technical University of Chemnitz [Dilger/Kassel 1993] which will be further developed together with the University of Würzburg into the INKAD (intelligent cooperative assistance system for disposition support in PPS systems) cooperative project [Hestermann et al. 1997] or the GEPROPEX research project and DE-PRODEX of the computer science research group B of the University of Erlangen-Nuremberg [Möhle et al. 1995]. The references contain further examples and details.

6.9 Summary

The application areas for intelligent agents can be divided into many possible specific applications. The assignment of the individual application examples follows the assignment into information agents, cooperation agents and transaction agents made in Chapter 3. Of the ten application areas introduced in these categories, the current state of development permits seven of these to be described. The majority of the shown examples are research projects and served to show the reader the basic concepts and architectures as well as the future potential. The currently used commercial applications of intelligent agents are characterized with a high user-friendliness and wide availability. They illustrate the possibility of work simplification for the user and the possible competitive advantages for decision makers through the use of these technologies.

7 The Future

Intelligent software agents have the potential to become one of the central components for the future information society. Although the developers of intelligent agents have primarily concentrated on the technologies and concepts, a change can be seen with the concentration on the commercial usage scenarios and service models. The technological basis for the commercial use of agent-based systems has been prepared. However, the final success of intelligent agents will largely depend on the acceptance of the new technologies by the end-user. Two complementary problem areas should be mentioned in this connection. A wide acceptance of intelligent agents is possible only when the social, ethical and legal reservations associated with the use of intelligent agent have become accepted, and also a wide range of agent-based services are available that provide direct benefits for the end-user.

The social and ethical questions are primarily concerned with the consequences the representation by software agents of the users will have for society and the use of electronic media. In which ways will agents interact with humans and other agents? How is it possible to ensure that an agent obey the wishes of its user and handles private data confidentially? What rules need to be defined for the social behavior of agents? And how can these rules be monitored or violations be punished? The central, legal problem for the use of intelligent software agents lies in the acceptance of the responsibility by software objects. The question of the responsibility must be unambiguously clarified if an agent performs actions on behalf of its user that have legal or financial consequences. A number of questions are still open here: to what extent can a software agent accept responsibility in a legal sense, to what extent is the user prepared to pass responsibility to his agents, and how can the user protect himself from the misuse of his agent. Only when all these questions have been satisfactorily answered, can a level of trust be built between humans and agents; the discussed application areas of intelligent agents must be realized on such a basis.

The second question regarding the development of a wide spectrum of agent applications can be answered only in the course of time. Chapter 6 of this book has shown how wide-ranging the possible uses of intelligent software agents are already and which specific services can be developed using the existing technologies. World-wide standards are a missing central component in the design of application scenarios. Although general standardization committees (for example the WWW Consortium or the Object Management Group), and also a number of purely agent-oriented committees, such as the Foundation for Intelligent Physical Agents (FIPA) or the Agent Society have been formed with the aim of the standardization of agents and agent systems, these developments are only at the beginning.

Unfortunately, recognized standards are a prerequisite for many applications. For example, the use of mobile agents is useful only when these have a large number of access points (i.e., computer systems) in the network. To permit the execution of the agents, all access points must provide the agents with a standardized runtime environment. A second example, the area of electronic commerce, can be mentioned here as representative for many other application areas. To produce a secure system, a number of standardized interfaces must exist in agent-based commercial systems [Zarnekow et al. 1996]. These include communications standards, negotiating standards, and security mechanisms. An inter-system standardization is required if an agent is to visit the electronic marketplaces of various suppliers.

We hope that this book helps to increase the acceptance and to provide a better understanding of the technologies and concepts of agent-based systems. Only this understanding will determine the further success or non-success of intelligent software agents.

Bibliography

[Agha 1986]

Agha, G., Actors: A Model of Concurrent Computation in Distributed Systems, MIT Press, London 1986

[Albayrak/Bussmann 1993]

Albayrak, S., Bussmann, S., Kommunikation und Verhandlungen in Mehragenten-Systemen, in: Müller, J. (Hrsg.), Verteilte Künstliche Intelligenz: Methoden und Anwendungen, BI-Wissenschaftsverlag, Mannheim e. a. 1993

[Albayrak 1996]

Albayrak, S., Intelligente Agenten: Grundlagen, Anwendungen, Werkzeuge & Sprachen, in: Foliensatz zur Vorlesung, Technische Universität Berlin, DAI Lab, Berlin 1996

[Aoun 1996]

Aoun, B., Agent Technology in Electronic Commerce and Information Retrieval on the Internet, in: Internet URL: http://www.ece.curtin.edu.au/~saounb/bargainbot/paper/ (Stand 1997)

[Austin 1962]

Austin, J.L., How to do things with words, Harvard University Press, Cambridge 1962

[Bean/Segev 1996]

Bean, C., Segev, A., Electronic Catalogs and Negotiations, in: CITM Working Paper 96-WP-1016, University of California, Walter A. Haas School of Business, Fisher Center for Information Technology and Management, Berkeley 1996

[Belgrave 1995]

Belgrave, M., The Unified Agent Architecture: A White Paper, in: Internet URL: http://www.ee.mcgill.ca/elmarc/uua_paper.html (Stand 1997)

[Bond/Gasser 1988]

Bond, A., Gasser, L. (Hrsg.), Readings in Distributed Artificial Intelligence, Morgan Kaufman Publishers, San Mateo 1988

[Booch 1991]

Booch, G., Object-oriented Design with Applications, Benjamin/Cummings, Redwood City, 1991

[Brenner/Zarnekow 1997]

Brenner, W., Zarnekow, R., Noch fehlt die schnelle, komplette Marktinformation. Elektronische Märkte – ein Überblick, in: Office Management, 45(1997)4, pp 15–18

[Brooks 1986]

Brooks, R. A., A robust layered control system for a mobile robot, in: IEEE Journal of Robotics and Automation, RA-2(1986)1, pp 14–23

[Brooks 1990]

Brooks, R.A., The Behavior Language; User's Guide, in: M.I.T. Artificial Intelligence Laboratory, AI Memo 1227, Cambridge 990

[Brooks 1991]

Brooks, R.A., Intelligence withour representation, in: Artificial Intelligence, 47(1991), pp 139–159

[Burmeister 1996]

Burmeister, B., Models and Methodology for Agent-oriented Analysis and Design, in: Fischer, K. (Hrsg.), Working Notes of the KI'96 Workshop on Agent-Oriented Programming and Distributed Systems, DFKI Document D-96-06, Saarbrücken1996

[Chavez/Maes 1996]

Chavez, A., Maes, P., Kasbah: An Agent Marketplace for Buying and Selling Goods, in: Proccedings of the First International Conference on the Practical Application of Intelligent Agents and Multi-Agent Technology (PAAM '96), London 1996

[Chavez et al. 1997]

Chavez, A., Dreilinger, D., Guttman, R., Maes P., A Real-Life Experiment in Creating an Agent Marketplace, in: Proccedings of the First International Conference on the Practical Application of Intelligent Agents and Multi-Agent Technology (PAAM '97), London 1997

[Coad/Yourdon 1991a]

Coad, P., Yourdon, E., Object-Oriented Analysis, Yourdon Press, Englewood Cliffs 1991

[Coad/Yourdon 1991b]

Coad, P., Yourdon, E., Object-Oriented Design, Yourdon Press, Englewood Cliffs 1991

[Coleman et al. 1994]

Coleman, D. et al., Object-Oriented Development: The Fusion Method, Prentice-Hall, Englewood Cliffs 1994

[Decker/Lesser 1992]

Decker, K. S., Lesser, V. R., Generalizing the Partial Global Planning Algorithm, in: International Journal of Intelligent Cooperative Information Systems, 1(1992)2, pp 319–346

[Decker/Lesser 1994]

Decker, K. S., Lesser, V. R., Designing a Family of Coordination Algorithms, in: Technical Report 94–14, University of Massachusetts, Department of Computer Science, Amherst 1994

[DeMarco 1985]

DeMarco, T., Structured Analysis and System Specification, Prentice Hall, Englewood Cliffs 1985

[Dilger/Kassel 1993]

Dilger, W., Kassel, S., Sich selbst organisierende Produktionsprozesse als Möglichkeit der flexiblen Fertigungssteuerung, in: Müller, J. (Hrsg.), Verteilte Künstliche Intelligenz: Methoden und Anwendungen, BI-Wissenschaftsverlag, Mannheim e. a. 1993

[Doran et al. 1997]

Doran, J. E., Franklin, S., Jennings, N. R., Norman, T. J., On cooperation in Multi-Agent Systems, in: The Knowledge Engineering Review, 12(1997)3, Internet URL: http://www. elec.qmw.ac.uk/dai/pubs/fomas.html (Stand 1997)

[Durfee/Lesser 1991]

Durfee, E. H., Lesser, V. R., Partial global planning: A coordination framework for distributed hypothesis formation, in: IEEE Transactions on Systems, Man and Cybernetics, 21(1991)5, pp 1167–1183

[El-Hamdouchi/Willett 1989]

El-Hamdouchi, A., Willett P., Comparison of hierarchical agglomerative clustering methods for document retrieval, Computer Journal, 32(1989)3, pp 220–227

[Fiedler 1996]

Fiedler, J., Intelligente Softwareagenten, Praktikumsbericht, IBM European Networking Center, Heidelberg 1996

[Fiedler 1997]

Fiedler, J., Mobile Agenten im Umfeld personalisierter Nachrichtendienste, Diplomarbeit, Brandenburgische Technische Universität Cottbus, Institut für Informatik, Lehrstuhl für Rechnernetze und Kommunikationssysteme, Cottbus 1997

[Fikes et al. 1971]

Fikes, R. E., Hart, P. E., Nilsson, N., STRIPS: A New Approach to the Application of Theorem Proving, in: Artificial Intelligence, 2(1971), pp 189–208

[Finin 1993]

Finin, T., Draft Specification of the KQML Agent-Communication Language, in: Internet URL: http://www.cs.umbc.edu/kqml/kqmlspec/spec.html (Stand 1997)

[Finin et al. 1994]

Finin, T., Fritzson, R., McKay, D., McEntire, R., KQML as an Agent Communication Language, in: Proceedings of the third International Conference on Information and Knowledge Management (CIKM'94), ACM Press, 1994

[Firefly 1997a]

Firefly, Building Intelligent Relationships: The Firefly Tools, in: Internet URL: http://www.
firefly.net/products/FireFlyTools.html (Stand 1997)

[Firefly 1997b]

Firefly, Collaborative Filtering Technology: An Overview, in: Internet URL: http://www.
firefly.net/products/CollaborativeFiltering.html (Stand 1997)

[Fritzinger/Mueller 1996]

Fritzinger, J. S., Mueller, M., Java Security, in: Internet URL: www.javasoft.com

[GeneralMagic 1996]

General Magic, An Introduction to Safety and Security in Telescript, in: Internet URL:
http://www.genmagic.com (Stand 1996)

[Georgeff/Lansky 1986]

Georgeff, M. P., Lansky, A. L., Procedural Knowledge, in: Proceedings of the IEEE Special
Issue on Knowledge Representation, 74(1986), pp 1383–1398

[Gilbert 1996]

Gilbert, D., IBM Intelligent Agents, White Paper, in: Internet URL: http://www.raleigh.ibm.
com/iag/iaghome.html (Stand 1996)

[Gilbert 1997]

Gilbert, D., Intelligent Agents: The right information at the right time, in: Internet URL:
http://www.networking.ibm.com/iag/iaghome.html (Stand 1997)

[Gray 1995]

Gray, R.S., Agent Tcl: A transportable agent system, in: Proceedings of the fourth International Conference on Information and Knowledge Management (CIKM'95), Workshop
on Intelligent Agents, Baltimore 1995, Internet URL: http://www.cs.dartmouth.edu/
~agent/papers/cikm95.ps.Z (Stand 1997)

[Gray et al. 1996]

Gray, R., Kotz, D., Nog, S., Rus, D., Cybenko, G., Mobile Agents for mobile computing, in:
Technical Report PCS-TR96-285, Department of Computer Science, Dartmouth College,
Hanover 1996, Internet URL: http://www.cs.dartmouth.edu/reports/abstracts/TR96-285/
(Stand 1997)

[Gray 1997a]

Gray, R., Agent Tcl architecture, in: Internet URL: http://www.cs.dartmouth.edu/~agent/architecture.html (Stand 1997)

[Gray 1997b]

Gray, R., Agent Tcl, in: Internet URL: http://www.cs.dartmouth.edu/~agent/agenttcl.html (Stand 1997)

[Green et al. 1997]

Green, S., Hurst, L., Nangle, B., Cunningham, P., Somers, F., Evans, R., Software Agents: A review, in: Internet URL: http://www.cs.tcd.ie/research_groups/aig/iag/pubreview.ps.gz (Stand 1997)

[Guilfoyle et al. 1997]

Guilfoyle, C., Jeffcoate, J., Stark, H. (Hrsg.), Agents on the Web: Catalyst for E-commerce, Ovum Reports, Ovum Ltd., London 1997

[Hansen 1996]

Hansen, H. R., Wirtschaftsinformatik I, Lucius und Lucius, Stuttgart 1996, 7. Auflage

[Harrison et al. 1996]

Harrison, C. G., Chess, D. M., Kershenbaum, A., Mobile Agents: Are they a good idea?, in: Internet URL: http://www.research.ibm.com/massive/mobag.ps (Stand 1996)

[Hayes-Roth 1971]

Hayes-Roth, B., A blackboard architecture for control, Artifical Intelligence, 17(1971)3, pp 211–321

[Hestermann et al. 1997]

Hestermann, C., Wolber, M., Wellner, J., Intelligentes kooperatives Assistenzsystem zur Dispositionsunterstützung in Produktionsplanungs- und -steuerungs-Systemen, in: Internet URL: http://ki-server.informatik.uni-wuerzburg.de/HTML...ann-puk-97/ (Stand 1997)

[Hestermann/Pöck 1995]

Hestermann, C., Pöck, K., Intelligentes kooperatives Assistenzsystem zur Dispositionsunterstützung in Produktionsplanungs- und -steuerungs-Systemen (INKAD) in: Klauck, C., Müller H. J. (Hrsg.), Künstliche Intelligenz und Verteilte PPS-Systeme, Interne Berichte Universität Bremen, Fachbereich Mathematik und Informatik, Bremen 1995, Internet URL: http://www.informatik.uni-bremen.de/grp/ag-ik/activities/ws-prog.html (Stand 1997)

[Hohl 1995]

Hohl, F., Konzeption eines einfachen Agentensystems und Implementation eines Prototyps, in: Diplomarbeit Nr. 1267, Universität Stuttgart, Fakultät Informatik, Stuttgart 1995

[HotBot 1997]

HotBot, HotBot FAQ, in: Internet URL: http://www.hotbot.com/FAQ/faq.html (Stand 1997)

[Hughes 1997a]

Hughes, M., Building a bevy of beans, in: Internet URL: http://www.javaworld.com/java-world/jw-08-1997/jw-08-step.html (Stand 1997)

[Hughes 1997b]

Hughes, M., JavaBeans and ActiveX go head to head, in: Internet URL: http://www.java-world.com/javaworld/jw-03-1997/jw-03-avb-tech.html (Stand 1997)

[Iglesias et al. 1996]

Iglesias, C. A., Garijo, M., Gonzalez, J. C., Velasco, J. R., A Methodological Proposal for Multiagent Systems Development extending CommonKADS, in: Proceedings of tenth Knowledge Aquisition for Knowledge-based Systems Workshop, Banff 1996

[Kalfa 1988]

Kalfa, W., Betriebssysteme, Akademie-Verlag, Berlin 1988

[Kassel 1996]

[Kassel S., Multiagentensysteme als Ansatz zur Produktionsplanung und -steuerung, in: Information Management, 11(1996)1, pp 46–50

[Kinny et al. 1995]

Kinny, D., Georgeff, M, Rao, A., A Methodology and Modelling Technique for Systems of BDI-Agents, in: Technical Report 58, Australian AI Institute, Melbourne 1995, Internet URL: http://www.aaii.oz.au (Stand 1997)

[Kirn 1996]

Kirn, S., Kooperativ-Intelligente Softwareagenten, in: Information Management, 11(1996)1

[Klauck/Müller 1995]

Klauck, C., Müller H. J. (Hrsg.), Künstliche Intelligenz und Verteilte PPS-Systeme, Interne Berichte Universität Bremen, Fachbereich Mathematik und Informatik, Bremen 1995, Internet URL: http://www.informatik.uni-bremen.de/grp/ag-ik/activities/ws-prog.html (Stand 1997)

[Knabe 1996]

Knabe, F., An overview of Mobile Agent Programming, in: Proceedings of fifth LOMAPS Workshop on Analysis and Verification of Multiple-Agent Languages, Stockholm 1996, Internet URL: http://matecumbe.ing.puc.cl/~knabe/lomaps96.ps.gz (Stand 1997)

[Koster 1995]

Koster, M., Robots in the Web: threat or treat?, in: Internet URL: http://info.webcrawler.com/mak/projects/robots/threat-or-treat.html (Stand 1995)

[Kraetzschmar/Reinema 1993]

Kraetzschmar, G.K., Reinema, R., VKI Tools und Experimentierumgebungen, in: Müller, J. (Hrsg.), Verteilte Künstliche Intelligenz: Methoden und Anwendungen, BI-Wissenschaftsverlag, Mannheim e. a. 1993

[Kurbel 1993]

Kurbel, K., Produktionsplanung und -steuerung: Methodische Grundlagen von PPS-Systemen und Erweiterungen, Oldenbourg, München e. a. 1993

[Labrou/Finin 1997]

Labrou, Y., Finin, T., A Proposal for a new KQML Specification, in: Technical Report TR CS-97-03, University of Maryland, Computer Science and Electrical Engineering Department, Baltimore 1997, Internet URL: http://www.cs.umbc.edu/~jklabrou/publications/tr9703.ps (Stand 1997)

[Lashkari et al. 1994]

Lashkari, Y., Metral, M., Maes, P., Collaborative Interface Agents, in: Proceedings of AAAI'94, Seattle 1994, Internet FTP: ftp://ftp.media.mit.edu/pub/agents/interface-agents/coll-agents.ps (Stand 1997)

[Lieberman 1997]

Lieberman, H., Autonomous Interface Agents, in: Proceedings of the ACM Conference on Computers and Human Interface (CHI-97), Atlanta 1997, Internet URL: http://lieber.www.media.mit.edu/people/Lieber/Lieberary/Letizia/AIA/AIA.html (Stand 1997)

[Maes 1994a]

Maes, P., Agents that reduce work and information overload, in: Proceedings of the CACM '94, in: Internet URL: http://paettie.www.media.mit.edu/people/paettie/CACM-94/CACM-94.pl.html (Stand 1996)

[Maes 1994b]

Maes, P., Modeling Adaptive Autonomous Agents, in: Artificial Life Journal, 1(1994)1+2, Internet URL: http://paettie.www.media.mit.edu/people/paettie/alife-journal.ps (Stand 1997)

[Magedanz et al. 1996]

Magedanz, T., Rothermel, K., Krause, S., Intelligent Agents: An Emerging Technology for Next Generation Telecommunications?, in: Proceedings INFOCOM '96, San Francisco 1996

[March/Simon 1958]

March, J., Simon, H. A., Organization, John Wiley, New York 1958

[Martial 1993]

Martial, v. F., Planen in Multi-Agenten Systemen, in: Müller, J. (Hrsg.), Verteilte Künstliche Intelligenz: Methoden und Anwendungen, BI-Wissenschaftsverlag, Mannheim e. a. 1993

[McCabe 1995]

McCabe, F. G., APRIL Reference Manual, Version 2.1, Department of Computer Science, Imperial College, London 1995

[McCabe/Clark 1995]

McCabe, F. G., Clark, K. L., APRIL – Agent Process Interaction Language, in: Wooldridge, M., Jennings, N.R. (Hrsg.), Intelligent Agents – Theories, Architectures, and Languages, Lecture Notes in Artificial Intelligence 890, Springer-Verlag, Heidelberg e. a. 1995

[Mertens et al. 1995]

Mertens, P, Bodendorf, F., König, W., Picot, A., Schumann, M., Grundzüge der Wirtschafts-informatik, Springer-Verlag, Heidelberg e. a. 1995, 3. Auflage

[Metral 1997]

Metral, M., MAXIMS: A Learning Interface Agent for Eudora. A User's Guide to the System, in Internet FTP: ftp://ftp.media.mit.edu/pub/agents/interface-agents/MAXIMSmanual.ps (Stand 1997)

[Möhle et al. 1995]

Möhle, S., Weigelt, M, Mertens, P., DEPRODEX: Denzentrale Produktionssteuerungs-experten, in: Klauck, C., Müller H. J. (Hrsg.), Künstliche Intelligenz und Verteilte PPS-Systeme, Interne Berichte Universität Bremen, Fachbereich Mathematik und Informatik, Bremen 1995, Internet URL: http://www.informatik.uni-bremen.de/grp/ag-ik/activities/ws-prog.html (Stand 1997)

[Möhle et al. 1995]

Möhle, S., Braun, M, Mertens, P., GEPRODEXS: Gesamt-Denzentrale Produktionsplanung-und -steuerungs-Experten: Kombination Wissensbasierter Ansätze mit ComponentWare, in: Klauck, C., Müller H. J. (Hrsg.), Künstliche Intelligenz und Verteilte PPS-Systeme, Interne Berichte Universität Bremen, Fachbereich Mathematik und Informatik, Bremen 1995, Internet URL: http://www.informatik.uni-bremen.de/grp/ag-ik/activities/ws-prog.html (Stand 1997)

[Montgomery 1997]

Montgomery, J., Distributing Components: For CORBA and DCOM it's time to get practi-cal, in: Byte, (1997)4, pp 93–98

[Müller 1993]

Müller, J. (Hrsg.), Verteilte Künstliche Intelligenz: Methoden und Anwendungen, BI-Wis-senschaftsverlag, Mannheim e. a. 1993

[Müller 1996]

Müller, J. P., The design of intelligent agents: a layered approach, Lecture Notes in Com-puter Science, Vol. 1177, Springer-Verlag, Heidelberg e. a. 1996

[Nickisch1997]

Nikisch, H., Zahlungssysteme für einen elektronischen Marktplatz, Diplomarbeit, Fakultät Informatik, Technische Universität Dresden, Dresden 1997

[Nwana 1996]

Nwana, H. S., Software Agents: An Overview, in: Knowledge Engineering Review, 11(1996)3, pp 205–244

[Nwana/Azarmi 1997]

Nwana, H. S., Azarmi, N. (Hrsg.), Software Agents and soft computing: Towards enhancing machine intelligence, Springer-Verlag, Heidelberg e. a. 1997

[Nwana/Wooldridge 1997]

Nwana, H.S., Wooldridge, M., Software Agent Technologies, in: Nwana, H. S., Azarmi, N. (Hrsg.), Software Agents and soft computing: Towards enhancing machine intelligence, Springer-Verlag, Heidelberg e. a. 1997

[OMG 1997a]

Object Management Group, A discussion of the Object Management Architecture, in: Internet URL: http://www.omg.org/library/omaindx.htm (Stand 1997)

[OMG 1997b]

Object Management Group, Java, RMI and Corba, in: Internet URL: http://www.omg.org/news/wpjava.htm (Stand 1997)

[Oustershout 1994]

Oustershout, J.K., Tcl and the Tk Toolkit, Addison Wesley, New York 1994

[o.V. 1997a]

o.V., Notes: The subsumption architecture, in: Internet URL: http://www.janus.demon.co.uk/alife/notes/subsump.html (Stand 1997)

[o.V. 1997b]

o.V., Methodological Assumptions of Subsumption, in: Internet URL: http://krusty.eecs.umich.edu/cogarch4/brooks/method.html (Stand 1997)

[Pinkerton 1997]

Pinkerton, B., Finding What People Want: Experiences with the WebCrawler, in: Internet URL: http://info.webcrawler.com/bp/www94.html (Stand 1997)

[Ranganathan et al. 1996]

Ranganathan, M., Acharya, A., Sharma, S., Saltz, J., Network-aware Mobile Programs, in: University of Maryland, College Park, Department of Computer Science, Technical Report CS-TR-3659, Baltimore 1996, Internet URL: http://www.cs.umd.edu/~ acha/papers/usenix97.ps.Z (Stand 1996)

[Rao/Georgeff 1991]

Rao, A. S., Georgeff, M. P., Modeling rational agents within a BDI-Architecture, in: Technical Report 14, Australian AI Institute, Carlton 1991

[Rao/Georgeff 1995]

Rao, A. S., Georgeff, M. P., BDI Agents: From Theory to Practice, in: Proceedings of the First International Conference on Multi-Agent-Systems (ICMAS), San Francisco 1995

[Rasmusson/Jansson 1996]

Rasmusson, A., Jansson, S., Personal Security Assistance for Secure Internet Commerce, in: Internet URL: http://www.sics.se/˜ara/exjobb/NSP/NSP.html (Stand 1996)

[Rosenschein et al. 1986]

Rosenschein, S., Genesereth, M., Ginsberg, M., Cooperation without communication, in: Proceedings of AAAI-86, 1986, pp 51–57

[Rumbaugh 1993]

Rumbaugh, J., Objektorientiertes Modellieren und Entwerfen, Hanser, München 1993

[Sandholm et al. 1995]

Sandholm, T., Lesser, V., Issues in Automated Negotiation and Electronic Commerce: Extending the Contract Net Framework, Proceedings of the First International Conference on Multi-Agent-Systems (ICMAS), San Fransisco 1995

[Selberg/Etzioni 1995]

Selberg, E., Etzioni, O., Multi-Service Search and Comparison Using the MetaCrawler, in: Proceedings of the 1995 World Wide Web Conference, Internet URL: http://www. washington.edu/research/projects/softbots/www/metacrawler.ps (Stand 1997)

[Selberg/Etzioni 1997]

Selberg, E., Etzioni, O., The MetaCrawler Architecture for Resource Aggregation on the Web, in: Internet URL: http://www.cs.washington.edu/speed/papers/ieee/ieee-metacrawler/ieee-metacrawler.html (Stand 1997)

[Shoffner 1997]

Shoffner, M., JavaBeans vs. ActiveX: Strategic analysis, in: Internet URL: http://www. javaworld.com/javaworld/jw-02-1997/jw-02-activex-beans.html (Stand 1997)

[Shoham 1993]

Shoham, Y., Agent-oriented Programming, in: Artificial Intelligence, (1993)1

[Smith 1980]

Smith, R. G., The contract net protocol: High-level communication and control in a distributed problem solver, in: IEEE Transactions on Computers, 29(1980)12, pp 1104–1113

[SUN 1997a]

SUN Microsystems, Java Distributed Systems, in: Internet URL: http://chatsubo.java-soft.com/current/index.html (Stand 1997)

[SUN 1997b]

SUN Microsystems, Component-Based Software with JavaBeans and ActiveX, in: Internet URL: http://www.sun.com/javastation/whitepapers/javabeans/javabean_ch1.htm (Stand 1997)

[SUN 1997c]

SUN Microsystems, Security: Safe-Tcl, in: Internet URL: http://www.sun.com/960710/cover/tcl-safe.htm (Stand 1997)

[SUN 1997d]

SUN Microsystems, Why Tcl?, in: Internet URL: http://sunscript.sun.com/tcltext.htm (Stand 1997)

[Sundermeyer 1993]

Sundermeyer, K., Modellierung von Agentensystemen, in: Müller, J. (Hrsg.), Verteilte Künstliche Intelligenz: Methoden und Anwendungen, BI-Wissenschaftsverlag, Mannheim e. a. 1993

[Sycara et al. 1996]

Sycara, K., Decker, K., Pannu, A., Williamson, M., Zeng, D., Distributed Intelligent Agents, in: IEEE Expert 1996, Internet URL: http://www.cs.cmu.edu/˜softagents/ (Stand 1996)

[Tanenbaum1989]

Tanenbaum, A. S., Computer Networks, Prentice Hall, Englewood Cliffs 1989

[Tardo/Valente 1996]

Tardo, J., Valente, L., Mobile Agent Security and Telescript, in: Proceedings of COMPCON '96

[Thomas 1995]

Thomas, S. R., The PLACA Agent Programming Language, in: Wooldridge, M., Jennings, N. R. (Hrsg.), Intelligent Agents – Theories, Architectures, and Languages, Lecture Notes in Artificial Intelligence 890, Springer-Verlag, Heidelberg e. a. 1995

[Vogel 1996]

Vogel, A., Java Programming with CORBA, OMG, John Wiley, New York 1996

[Wavish/Graham 1996]

Wavish, P., Graham, M., A Situated Action Approach to Implementing Characters in Computer Games, in: Applied AI Journal, (1996)1

[W3 1997]

World Wide Web Consortium, HTML 3.2 Reference Specification, in: Internet URL: http://www.w3.org/TR/REC-html32 (Stand 1997)

[WebCrawler 1997]

WebCrawler, Help – How WebCrawler Works, in: Internet URL: http://www.webcrawler. com/WebCrawler/Help/AboutWC/HowITWorks.html (Stand 1997)

[Weiß 1997]

Weiß, G. (Hrsg.), Distributed Artificial Intelligence meets Machine Learning – Learning in Multi-Agent Environments, Lecture Notes in Artificial Intelligence, Vol. 1221, Springer-Verlag, Heidelberg e. a. 1997

[Weiß/Sandip 1996]

Weiß, G., Sandip, S. (Hrsg.), Adaption and Learning in Multi-Agent Systems, Lecture Notes in Artificial Intelligence, Vol. 1042, Springer-Verlag, Heidelberg e. a. 1996

[White 1996]

White, J. E., Mobile Agents, in: Bradshaw, J. (Hrsg.), Software Agents, AAAI Press / The MIT Press, Menlo Park 1996, Internet URL: http://www.genmagic.com/agents/White-paper/whitepaper.html (Stand 1997)

[Wildstrom 1997]

Wildstrom, S. H., A way out of the web maze, in: Business Week, 24.02.1997, pp 94–107

[Winston 1987]

Winston, P. H., Künstliche Intelligenz, Addison-Wesley, Bonn e. a. 1987

[Wirfs-Brock et al. 1990]

Wirfs-Brock, R., Wilkerson, B., Wiener, L., Designing Object-Oriented Software, Prentice-Hall, Englewood Cliffs 1990

[Wittig 1995]

Wittig, H., Agents and Intelligent Agents as DAVIC Applications, Seventh DAVIC Meeting, London 1995

[Wittig/Griwodz 1995]

Wittig, H., Griwodz, C., Intelligent Media Agents in Interactive Television Systems, International Conference on Multimedia Computing and Systems, Boston 1995

[Wooldridge/Jennings 1995]

Wooldridge, M., Jennings, N. R., Intelligent Agents: Theory and Practice, in: Knowledge Engineering Review, 10(1995)2

[Yourdon 1991]

Yourdon, E., Modern Structured Analysis, Yourdon Press, Englewood Cliffs 1991

[Zarnekow et al. 1994]
Zarnekow, R., Wittig, H., Meyer, A., Agent Standardization Issues in Electronic Commerce Systems, Proceedings FIPA Opening Forum, Yorktown 1996

[Zelekwski 1997]
Zelewski, S., Elektronische Märkte zur Prozeßoptimierung in Produktionsnetzwerken, in: Wirtschaftsinformatik, 39(1997)3, pp 231–243

[Zlotkin/Rosenschein 1996]
Zlotkin, G., Rosenschein, J. S., Mechanisms for Automated Negotiation in State Oriented Domains, in: Journal of Artificial Intelligence Research, (1996)5, pp 163–238

Index

Springer
and the
environment

At Springer we firmly believe that an international science publisher has a special obligation to the environment, and our corporate policies consistently reflect this conviction.

We also expect our business partners – paper mills, printers, packaging manufacturers, etc. – to commit themselves to using materials and production processes that do not harm the environment. The paper in this book is made from low- or no-chlorine pulp and is acid free, in conformance with international standards for paper permanency.

Springer

Printing: Saladruck, Berlin
Binding: Buchbinderei Lüderitz & Bauer, Berlin